Critical New Perspectives in Early Childhood Music

Exploring and expanding upon current understandings of early childhood music education, this book provides a much-needed response to the rapid social, cultural and technological developmsents affecting children's experience of music today.

Critical New Perspectives in Early Childhood Music returns to the core question of how children engage, participate and learn through music, and how we are to best harness musical resources to their benefit. Chapters move beyond conservative or traditional models of practice and draw upon new and emerging insights from the fields of childhood studies, neuroscience, psychology and sociology. In-depth analysis of research and real examples from practice illustrate the strengths and possible shortcomings of each approach and acknowledge the diverse impacts of digitisation, increased child autonomy, intensive parenting practices, and cultural and economic diversity on the child's experience of music.

An invaluable theoretical overview of current thinking in relation to contemporary musical childhoods, this book will support and challenge students and early childhood music educators as they rethink practice for the present day.

Susan Young has recently retired from her position as Senior Lecturer at the University of Exeter, UK. She is internationally recognised as a leading authority on early childhood music education.

Critical New Perspectives in Early Childhood Music

Young Children Engaging and Learning Through Music

Susan Young

LONDON AND NEW YORK

First published 2018
by Routledge
2 Park Square, Milton Park, Abingdon, Oxon OX14 4RN

and by Routledge
711 Third Avenue, New York, NY 10017

Routledge is an imprint of the Taylor & Francis Group, an Informa business

© 2018 Susan Young

The right of Susan Young to be identified as author of this work has been asserted by her in accordance with sections 77 and 78 of the Copyright, Designs and Patents Act 1988.

All rights reserved. No part of this book may be reprinted or reproduced or utilised in any form or by any electronic, mechanical, or other means, now known or hereafter invented, including photocopying and recording, or in any information storage or retrieval system, without permission in writing from the publishers.

Trademark notice: Product or corporate names may be trademarks or registered trademarks, and are used only for identification and explanation without intent to infringe.

British Library Cataloguing in Publication Data
A catalogue record for this book is available from the British Library

Library of Congress Cataloging in Publication Data
A catalog record for this book has been requested

ISBN: 978-1-138-23996-8 (hbk)
ISBN: 978-1-138-23998-2 (pbk)
ISBN: 978-1-315-29457-5 (ebk)

Typeset in Bembo
by Out of House Publishing

To my grandchildren – Alice and Harry, Charlie and Ted.

Contents

Preface ix

1 **Some windows and a map: early childhood music in new times** 1
   Young children in changing times 4
   Contemporary practice in early childhood music 11
   Conservatism 12
   Is there a need for theory? 15
   Introducing childhood studies 18
   About this book 21

2 **Shaky eggs and hello! songs: the view from childhood studies** 25
   Vignette 25
   A new paradigm 31
   Children's own experiences and agency 33
   Children's music 35
   Interpretive reproduction 36
   'New wave' childhood studies 38

3 **Bone pipes and brain cells: biological perspectives** 42
   Vignette 43
   10,000 hours 45
   Evolutionary origins 46
   Sociable music 47
   Mother-baby interaction 48
   Attachment 49
   Neurological magic? 52
   Neuroscience methods 57
   Future promise 59

Determinism 60
Conclusion 61

4 Pathways and pigeonholes: the view from developmental psychology   62
Vignette 64
Developmentalism 65
Issues and questions 67
Theoretical conceptions of musical development 74
Piaget again! 75
Philosophical approaches 76
From philosophical to scientific approaches 80
Development in a social and cultural context 82
Coming to the present 84

5 Karaoke kids and digi-tots: sociological perspectives   87
Vignette 87
Children's music-making in social contexts 90
The home, family and parenting 92
Digitised music, new technologies and media 97
Pink and blue 103

6 Paper sheep and camels: the view from other places   108
Vignette 108
Anthropological perspectives 111
Cross-cultural studies 111
Insights into children's music from other places 113
What counts as children's music? 115
Ethnomusicologies of music for children, lullabies in particular 121
Authenticity 124
Communicative musicality: an anthropological perspective 124
Diversity 129
A Somali tale 132

Afterword   133

References   135
Index   153

Preface

> without theory, practice is impoverished, and vice versa
> Lucy Green, 2014:ix

Present-day early childhoods and present-day music are changing. The pace of change and the nature of these changes may be contested, but that they are changing is not in doubt. Contemporary children and their parents are inventing what it is to have a musical childhood now, with its embedded digital musical practices, cultural diversity, the rise of intensive parenting practices, the widening gap between rich and poor, and, in so doing, are introducing the rest of us to new ways of thinking, doing and being musical in childhood. We need to pay much more attention to musical babyhoods and childhoods as they are lived and experienced by young children, now, in *their* present. The aim of this book, therefore, is to expand our thinking on the topic of present-day musical childhoods, to bring together what we know, to suggest what we need to consider and reconsider, and to point out important, emerging insights that we need to take into account.

This is not a book that will provide a set of tidy answers or recipes for practice. My aim is to be explorative and propositional, not conclusive or prescriptive. I ask readers to go back to core questions of how we understand childhood and children musically. No one perspective that I explore in this book will hold the key, but all of them start to combine into a theoretical map, and a map marking out some terrains that are familiar but others that have been, until now, less explored in relation to early childhood music education.

The field of early childhood music has grown considerably in the last fifteen to twenty years to become an energetic, active field of practice in its own right. Yet there are no professional career pathways and, at least in the UK, no university or higher education presence for early childhood music, unlike other sectors of music education. As a result, there are no institutional structures that support the development and dissemination of theoretical knowledge. There are short, 'quick fix' training days aplenty, but these focus on what to do, not how to *think*.

So I wanted to write a book that would encourage thinking. The field of early childhood music education is held back either by conservative, traditional models of practice or by lightweight, for-profit approaches, both combined with a reluctance to recognise and examine the underlying ideologies of musical childhoods, which, as I will go on to argue in this book, are out of step with twenty-first century children. I am less willing, these days and in these times, to accept doctrinaire positions, and this book may be penetrating and uncompromising at times in its critique of ideas and practices that I think need to change. I feel a sense of urgency as I write it. Yet this is fundamentally a positive, optimistic and affirmative book.

'Speak from where you are' says the feminist philosopher Rosi Braidotti. And this is where I am. I have been involved in music education for over forty years, focusing on music in early childhood for a large proportion of that time. I started with formal training in classical piano and musicology, followed by a year studying Dalcroze eurhythmics at the Institut Jaques-Dalcroze in Geneva. Over the years I have taught children and then students across the whole age range, shifting my teaching approaches from Paynter-inspired creativity to Kodály-inspired pedagogies, always with that solid grounding as a pianist and in Dalcroze eurhythmics behind me. My PhD research focused on three- and four-year-olds and adopted the 'music is play' and social developmental approaches that were current at the time. Formative in my experiences were enjoyable periods as a lecturer at Roehampton University, which incorporates the Froebel College with its strong traditions in early childhood and play, and then Exeter University, where I coordinated a childhood studies programme. As I moved into retirement, I took a break away from music and education and returned to university to study biological anthropology, focusing on babyhood and parenting. My new-found anthropological interest will be evident in this book.

It is a chequered career therefore, in many ways typical of women who combine childcare and family life with building a professional career, and typical of the early childhood music field which cannot provide a living in itself but needs to be supplemented with other activities. It has also shifted theoretically from music performance and musicology, through music education theory and the embodied knowing ideas of eurhythmics, to developmental psychology, childhood studies and anthropology. I draw on this mixed theoretical background in writing the present book.

The impetus for writing this book grew out of working with students who were studying for a Master's degree that specialised in early childhood music. Although we provided students with lengthy lists of reading, there were no books which gave an up-to-date theoretical overview to support the students or which challenged them to rethink the fundamental premises of their work. The students wanted to complicate what they do, were not satisfied with simple formulae, did not seek firm answers but wanted to trouble their practice to find new ways forward. It is those students – their intellect, warmth, enthusiasm, integrity, laughter and their continuing friendship – whom I held in mind as I wrote this book. I thank them warmly, and the many research students, educators, artist-pedagogues, parents and children whom I have had the privilege to work with over the years, for all that I have learnt from them.

1 Some windows and a map
Early childhood music in new times

> What I propose is very simple: it is nothing more than to think what we are doing.
>
> Hannah Arendt, 1958:5

Imagine a nursery somewhere in central London where three-year-old Aya is singing to herself while playing on the floor with some toy cars. An educator passing through the room might notice that she is half-singing, half-speaking, and then recall a model of singing development that positions Aya at the stage of 'has started to use a singing voice'. Another adult listening in might notice that Aya's friend Ahmed begins to join her singing, and be reminded of ideas about music and learning as taking place in social interactions with others. Another eavesdropper on Aya's singing might recognise the words and half-formed tune as a children's popular media theme and be curious about how children's everyday experiences beyond the nursery are incorporated into their spontaneous singing play. She might also know that Aya's family arrived recently as refugees from Syria and wonder how Aya weaves her songs between her musical background, recent experiences and her new life in London. Another watching adult may notice that the educator responsible for this preschool classroom does not appear to hear Aya and Ahmed's singing at all, but unthinkingly shushes them both and ushers them across to a number activity on the nearby table. She may reflect on the educational policy decisions that result in educators unthinkingly giving higher value to numeracy skills, even for three-year-olds, at the expense of their singing.

Maybe the adults briefly pausing to listen to these two three-year-olds shuffle quickly through many different viewpoints and recognise that each spotlights a different aspect of this small musical happening and each reveals a different version of Aya as musical. Each theoretical window creates and allows for different ways in which she can be and become musical. How parents, educators, therapists, artists 'see' children as musical determines what experiences and opportunities they offer, what they encourage, foster and teach. Viewpoints drawn from different theoretical perspectives help to bridge the gap between what we observe and hear, how we understand it, and then how we act in response and design experiences. In my imaginary scenario, the children's own singing could flourish only in the moments when they were left to play freely and the formalised curriculum did not hear it. So while each spotlight illuminates one aspect, it can throw others into shadow. A developmental viewpoint that looks only at Aya's singing skill, for example, may overshadow those aspects that are part of her home and background experiences and that vividly colour how she sings. Equally, when there are many viewpoints, one may unsettle another. Reflecting on Aya's hummed song as perhaps echoing a children's popular media tune provokes questions about the connection of Aya's everyday musical experiences with those traditionally provided in nursery settings, and may throw up tensions between popular and traditional songs for children. Alternative theoretical viewpoints may suggest new and valuable combinations. A viewpoint that is very attuned to cultural variations, drawing on anthropological perspectives, for example, may then combine with others to create new ways of seeing, and reveal new hearings of Aya's singing and how she participates in the educational environment of the nursery. So a well-rounded understanding of Aya as a singer requires the combination of many viewpoints drawn from a multifaceted theoretical approach.

This one small incident (of which there are many in a typical preschool day) can therefore be viewed from many different – and also complementary, overlapping and at times challenging – positions. In short, there are alternatives, many discourses or narratives, arising from different theoretical perspectives, that can be told about young children's music. No one single perspective can capture Aya's singing in any complete way. And the story – or stories – we tell ourselves about Aya's singing creates an image of her as musical, configures both the child and childhoods as musical and determines how she can *be* musical and how we *act* musically in relation to her. That is the core theme of this book.

A wide range of possible stories is to be welcomed. Different views can provoke experimentation and result in conceptual creativity and theoretical vitality. But the field of early childhood music education is barely listening, preferring to stick to well-trod theory and practice pathways and holding onto outdated images of musical childhoods. Lively discussions are taking place elsewhere, in the general field of early childhood and the broader field of childhood studies, but are not yet impinging on or being integrated into the field of early childhood music. While the field should be vibrant with debate and open-minded discussion, it remains conservative and, dare I say, hidebound by a few dominant perspectives held in place by traditional methods and narrow discussions of 'what works' or even, increasingly nowadays, 'what sells'.

From that small vignette of Aya's singing, it is obvious that not all perspectives or narratives have equal voice. The voice in the educator's ear was not Aya's singing but an urgent voice telling her to hustle the two children over to the number activity table. In England, as in many countries, early-years education is perceived as instrumental in raising standards of academic achievement. This has resulted in a narrow, skills-based view of curriculum content and learning that gives priority to literacy and numeracy. These are the dominant narratives of early childhood currently shaping and defining early childhood practice.

Expressive and aesthetic areas – including the arts – have been marginalised and even silenced (Osgood, 2017). A cluster of theoretical approaches described as 'postmodern' or 'critical theory' seek to expose and challenge the dominant narratives, to quieten them so that other voices can be heard, and to reveal how they are not 'truths' about early childhood but stories and narratives built on particular worldviews that give privilege to certain versions of reality (e.g. Yelland, 2005). The postmodernist or critical-theory position points out that interpretations arising from different theoretical perspectives are never objective; rather, knowledge is socially constructed and built upon partial and subjective interpretations. So, for example, understanding children's development as progressing in certain stages is not a 'truth' about their capabilities and competences, but an interpretation, a story, or a narrative. Crucially, it is the interpretations of the powerful groups and individuals – white, middle-class, able-bodied (Osgood, 2017) – that become embedded in prevailing ideas about music, children, education and what is valued – or not. It is this worldview, for example, which privileges maths over music.

The educator, deaf to Aya's singing and giving priority to the number activity, implicitly accepted the dominant narrative about early childhood and what it is telling her about the value of an early start for school readiness, built on developmental theories, objective measures of recording children's progress and the need for 'evidence' to monitor, measure and prove. What if the adults in my imaginary nursery room had paused for a moment, heard the quiet voices of the children's singing, questioned their own actions, and asked themselves from where and why these dominant narratives have come into place? What if they had asked themselves who stands to gain, who will lose, who holds the power to decide, and what are the full implications for children's education if their singing is silenced? They might then have paused to listen to Aya and Ahmed's singing, encouraged them to sing more, heard the echoes of a Syrian lullaby, a TV theme or current UK pop tune, or whatever was musically buzzing in these two children's heads at that moment, and imagined what their singing might have meant for them as they weaved imagination around the toy cars, affirming their friendship and sharing song scraps. A critical perspective aims to make explicit the underlying motives, assumptions, and how policies, practices and curricula operate. It tries to dislodge many of the established ways we have come to think about children musically. The critical edge is there to provoke, to cause trouble and deconstruct some of the commonly held truths and taken-for-granted assumptions that are held about children, music and their music education. Therefore, my aim is not only to introduce a wider range of viewpoints, but also to engage critically with images of musical childhoods and the larger structures that shape those childhoods.

So, in this book, I will discuss how an expanded range of perspectives drawing on different background theories can illuminate and explain young children's musical experiences and, at the same time, I will be filtering them through a critical lens. Hopefully, this process will prompt alternative understandings that will then call for creative adaptations in practice. However, I am less concerned with the small part of children's musical growing-up that takes place in formal educational settings, which may surprise some readers for a book that hopes to have much to say for early childhood music education. But I am very concerned with how babies and young children grow up being musical through a whole mosaic of different experiences in different contexts, and with how we understand contemporary musical children and childhoods, and only then do I move on to consider how that may impact on the educational practices we design for them.

This brings me to another core theme running through this book, which is that the nature of music and musical childhoods has changed profoundly in recent years, and that – crucially – music education needs to keep in step with those changes. To enable it to do so, we need to turn our attention to understanding those changes from within. And for that, we need theoretical approaches that allow us to study children's everyday contemporary musical lives and, at the same time, to consider and conceptualise the wider contexts – social, material, technological, economic and cultural – that are shaping their musical lives. We need approaches which recognise the detail of children's lives as they are situated in specific times and places. These theoretical approaches are to be found mainly in the direction of childhood studies strongly influenced by sociological and anthropological thinking, hence the emphasis on these disciplinary viewpoints in this book.

Another core argument is that the contemporary world for very young children – both generally and in terms of music – is changing. These changes are full of exciting new possibilities, but are also fraught with contradictory developments. Much is new, and somewhat confusing, and cannot be accounted for with old theoretical concepts. Heeding Rosi Braidotti (2011), we need new theories, new concepts and new terms that can engage with the present time, and we need to learn to think differently and to think differently more quickly, on our feet. To explain what I have in mind, let me move on to talk about the present time for young children and their musical experiences.

Young children in changing times

We only have to look back a generation or two to recognise that children's lives are continually changing in response to social, cultural and political situations. My 1950s childhood is a world away from that of my grandchildren. The present period, many are suggesting, is marked by both the accelerating pace and the nature of the changes (Sommer, 2012). If I spell out the most obvious widespread changes, these are changing patterns of family life and parenting practices, innovations in technology and increasing migration resulting in cultural diversity within societies. At the same time, we must immediately pause to remember that, viewed globally, the changes differ across diverse groups of children. Only one third of households across the world have electricity, for example, so up-to-date innovations in technology may be meaningless for a majority of children worldwide. If we look more closely at the structural changes to babyhood and early childhood in what is often referred to as the 'minority' world (the affluent countries of Europe and North America, in particular), the birth-rate is falling, families are smaller, the survival rates of babies and their health are much improved, family groupings are much more varied, more mothers are employed outside of the home and many more very small children are cared for and educated by professionals (Boocock & Scott, 2005:52–56).

Focusing on musical childhoods, we live in an exciting age in which new technologies are transforming musical lives. The digitisation of music and multimedia has brought far-reaching changes to the nature of music and musical practices. Young children hear considerably more music than generations before and they can hear it repeatedly, the same each time. The sheer richness and variety of music and how it can be accessed now means that a tapestry of every kind of music can be downloaded into young children's lives, portable in tiny devices and instantly accessible wherever they are, whatever they are doing. Young children can now be surrounded by music and musical sounds: at home, in the car, in waiting areas, as they go shopping; embedded in toys, smartphone apps, video games and video clips accessed via touchscreen devices. Music pops out from everywhere. My dishwasher plays a tiny tune for each of the function buttons, which has become a fascinating plaything for all the small children who visit my house. A large number of homes in the minority world contain a wide range of digital devices that include TVs, mobile phones, computers, iPods, mp3 players, digital cameras, interactive toys and games, and video game consoles (Ilari & Young, 2016). There has been a key shift from fixed technology (e.g. music centre, TV) to handheld, touchscreen devices (e.g. mobile phone, tablet), many of which young children, even babies, can now manipulate for themselves (Holloway, et al., 2015; Hourcade, et al., 2015). Young children are growing up immersed in a digital world that changes at lightning speed. Touchscreen technologies have brought about a very recent *major* revolution in early childhood technology use that I will discuss further in a later chapter. It is also clear that not only have the devices moved on and will continue to do so, but so too have the kinds of musical activities they enable. Media forms are now multimodal and integrated, with music as just one embedded element. New kinds of musical practices, musical play and ways of using and engaging with music are possible (Katz, 2010). As Andrew Brown writes, digital technologies enable us to 'amplify our musicality' and 'the globalised technoculture in which we find ourselves calls for a re-examination of the musical life of today's child' (2015:18). The changes strike me as profound if I think back to my own 1950s non-digital, screen-free childhood with only occasional light music programmes from a large fixed radio in one room and my mother's playing on an old piano. It must have been a surprisingly silent childhood. Children bring all their musical experiences with them into the music session. Those experiences are there, present in the ears, bodies and musical memories of the children we work with. And so what does this mean for how we design educational practices with young children?

What is more, even the youngest children can be active in selecting and activating these musical sources independently, particularly via touchscreen devices, making them highly personalised and interactive. Parents encourage children to have autonomous preferences and express those preferences as early as they are able, looking for signs and attributing preferences in the non-verbal actions of babies. Vast quantities of commodified music, apps and video clips for very young children are produced, bought and sold. This leads, in turn, to unprecedented possibilities for consumption and, while very small children may not be targeted directly as consumers, they are targeted indirectly through their parents (Cross, 2016). Patrick Hughes (2005) describes the way that parents are targeted by baby and toddler product companies – and we can include franchises selling musical products here – which redefine babies as learners whose potential to learn will be stimulated by these products. Thus, in a consumer society, private music providers and companies sell not merely musical products but the promises which their products embody.

Parents are having fewer children and at later ages. Not only that, but they want 'higher quality' children, investing more time, money and emotion in those children. In certain groups of the population, in particular the middle classes, an intensive form of child-rearing has emerged that involves the early cultivation of children's cognitive skills (Gopnik, 2016; Hays, 1996; Lareau, 2003). Children have become a kind of project involving work, replacing relaxed family spontaneity and love with a long 'to do' list. This intensive child-rearing falls primarily on the mother, resulting in a tendency to over-emphasise the mother-child relationship and downplay the many other relationships in a child's life. These characteristics of contemporary childhood are immediately apparent in what has become a focus of interest and emphasis in both music theory and practice. Musical parenting (a relatively recent term) and music as a medium for interactive exchanges between babies, toddlers and their mothers have become primary topics of research and a main plank of early childhood music theory. This is something I will contest later in this book. It is also evident in all kinds of provision of early childhood music, and particularly in the rise of private music sessions, whose promotional materials often seek to appeal to this image of intensive parenting. The rise of the word 'parenting' came with the rise of this particular cultural image of being a parent and the belief that the job (and it has become more of a 'job', less a relationship) of a parent – invariably the mother – is to gather expertise and information, as well as items and equipment, to help shape their child.

At the same time, mothers with preschool-aged children are returning to work, which results in more young children in childcare and early education. Young children are increasingly taken care of, supported, but also monitored, outside of the home within care, educational, welfare and health institutions which, in the UK and many other countries, have a wider reach and influence than hitherto. At the same time, certain parents – those considered to be experiencing forms of social disadvantage – are often deemed to be 'in need' of extra support and intervention from welfare services (Gillies, 2014). Here, too, the impact on early childhood music education is apparent, with early childhood music that receives state or charity funding often designed as a means of supporting parents and children deemed to be in need. Increasingly in the UK, the result is a two-tier system of music education provision, with private music sessions for middle-class mothers who can afford to pay and free music sessions as support for so-called 'vulnerable' and 'disadvantaged' children and their parents (Young, 2017a).

Attitudinal and ideological shifts accompany these demographic, economic, technological, commercial and musical changes to childhood. Young children are watched and worried over. Much has been written about the anxieties that have become a hallmark of middle-class parenting. Anxiety about the risks to children outside the home result in greater restrictions on children's freedom of movement, fewer opportunities to play out-of-doors and to play independently in mixed-age groups (Frost, 2009). In common with all children of my generation, I walked to school independently at the age of five, joining with all the neighbouring children in small mixed-age friendship gaggles and getting up to playful adventures en route. Now, as a result of restrictions on movement, adults manage and organise children's time and space – seen clearly in the rise of the private music class – and provide more home-based activities (Valentine, 2004:70). At home, even for very young children, bedrooms are typically set up as a play and entertainment space making use of home-based technological activities and media. But it can be a solitary childhood, with fewer siblings, parents who work, and little opportunity for outdoor play with friends. It dawned on me, during a study I made of young girls singing at home with karaoke, that the equipment (along with a plethora of other playthings) had been provided by parents as a means of occupying their children safely indoors, in solitary play, and in two cases releasing parents to work in home-based offices (Young, 2012).

The changes to early childhood have resulted in mixed responses. It has even been argued that childhood, or childhood as we want to imagine it, is disappearing. 'Too fast, too soon' is the cry from those who claim that children are missing out on the genuine experiences of early childhood and growing up too quickly. Young children can use modern-day technologies independently (even babies can swipe touchscreen technologies), accessing YouTube clips and imitating the dancing and singing of adult popular music. Sue Palmer, in her book *Toxic Childhood*, adopts an even stronger standpoint, arguing that rapid, and what she sees as negative, changes are damaging and destroying childhood (2016). Fears and anxieties about the negative impacts of changes to childhood circulate in the popular press and in everyday conversations. These fears, as listed, for example, by the Save Childhood Movement on its website of the same title, focus on the changing nature of family life, the disconnect between children and the natural world, the downward pressures of the schooling system, the influences of commercialisation and the advances of digital technology. The consequences are framed as stress and lack of well-being. Very often the anxieties are based more on opinion and supposition than research that provides accurate information as to the impact and consequences of these changes. That is not to deny the importance of carefully considering the impact of contemporary changes to early childhood, nor to dismiss these serious concerns. But the 'risk' society can tend to jump to exaggerated conclusions before we have enough information on which to base conclusions. Such views tend also to perpetuate a traditional image of childhood as playing out-of-doors in the natural, non-technological world, as free of influence from new media and commercialism, and as living in conventional, two-parent families. The construction of the idealised, romantic childhood is identifiable in such texts and movements – and indeed, as I will go on to explain as the book pages turn, also identifiable in our music education practices.

One change affecting present-day childhoods at the broadest level is profound, indisputable and must be addressed seriously, namely, the increasing disparity between the rich and the poor, both within countries and between countries (Penn, 2005). We all have a responsibility to face up to the fact that the global economy is increasingly inhumane, resulting in structural injustice, inequality, oppression and increasing poverty. Grinding poverty, political unrest, war and ethnic tensions result in large swathes of certain populations moving across national borders. We need to recognise that there is no fixed or unchanging culture, whether defined by country or region, and that diversity is a reality that must be accommodated and welcomed. Diversity and disparity are both issues that early childhood music education needs urgently to address. The music session may appear to be a small, self-contained activity, but it does not take place in a social void and should be responsive to the widest social issues affecting all children.

Yet, while I have been drawing attention to changing childhoods, others insist on keeping a sense of proportion. In a seminar discussion led by the educational philosopher Gert Biesta, he argued that while there is a story that circulates of rapid and dramatic change in childhoods, of increasing diversity and variation, the reality is that much stays the same. As we discussed in that seminar group, from a biological point of view, babies share the same physical characteristics and biological requirements, and young children mature physically in much the same way, notwithstanding the environmental variations in diet, hygiene, health and stress that can impact on children's physicality in profound ways. Play is another aspect of childhood which remains constant, as does the role of caring adults. Dion Sommer suggests that, at the micro level of everyday life, families strive to filter out change and uncertainty in order to create stability, order and gradual change through everyday routines that he calls 'plain traditions' (2012:90). So, at the level of their own experience, children move through the day in regular and familiar patterns and routines, often marked with music, songs and rhythmic games. We are all familiar with how small children seek to bring repetition and familiarity to their lives by asking for the same stories and songs, the same pieces of music. 'Again' is one of the first words a baby learns, enjoying the sense of stability and independence that repetition bestows. And in planning their music sessions, early childhood educators typically seek to combine repetition and familiarity with gradual change.

Yet the notion, whether real or imagined, that we are living in a complex and permanently changing society breaks the generational continuity of family practices which, as Nancy Vansieleghem points out, legitimises greater recourse to expertise and 'an expansion of measures to manage the inner life of families' (2010:341). In what some are calling the invasion of the experts, music for very young children has readily joined in, finding connections with the rhetoric by simply adding a musical slant. Comments posted on social media pages dedicated to educators providing music for babies refer to 'musical baby bonding' and 'musical parenting'. The educators discuss approaches through which 'parents' (mothers, that is) are to be instructed and guided on how to interact musically with their babies and how to use music beneficially in the upbringing of their children. The music leader becomes the expert, bestowing guidance and knowledge to the 'mums', as they are typically referred to (a diminutive term which is indicative of the expert-novice relationship). There is an overall assumption that scientifically informed support is required to tell parents about correct parenting procedures. Music in babyhood has been reframed as something that needs to be mediated through experts. Paradoxically, it is claimed to be natural, intuitive parenting, but on the social media pages all kinds of reasons are drawn up for why parents no longer know how to do it or do not care to do it, thus further endorsing the need for experts. In this way, expertise seeks to intervene in the most intimate relationships of family life. As Jan Macvarish points out, it pathologises babyhood/early childhood and intimacy, and makes dysfunction appear widespread and almost inevitable unless great care is taken (2016).

So, opinions vary as to the nature and pace of the changes to early childhood that have occurred, and as to their extent and depth – whether they take place at the structural level of childhoods viewed from the perspective of adults, or at the level of young children's everyday lives as they themselves experience them. Moreover, opinions vary as to whether the changes are viewed with an air of optimism as a good thing, or with pessimism as toxic and damaging and requiring intervention. What these contrasting opinions do reveal, irrespective of the clash of views, is the attention and focus that early childhood now attracts, and how intense that attention can be, often arousing strong emotions between advocates of one position or another. One only has to read some popular newspaper headlines or the chat on popular parenting websites to perceive the intensity of emotions that issues around very young children can raise.

The emotional response is generated by a particular ambiguity in how early childhood is viewed (Gillis, 2009). On the one hand, the first years of life are viewed as having a uniquely important character in that they determine lifetime outcomes. This view then justifies attention, concern, investments and interventions, but also fuels fears and anxieties that foundations not properly laid will lead to later problems, weaknesses and deficiencies. There is a 'now or never' anxiety that resonates in the arguments, which carries significant consequences for the way that young children are treated and understood. Developmental theory and theories of attachment, in particular, are largely responsible for this emphasis and the sense of urgency that surrounds early childhood. Music in early childhood has become closely bound up in these ways of thinking, drawing in extra support from recent evolutionary and biological theories of music. These ideas have been yet further bolstered by contemporary neuroscience, which has played an increasing pivotal role by (apparently) providing biological evidence for the cruciality of the earliest years to preventing later problems – much more on this in the pages to come.

The sense of urgency surrounding the earliest years has become further entangled in arguments framed by human capital theory. These arguments rest on the rationale that investment in the very young will reap benefits by creating individuals who contribute to, rather than take from, the national economy. This rationale has been taken up with enthusiasm by politicians. The picture of gold bars alongside images of a shrunken child's brain on the cover of a UK government policy document brazenly and crudely symbolise human capital theory with the title, 'Early intervention, smart investment, massive savings' (Allen, 2011). Music, looking for justification in an early education system increasingly focused on core skill areas, has latched onto these arguments and frequently justifies its place in early education on the grounds of wider 'benefits' and, by implication, with reference to these economic rationales. Yet the evidence for non-musical gains from musical interventions for preschool children is still very inconsistent and, as is frequently argued, the 'benefits' claims reduce music education to a means to an end rather than being intrinsically valuable for its own sake (Mehr, *et al.*, 2013).

So the previous paragraphs have opened windows onto contemporary early childhoods that I will develop as I progress through the book. There is much to unpick, discuss and deliberate thoughtfully. I will, however, often have to tread a careful path, for I am not minimising the value or positive qualities of early childhood music practice, nor wishing in any way to disparage the work of others or diminish the importance of preventing neglect and disadvantage to very young children. Quite the opposite, I recognise that there are different agendas and powerful voices around early childhood and music. Work in music with young children is often imbued with an idealised and emotion-invested aura, which is compelling and attractive on the one hand, but also results in surprisingly closed and sometimes staunchly defended attitudes. As I have discovered from experience, to challenge these ideologies is to risk my motives being misunderstood. I hope to show, through carefully constructed arguments drawing on wide reading, how these ideologies can cloud open-minded and honest appraisal.

So if society, culture, families, early childhoods, technologies and the nature of musical experience are changing, albeit not as rapidly and profoundly as some claim, then early childhood music education has to place itself inside those changes and be responsively part of them. It is essential to recognise the whole host of wider social, cultural and political issues and interests that impinge on childhoods in our present day and the complicated relationships between biological, material, social and cultural factors that construct musical childhoods in ways that I will go on, as best I can, to describe and discuss. These changes do, and indeed must, provoke established fundamental beliefs about young children and how we work with them in music, and challenge the theories underpinning our work. In the light of these changes, we have to grapple with their complexity and work out how to reshape the theoretical bases and reshape early childhood music education practice. We must be in tune with the times, not several steps behind, open-minded to the realities and positive about their creative potential.

Contemporary practice in early childhood music

Over the last ten to fifteen years, early childhood music education has expanded considerably to become an energetic field of activity in its own right. The most marked expansion is the shift downwards in age to encompass the birth to three age phase brought about by, among other things, an important paradigm change in how babies and toddlers are viewed – no longer as incompetent and living in a confused perceptual world, but as possessing musical competences from birth. A wealth of interesting experimental studies have revealed the range of musical competences possessed by babies (Trehub, 2010, 2015). I can remember in the early 1990s attending a conference presentation by Esther Beyer describing Brazilian mother and baby music groups and being surprised that anyone would consider it worthwhile to provide music sessions for babies (Beyer, 1996; Pecker, 2014). I still at that time held on to the prevailing view that characterised babies and very young children as 'not yet' able to do anything musically of any worth or interest. How wrong I was! At that time, early childhood music education usually spanned the three to eight age phase. Nowadays, baby music classes are commonplace and the field usually encompasses the birth to five years age phase. That is certainly the age range I have in mind for this book. It is important to remember how recently and rapidly work with under three-year-olds has developed.

The expansion has also taken early childhood music into many different modes of activity. Music for young children has proliferated into a fragmented, complicated and energetic area of activity driven by varying aims and agendas and all the different types of music provision it covers cannot be neatly circumscribed. It spans therapy, education, entertainment, performance arts and community music. It takes places in a range of contexts: schools, nurseries, playgroups, libraries, museums, arts centres, theatres, concert halls, hospitals and private classes in rented premises and homes. It can involve babies and children with their parents, carers or early childhood educators, or young children in small groups on their own. It spills over and is integrated into the wider structural aspects of early childhood – the play settings of nurseries and kindergartens, as well as into families, communities, and private and public provision – and can be designed around a range of purposes that combine music with social intervention or thinly disguised for-profit, commercial motives. A distinctive aspect of this expansion has been the rise of the private music session provided by individual entrepreneurs, many spreading under franchise banners, and the consequent need to create, market and make a profit from the music session as a product. This has shaped practice in very distinctive ways. The growing popularity of these types of music classes demonstrates changing parenting practices, at least among a certain middle-class tranche of mothers.

Early childhood music sessions might be led or guided by early childhood practitioners, community musicians, performing artists linked to arts organisations, music therapists or teachers, all of whom might be working in state-funded provision or privately. From what I have observed, everyone falls into early childhood music from somewhere else, often by chance or as an employment option in combination with caring for small children. No one declares at the start of their career that their professional ambition is to become an early childhood music educator, not least because there are no formal qualifying and professional pathways. Early childhood music 'people' may have a wide range of backgrounds, often including early childhood music with a portfolio of freelance teaching and performing activity. Some may have qualification backgrounds in music, education and to postgraduate level. Others may have no more qualification than a confidence to sing and have bought into a franchise which provides sing-along CDs and ready-made session plans. Given the absence of professional pathways, everyone learns 'on the job' in ad hoc and largely self-guided ways. There are numerous decentralised and loosely connected networks, as well as many informal, practical training opportunities, and early childhood music educators must learn to navigate a wide range of different working contexts, with varying values, systems and expectations.

Conservatism

However, in spite of this rapid expansion in practical activity, early childhood music education has not, generally speaking, kept abreast of the innovative theoretical ideas around young children and early childhood that have burgeoned in recent years. In conferences and professional articles, the field is overwhelmed by descriptive accounts of practical projects and empirical accounts of young children's musical actions and experiences, but underwhelmed by the theoretical debates that underpin them. The field tends to recycle its own internal theories and narrow its discussions, remaining complacent and uncritical on a more theoretical level. For the most part, early childhood music education sails on unconcerned by the circulating theoretical dilemmas and, in so doing, holds onto traditional models of practice and conventional ways of understanding children and childhood, and so has become ill-equipped to deal with present-day dilemmas and challenges.

There are a number of reasons why early childhood music education remains conservative in both practice and research and these are interrelated. They are also understandable. While I explain and explore them, I do have empathy for the genuine difficulties and constraints they represent. Many are associated with the low status, marginalisation and underfunding of the field, coupled with the lack of professional qualifications and salaried positions. One obvious reason is linked with the rapid expansion of practice. There has been barely time to catch breath and little time to research, deliberate and evolve contemporary models of practice, particularly with under-threes and their parents/caregivers. When funding is tight and freelance hourly-paid employment the only option for many, it is unsurprising that time is given to the work itself and not to researching, exploring and deliberating over practice. As a result, the expansion has not been accompanied by exploring, experimenting and evaluating the underpinning theoretical frameworks. There is a general and widespread belief in the value and usefulness of music for babies and very young children and a shared, if unexamined, belief that it contributes to essential foundations in key areas, and this has driven the expansion of activity. If you pick up the tentative tone of that last sentence, it is because in later sections of the book I critique these beliefs.

Yet, at the same time, there is a widely-held assumption that practice is easy and unskilled. Because the children are very young, a developmental view equates their age with musical simplicity, and musical simplicity is assumed to require little skill on the part of the adult. Becoming a practitioner is thought to consist of little more than collecting an age-appropriate repertoire of attractive children's songs with accompanying movement actions and props. When traditional models of practice position the adult as music leader and performer, the musical skills required may indeed be undemanding if assessed only in terms of musical complexity. When, however, the model of practice is understood as requiring detailed understanding of children's musical capacities, and of how to engage with young children and foster, support and extend their musical learning and, sometimes, how to work with parents as well – *and* to do all this across an age range marked by huge developmental changes – practice is far from easy. In reality, practice is highly skilful and requires complex and far-reaching knowledge. Yet this is poorly appreciated, and assumptions that practice is unskilled perpetuate low-level and conservative practice.

Conservatism is also a consequence of the shortage of innovative research, particularly larger-scale research studies, which is likewise linked with the low status of the field. Early childhood music education is not a field that attracts generous funding for research. Specialist academics are few and far between. Handicapped by the low status of their field, academics tend to occupy more lowly positions in their institutions and typically have big teaching commitments alongside the requirement to produce academic output. What research takes place is often small-scale, carried out on tiny budgets, or by students studying for Master's and PhD degrees. Many of these studies are excellent and informative. I certainly value them and have spent much time searching them out from obscure sources in order to draw on their insights in this book. But, generally speaking, research in early childhood music education is either small-scale in the hands of experienced academics or novice studies for postgraduate qualifications. There are also some very active areas of research that have considerable relevance for early childhood music – the laboratory studies into infant musicality, the adult-infant interaction research, ethnomusicological fieldwork of children's music in different societies – but the findings need to be sorted and the implications identified if they are to have relevance and application for practice.

Conservatism is only too apparent in the fact that approaches originating in the social and political conditions of early- or mid-century Europe – the 'big three' known by the names of their (male, dead, white, European) originators Dalcroze, Orff and Kodály – still have a very strong grip on practice. It is ironic, but perhaps revealing of current anxieties around change and loss in musical childhoods, that methods devised for such different social, musical and political situations from those children experience now continue to perpetuate retrospective versions of musical childhoods. Educators often align themselves with a particular method marked out by philosophies, pedagogies and understandings of music and musical learning that lead to specific curricula and particular types of educational activities. At the start of this chapter, I described how a particular 'window' or viewpoint creates a version of musical childhood. Each of these methods encapsulates a strictly defined and distinctive image of musical childhood and what children should become musically. Allegiance to a particular method often becomes an important element of professional identity. The demarcations are clearly drawn and sometimes, unfortunately, the outlooks are territorial and dogmatic. Devotees of key methods can show inflexibility and even a lack of curiosity for anything that sits outside *their* approach. This is something Thomas Regelski (2002) has labelled 'methodolatry', a term he has coined to denote the unquestioning devotion to a given way of practising music education, a dutiful repetition of traditions. The methods are often underpinned by philosophies that have been in place for a long time and, although they are weak in empirical evidence to back them up, they are strong in beliefs that are perpetuated by authoritative, expert teachers. Some newer approaches, promoted as methods, have evolved into franchises that are territorial for commercial reasons. Among franchise owners, protecting 'professional turf' serves to safeguard profits. Such narrow interests, whether attached to traditional methods or newer, franchised methods, do not encourage the healthy climate of collaboration, sharing and open-minded critique and the moves towards centralisation rather than fragmentation that the field of early childhood music education so badly needs.

On the other hand, 'the methods', if approached in a spirit of open-mindedness, point to traditions of practice and a pedagogical heritage from which we can all learn, and in the hands of alert, thoughtful educators they have evolved in keeping with social change. But they need to be critically examined, adopted selectively and reimagined in relation to contemporary situations and not blindly followed. I have studied Kodály and Dalcroze approaches in parent institutions within their respective countries of origin and have qualifications in both. If a group of four-year-olds stood in front of me, I would still probably work with them in a way that echoes both these approaches, using voices and embodied movement in creative ways. At the same time, I strongly argue that contemporary changes in the nature of childhood and music weaken these pedagogies, which originated in other times and places, and certainly challenge the images of musical childhood they embody.

Conservatism is also understandable in the current financial and political climate, which has created an era of uncertainty that gives rise to anxieties around childhood and to even greater insecurities of employment for professionals, neither of which are conducive to experimentation. Many countries, like the UK, are experiencing a time of austerity. Conservatism is possibly a form of response in the face of austerity, uncertainties, changing childhoods and changing musical practices. It may represent a retreat from expansive and adventurous thinking into less risky and familiar approaches. I suspect there may be reassurance in creating a pre-digital, non-political world of innocent, natural childhood that can hide from the complexity of these changes. Some models of practice, particularly those evolving in private music classes, seem to be an attempt to preserve and uphold certain traditional, timeless qualities and images of childhood mediated through the songs, music, resources and activities. But it makes little sense to continue to peg our pedagogical practices to norms, values and images of childhoods from the past. Music education should be constantly adapting to contemporary situations, reappraising and renegotiating the values and purposes of its practices, alert then to the reasons why conservatism seems to prevail and why open-minded thinking seems to be in short supply. Thus, I argue, practice should not be defined by fixed 'methods', franchise materials or canonical repertoires held in place by anxieties and cautious thinking, but be constantly evolving. I would like to see early childhood music practice created by those we work with and generated by the actual processes of how music is made, participated in, enjoyed and learned about. My optimism is for an openness to the improvisational, adventurous nature of practice: responsive, dynamic and evolving – a music education for the present.

Is there a need for theory?

In setting out the aims and rationales that motivate this book and the issues and arguments that drive it, I may be running ahead of myself and need to put in place a foundational argument for the place of theory. There can be a temptation to think that practice is the 'real thing' and that theory is an optional add-on. A significant quantity of writing about early childhood music is practice-orientated and focused on what to do, rather than why. Theory and practice are thought to be separate, involving different people in different places, with a gap between them that is difficult to bridge (Gluschankof, 2007). There can even be resistance to theory, in the belief that it is overly academic, elitist and obscure. I have encountered the view from managers and administrators that academics, particularly those orientated by critical theory, tend unnecessarily to complicate matters and do not come up with the concise practical solutions that are most needed. Practice dominates and, for the most part, is thought to be straightforward and unproblematic.

I would agree that many accounts of research studies and theoretical texts are written in a specialist language that is sometimes jargon-ridden and unnecessarily complex, and can require time and thought to read. They are published in journal articles and books that are prohibitively expensive and difficult to access. Moreover, the original accounts of research rarely provide the kind of certainty and 'ready to go' knowledge that educators, managers and policymakers typically seek. Research reported in academic journals explains the study procedures and findings in detail and is tentative, conditional and provisional. For those who want their research as an add-on, usually for advocacy purposes, it is ideally delivered in sound bites that have been reduced and repackaged. These research sound bites crop up in newspaper articles, web pages, blogs, social media, in executive summaries, handbooks and popular texts for practitioners, where they are often recycled verbatim and without recourse to the original source. They typically begin with 'research has shown', which gives a ring of authority to what follows. All too often, any tentativeness in the original research becomes certainty, possible correlations become causal relationships, and claims are exaggerated. We will see how this takes place when I discuss later in the book the way that findings from neuroscience are reported and used. Are journalists and bloggers sensationalising research findings to attract readership, or are researchers tempted to exaggerate the importance of their findings? Probably a bit of both according to Samuel Mehr (2015). Going back to read the original accounts of research, reading theoretical texts to frame the research, reflecting on practice and imagining alternatives takes time, energy and resources, and these are understandably in short supply. But this we must do to avoid being duped by 'fake news'. Moreover, for those educators who work in their own private practice, experimenting with theory-inspired modifications to practice is risky; it may work, it may not, and when income is dependent on loyal purchasers, it may be prudent to stay with the tried and tested. Little wonder, then, that theory gets sidelined and practice remains conservative.

Yet practice is always underpinned by a working theory, even if this is implicit rather than explicit. To declare, as some do, that theory is not necessary and that real-world experience and practice are all that matters is, in itself, a theory for practice. Everyone working with small children and music holds a set of ideas about how the work should be carried out, what they are aiming to achieve, what the work should look and sound like, and how the children, or babies, and adults should participate. This is their working theory. Working theories are often handed from professional to professional in training courses and written materials, and rarely subject to hard scrutiny. The problem is that taking the theoretical side of practice for granted means that educators may be working with beliefs and assumptions that are biased and out-of-date. They can even, unwittingly, disadvantage the very children educators aim to benefit. Implicit theory can become a set of blinkers that prevents practice from growing, expanding and improving. Most importantly, theory that has a critical edge engages with questions, issues and values that are crucial to good practice and – let me stress this essential point – good practice that strives to serve all children, today's children, equitably and to maximise their opportunities.

There is also the serious risk that without firm theoretical footings educators are not thinking and acting independently as professionals, but bending in the wind with every new fashionable idea or policy pronouncement. At a time when the grip of policy-driven practices is tightening and when convincing and enticing sound-bite ideas circulate on the Internet, independent thinking becomes even more crucial. My hope in writing this book is that it might help early childhood music educators to become thinking professionals: independent, knowledgeable, ethical and imaginative.

The concept of theory in this book is not, however, knowledge as a set of facts or information, or a recipe that is simply to be applied to practice. It is certainly not prescriptive or dogmatic. The concept of theory in this book is active and interactive, a tool to use in the process of interpreting, analysing, evaluating and critiquing practice within the context of every educator's own individual circumstances. Every working context consists of many interacting and reciprocally influencing dimensions: the children, parents, other adults, the space, the time, the location, even the climate, and the wider political, social and cultural context framing the music work, the music itself, all the embodied sounds, movements and gestures of those taking part, the materials, instruments and technologies, so that the whole dynamic system takes on situated meaning. Theory must therefore be adaptive to every educator's individual working situation.

Theories are themselves part of something bigger; they are framed by a particular paradigm or discourse. A paradigm is a set of ideas, beliefs and values, an overarching frame that determines the basis, focus and boundaries of a theory. As such, a paradigm can exert a powerful influence on how we see the world, on how we see young children as musical for instance, and on what priorities for action we set and how we decide to act musically in relation to young children. It provides the framework within which knowledge can be evolved, but it also imposes certain limitations and constraints.

Paradigms vary according both to historical period and to place. There are certain strong traditions of theoretical thinking that prevail at any one time, coloured by the current society, culture, politics and economics. Therefore, it is always important to ask from when and where a particular theorist or set of ideas originates and then to position them within a paradigm of thinking. This is not to say that historical ideas or ideas from other cultural contexts do not have relevance; indeed, they can be extremely valuable and illuminating. But, for example, in drawing on historical music education theories and methods they need always to be understood as 'of their time and place'. Equally, it is important to recognise that research from other countries is 'of its place' and hence does not automatically import to other national contexts. For example, research and theorising from Scandinavia is grounded in a welfare state deeply imbued with social democratic values. While we, in the UK, find Scandinavian ideas inspirational, the politics of neoliberalism and the permeation of market principles into current understandings of childhood, education and arts organisations would make it difficult to import theoretical ideas from our Scandinavian colleagues without adaptation (Young, 2017a). So, research and theoretical writing are not neutral, but always set within particular contexts, paradigms and worldviews – indeed, as is my writing of this book.

The paradigm of 'positivism' has dominated early childhood education and remains strongly influential on both policy and practice. Positivism prioritises rational objectivity and believes that children and childhood can be understood through the discovery of universal unchanging rules or laws. These rules are arrived at through processes of scientific research based on processes of testing and measurement that aim to reduce and simplify all the complexities of real life in order to arrive at clear-cut conclusions. Positivism has given rise to models of development that assume there can be universal pathways of children's development across many different domains: cognitive, social, physical – and indeed musical as well. Positivism also gives authority to experts who are able to provide the evidence to (supposedly) reveal to us exactly how things are, and then to suggest and justify what action we must take to improve things (Dahlberg, *et al*., 2007).

In the late 1990s an important change of paradigm regarding how children and childhood are understood took place (Kehily, 2009; Wyness, 2006). A 'new' sociology of childhood emerged in Scandinavia and the UK, which challenged the dominance of the positivist paradigm and the belief in developmentalism that it had given rise to. This paradigm shift proposed alternative ways of understanding and thinking about children and childhood, and it initiated a field of academic activity that has come to be known as childhood studies. The important theoretical developments that scholars working in this field have introduced will be the topic of the next chapter. Here, I go on to discuss the core idea of interdisciplinarity, which has been central to childhood studies and is also central to this book.

Introducing childhood studies

Childhood studies has emerged as an energetic field that originally combined sociological and anthropological approaches with a children's rights agenda. It has gradually acquired more theoretical bedfellows, eventually moving towards a broad multidisciplinary approach that seeks to bring together biological, psychological, sociological and anthropological perspectives. Childhood studies scholars argued that the study of children has been, and indeed largely continues to be, compartmentalised within psychology, education, medicine and sociology, and that communication between the fields is limited. The result is a fragmented child, differently viewed through each disciplinary window. An interdisciplinary childhood studies approach, it was proposed, offered a meeting place for diverse perspectives on (early, musical) childhood to come together.

Another founding principle of childhood studies has been a move away from 'grand theories', particularly the 'one size fits all' theories of psychology or sociology, which sought to explain everything under one sweeping theoretical model that could be applied to all children universally. Instead, they argued strongly that all children are different and therefore theoretical frameworks are needed that are sensitive to and can accommodate variation. This revised view of children recognises that our knowledge of childhood is historically and culturally situated and that only multidisciplinary – and ideally interdisciplinary – approaches can capture the multiplicity and complexity of children's (musical) childhoods. Again, my opening vignette of Aya's singing aimed to illustrate this.

The 'new' sociology of childhood argued that, as a result of the dominance of the positivist paradigm, all theoretical viewpoints are not heard as equals. In policy and in many mainstream approaches to educational practice the dominant discourse of developmental psychology still holds sway (in spite of trenchant challenges) and its assumptions and beliefs remain deeply imbricated in education discourses and practices. Therefore, this book has the difficult task of not only expanding the range of theoretical perspectives but also realigning them in relation to one another. Those perspectives that are more powerful and dominant are carefully reassessed and repositioned within a broad and multitheoretical framework for understanding children's musical experiences and musical childhoods. Those that are marginal are given more prominence to rebalance the theoretical landscape. Importantly, I do not suggest we toss out the psychological, and particularly developmental, approaches, but propose that these should be critiqued, evaluated and repositioned. This also means careful appraisal of the biological, neuroscientific and genetic research that is currently gaining such attention. I 'put the brakes on' and urge more caution. I call for more debate about the possibilities of this research, more honesty about its limitations and more awareness of the potential dangers of over-hasty take-up of its findings. So, overall, if I am critical of certain ways of thinking about musical childhoods, it is not because I think we should abandon those ways of thinking, but because they need to be reconstructed within new disciplinary landscapes. I want to make the case not only for a broader creative approach, theoretically, to early childhood music, but also one in which sociological and anthropological perspectives and critical-theory perspectives occupy a stronger position.

Not that bringing together theoretical perspectives in a multiple or interdisciplinary approach is straightforward or easy. Different theoretical traditions use different research methods and have different conceptual languages. Simply stitching together different theoretical ideas is not enough. There is a risk that a 'bolt on' approach will result in a patchwork of ideas and confusion and lose touch with the ontological bases in which concepts are rooted and gain stability. For this reason, four chapters each cohere around one disciplinary tradition – biology, psychology, sociology and anthropology – so that the disciplinary grounding is firm. However, a truly interdisciplinary approach requires some concepts that can bridge between disciplines so that disciplinary boundaries can soften and become receptive to questions, research methods and concepts that may conventionally sit outside a discipline. While I do not claim to have made any kind of interdisciplinary synthesis, I have brought many different theoretical viewpoints together to 'speak' to one another and, in doing so, have hopefully moved early childhood music education further along an interdisciplinary pathway.

One important aspect of working towards an interdisciplinary approach is to recognise the different levels of explanation. Neuroscientists work at microscopic levels of brain activity; sociologists work at the wide level of social structure. Scaling across these different levels on the explanatory ladder from micro through to macro levels and being able to apply multilevel explanations of practice can only lead to richer understanding. This also helps to make meaningful interconnections between theory and practice. Maria Wassrin (2016) provides a valuable example of research that weaves across three levels from microanalysis of actual musical interactions between children and Swedish pedagogues to a political-philosophical 'macro level'. She emphasises that at all three levels her analysis is practice-connected, not just at the micro level of musical interactions between children and pedagogies, and furthermore that all three levels are interconnected. Like Maria Wassrin, I do not advocate a simple reductionist approach, however, where the lowest level considers biological explanations (for instance, behaviour is explained in terms of genes and brain structures), a middle level considers psychological explanations, and the highest level considers social and cultural explanations framed in terms of the influence of social groupings. As Alan Prout suggests, we need to think in terms of 'complex systems' which 'contain different levels' and that 'reciprocal relations' take place between these different levels' (2005:94). I can very simply illustrate these levels and how they may be brought together by returning again to three-year-old Aya. How Aya is learning to pitch her voice to sing may be better understood with additional knowledge about the biology of the vocal mechanism and how it matures, and about the psychological processes of pitch perception gathered from precise experimental studies. But, at the same time, Aya comes from a family and wider social group where singing is practised in certain ways that may make a difference to *how* she sings, including how she uses her voice physically, as well as how she can access singing socially in her nursery. Aya's family migrated from Syria. Unfortunately, there are no studies of Syrian children that I can call upon to ponder how her early experiences of Syrian music might affect how she attunes to non-Syrian music, but I can refer to an example of babies from nearby Turkey who were found to have already become accustomed to the musical characteristics of Turkish music (Soley & Hannon, 2010). We might, then, wonder how Aya's early attunement to music in her native Syria would impact on her pitch perception and how she participates in singing conventional nursery songs. So, by combining and integrating diverse forms of understanding at different levels and plotting the relationships between them, we can arrive at a more complete picture. To adopt a multidisciplinary perspective is to understand what level of explanation a theoretical perspective is providing and what it can and cannot tell us. We can then consider how we might use different perspectives in combination in the search for a fuller understanding of the complexity that even this one small singing incident represents.

Having originated in the 1990s, the field of childhood studies is now weathering conflicts and controversies that have arisen more recently and there has been a move into what some have termed 'new wave' childhood studies (Ryan, 2011). A general view emerged that certain tenets of childhood studies had started to become stuck and unproductive, particularly some of its originating bedrock concepts (Tisdall & Punch, 2012; also Prout, 2011). The new wave is reviewing some of the earlier principles and giving impetus to new possible ways of understanding childhood. Within an overall aim to bring early childhood music education theory up to date, it might be thought contradictory to spend time explaining childhood studies in its earlier forms and relating them to music education. However, this chronological approach is necessary because the theoretical foundations need to be in place before I can explain the most contemporary modifications. But that discussion continues later; for now, in this final section, I need to provide some 'nuts and bolts' information about the chapters that follow.

About this book

The first thing to say is that this is intended to be an academic book, but I have tried to keep my explanations clear and to write in an accessible style, with illustrations and anecdotes, while also staying true to the main purpose of academic activity, which is to enhance knowledge by raising and delving into difficult and knotty issues. I talk mainly of 'education', but have asked myself often if this is the right term to use for this burgeoning range of activity in music designed for early childhood – or is it too narrow and does it carry too many ready-made and unhelpful assumptions? Many who align with community music, participatory arts practice or therapy with very young children consider that terms such as 'education' and 'teaching' impose limiting structures and assumptions on their work and would wish to shake off those limitations. I dodge the issue of naming this mixed area of practice by sometimes referring simply to early childhood music, to 'work in music' with children, or even just to 'provision'. But then, seemingly in complete contradiction with my aim of broadening the narrowness of the term 'education', I then refer mainly to 'educators'. There is a clear reason for doing this: to bestow upon the role the professionalism which it deserves but so rarely receives. I ask readers to recognise, however, that I intend the term 'educator' to denote a role that is also broad and loose enough to embrace many different types of work in music with young children.

I mostly refer to 'babies' rather than infants. Although infant is the academic term, and this is intended to be a book that takes theory seriously, the term 'infant' creates a distance and formality that I want to avoid. For the same reason, I refer to 'toddlers' as a useful shorthand, even though I am aware that some consider this to be a demeaning term for young children. I also, somewhat reluctantly, use the term 'Western' here and there to encapsulate the affluent developed countries of Western Europe, North America, Australasia and parts of Asia. There are so many problems with this term, but it is a quick, if rough-edged, catch-all, and the other terms that are sometimes adopted such as north/south or various shades of 'developing' are equally problematic for different reasons. Occasionally, the context allows me to talk of majority- or minority-world children, and this distinction I prefer.

Although I broadly describe the early childhood music education field as conservative, there is innovative research and literature to be found, but they are tucked away in conference proceedings, reports of projects or dissertations and theses. As a marginal topic, the occasional article may appear here and there in psychology of music, music education or early childhood education journals, but it needs persistence to dig out relevant work. The general broadening of interests around childhood and children's experiences that has taken place has given rise to some focused work on young children's musical lives and closely related fields such as new technologies, media and cultural studies. But this work, too, is dispersed. Another aim of this book, therefore, is to draw together examples of this disparate and scattered literature in order to introduce music educators to the range of academic activity that can inform practice. This book is not intended to provide a comprehensive review of research and literature; it is selective in the research it references, using studies to illustrate or expand ideas, sometimes referring to quite obscure sources in a deliberate attempt to model an approach to citing literature that does not simply reach for the usual sources. Therefore, the bibliography is deliberately wide-ranging. On the other hand, academic texts can be stuttering to read if every short statement is followed by a laundry list of references, so the references in the text itself are kept deliberately light, with most literature being tagged only once or twice and only the first author being named when there are several. Readers versed in the formal conventions of academic writing and referencing may wag a finger at this approach. However, in this way I hope I have networked the book into a wealth of very diverse literature, grounded the book theoretically and also correctly acknowledged the very valuable work of others on which I draw, and achieved all of this without clogging up the text.

I am also very mindful, as Alexandra Kertz-Welzel from Germany tells us, that English is the dominant language and that Anglo-American terminology and music education concepts tend to dominate (2016). There can be a tendency for English language sources, particularly those from North America, to be cited and then re-cited, causing them to rise to the surface while other equally important and informative, globally dispersed sources sink with little trace. In this way certain narratives get told and retold, and certain views and ideas start to solidify, contributing to the conservatism, inertia and narrow outlook that I have described. Citation also affects what is researched and discussed: pathways of research become more established, commitments to particular lines of thinking harden and the funding and support follows. Heeding

Alexandra Kertz-Welzel, it is very important to develop sensitivity towards the diversities of music education and research traditions. I have endeavoured to read and cite as much as possible from international sources. Much work is published in English, but there is also a wealth of very valuable work published in other languages and web-based translation tools now offer simple, if clumsy, translations that can serve well enough.

Childhood studies often includes a strong focus on the historical, explaining how children have been differently understood and viewed in times past in order to better understand key shifts in our perceptions of contemporary childhoods. While it would have been informative and fascinating to explore an extended historical perspective in relation to musical babyhoods and childhoods, I have no expertise in historical research and so, apart from some discussions where I trace the chronological sequence of an idea into the recent past, the book does not include a chapter specifically discussing a historical perspective. At several points in the book I make reference to the fact that the political and economic context is an important perspective to take into account. The 'macro' sociological context impinges on practice in many significant but maybe less obvious ways. However, again, I do not include a specific chapter on policy, economics and political perspectives, but bring these dimensions into play here and there.

Childhood studies also includes a strong focus on anthropological perspectives. This domain *is* within my expertise and interests and so I include a chapter written from this standpoint. Anthropology is concerned with expanding our understandings of children across 'space' and cultures, and the diversity of contemporary childhoods requires this. The sister discipline of ethnomusicology, which is essentially the anthropology of music, similarly expands our understandings of music and musical practice. I also use an anthropological stance to provide a critical edge at certain points through the book.

The examples of musical activity that ground the book and illustrate how theoretical viewpoints can be applied to real situations are all drawn from my own experiences here in the UK. I hope these examples have enough generality to be easily translatable to people and practice contexts in other countries. Inevitably, some of the issues I discuss may be framed by national characteristics of early childhood music education in England. I realise, of course, that the social, cultural and political contexts make a significant difference to policies on practice and how it is enacted, so the examples may need to be reframed in relation to other countries, their policies and systems.

All books have omissions. This book draws on children and childhoods as they are perceived and experienced in a number of societies located in the minority world, for this is where the early childhood music experience and practices that this book primarily addresses take place. I acknowledge the variation, the complexities and – most worrisome – the inequalities of childhoods lived across the world. However, drawing on childhoods more widely across parts of the majority world would have introduced enormous complexities around how these childhoods are conceived musically, experienced by children and understood by others, as these children live in different cultural contexts, with different histories and different economic and political backgrounds. Sometimes I make forays into wider world contexts, drawing in examples of musical childhoods, making comparisons and introducing theories that may have been generated by anthropologists. My aim in doing this is to expand horizons, and therefore these forays are highly selective, hopefully very respectful, and intended to be specific, not representative.

I am also aware that I do not include specific discussions about working with children who have diverse physical or mental abilities. Again, this is because I have had to make selections about what to include and exclude. It is not to imply that these aspects of childhood are not important. However, I take reassurance from Kay Tisdall's arguments that many of the prominent themes in childhood studies – the recognition of diversity, of children's voice and agency – are inclusive of all children and of benefit to children experiencing disabilities (2012).

The next chapter introduces childhood studies in more detail. Thereafter, the chapters each take different perspectives which broadly equate to biological, psychological, sociological and anthropological viewpoints. There are some key topics that I eventually placed in certain chapters – gender and technologies, for example – that did not belong definitely in any one chapter and sometimes migrated from chapter to chapter as I wrote this book. These topics help to loosen the theoretical narrowness of certain chapters and also fill out the middle ground between theories and real-world experience and application. By separating the theoretical perspectives I risk giving the impression that they are discrete and sharply delineated. This is not so. Theories overlap, merge, grow out of and into one another. However, I held in mind that this book aims to provide a working and up-to-date theoretical map for those who are wanting to increase their professionalism in early childhood music. Any map marks out the boundaries. Readers plot their own journeys.

Here are the main themes that thread through this book:

- *Contemporary early childhoods are changing and diversifying.*
- *Digital technologies and the commodification of music, coupled with changing parenting practices, are profoundly changing the nature of music and musical experience in early childhood.*
- *Babies and young children have the capacity to act and interact in shaping their musical childhoods.*
- *Babies and young children's participation in families, peer groups, with carers and educators, in communities and cultures constitutes their musical lives.*
- *An approach that brings together multiple theoretical perspectives can provide a multifaceted picture of young children's musical experiences and musical childhoods.*
- *Contemporary practice in early childhood music education should be responsive to the present and current developments in music, childhood and parenting culture.*

2 Shaky eggs and hello! songs
The view from childhood studies

Vignette

Picture a typical music session for three-year-olds with their parents. I write 'parents' but the parents are almost certain to be exclusively mothers. The young children and their mothers sit in a neat circle on brightly coloured floor cushions in a spacious hired hall. The session leader starts with a 'hello' song and then introduces children's songs, one after another, for all to join in. Typically, the songs are about little animals, hopping bunnies, frogs and ducks, associated with a pastoral lifestyle which is quite removed from the reality of most children's lives. The songs might also be associated with a retrospective, traditional childhood of currant buns, winding bobbins and riding on buses. There may be props, soft toys or puppets and light fabric scarves to swish, swirl and hide behind. There are small, highly safety-conscious instruments, probably one for each child to hold, such as shaky eggs and rhythm sticks. There may be surprise, a sense of wonder, combined with softness and happiness, conjuring up a certain image of these small children with their mothers.

We are so used to this early childhood image of playful innocence mediated through the various elements of the early childhood music session – the songs, activities, instruments and materials – and conveyed in the way the session is run and the parents and children are addressed that it may seem self-evident, uncontentious and difficult to imagine how it could be otherwise. Phil Jones writes that contemporary society creates a separate set of images to accompany children in their lives and that this is now so much a part of society that we assume it to be normal, whereas it is, in fact, a remarkably recent phenomenon (2009:77). Indeed, many might argue that we need to preserve this image, that children need to be nurtured in a warm environment, expressing an 'eternal' childhood that is set apart and protected, particularly in the face of the world at large, with all its risks and negative influences. Sharon Hays, describing contemporary motherhood, writes of 'sacred children, sacred mothering' in which children are seen as precious (1996). But the image of the close-to-nature, happy, playing, vulnerable child is a dominant image created by adult attitudes, ideas and values of childhood, here and now, not a truth about how children intrinsically are. From a sociology of childhood perspective, the varying images of childhood are described as social constructions, that is, how, in a particular time and place, childhood is represented and understood. Erica Burman writes of a traditional, romantic, European model of childhood innocence, the natural and pure child that is in need of our protection and 'swathed in the golden light of nostalgia' (2017). This discourse of children as close to nature, wrapped in nostalgic romanticism, has a long history in European thought, largely attributed to Rousseau and his philosophy of the natural child (see Hendrick, 1997; Taylor, 2013).

It is easier to recognise how childhoods further removed from us in time and place are socially constructed, but much less easy to see the same process at work close to home (Jenks, 2005). It is obvious that a childhood lived over 150 years ago is quite different from the present day, not just in material and technological aspects, but in the way that children were viewed and 'seen'. Victorian children in England were subject to strict authoritarian parenting and rigid schooling. Some young children had to work in gruelling conditions in the industries – indeed, as they still must do in some countries. Travelling the world, it is not unusual in countries where poverty is rife to see even quite young children involved in earning money for the family by selling. My own travels have included seeing children selling toothpicks at an Addis Ababa bus station, dodging traffic to sell snacks at the lights in Havana or selling their music by busking in streets. In many traditional societies children are 'useful' in contributing to the work and income of the family. Travelling in South America, I watched two very small Guatemalan twin boys, perhaps only three- or four-years-old, dressed in traditional Guatemalan outfits, playing chinchines (Guatemalan maracas) as they busked in the street with their marimba-playing father to earn money from tourists. I would guess that their father had selected traditional melodies that would catch the tourists' ears, adapted to provide a musical role for his small children. No doubt the presence of small twins in 'cute' matching Guatemalan dress was part of a deliberate appeal to the mainly North American and European tourists. The twin boys were certainly attracting attention, photos and smiles. Let's imagine their British counterparts, given shaky eggs to play in a music session, keeping the beat to a recording of traditional Guatemalan music, but within a very different framing of the activity, as play rather than work, as artificial activity rather than embedded in real life, enrichment rather than necessity, useless rather than useful. I expect that poverty had required the Guatemalan family to seek a means of making money, moving perhaps from the rural regions to a city popular with tourists. Affluence enables the British mother to seek out the private class to provide a musically similar activity for a very different purpose.

By contrast, where children are in nursery or school and are an economic cost to the parents, rather than an economic asset, their child 'work' and contribution to family livelihood becomes negligible (Rogoff, 2003). It is in this context that childhood is given a special, distinctive status that some have described as 'sentimental idealization' (LeVine & White, 1986). The key shift in socio-economic cultural contexts is from an emphasis on the value and usefulness of the child for the needs of the family to her value in and of herself and to the needs of the child, a frankly 'useless' child (Zelizer, 1985). The Guatemalan twins' performing contributes to the family income, whereas the musical activity of their British counterparts depletes the family income because attending the music session costs money. The change is from a parent-family-centred outlook to a child-centred outlook. The developments from the useful to useless child gradually led to fewer children receiving greater attention over a longer period of their lives than had been – or is – typical in traditional agricultural societies, or even the earlier industrial societies of England. The term 'high-investment parenting' has been coined to describe recent parenting practices in the affluent middle class, where parents pour time, finances and energy into 'project children' (Maxted, 2014). Private music classes are typically purchased by 'high-investment' parents and marketed to appeal to their expectations and desires.

So it is adults who construct a musical image of early childhood according to the prevailing ways that childhood is organised in the wider culture. Musical activities provided in early childhood sessions, whether private or school/nursery-based, have a particular aesthetic, a distinctive style that is typically happy, animated, cute and affectionate. The act of selecting songs, providing resources and modelling actions may seem neutral and uncomplicated, yet ideologies of both music and childhood are deeply present within them and in how adults behave with children in relation to them. Many parents and those who work with young children identify closely with the discourse of the romantic, natural, pure child and may defend it staunchly. Indeed, mothers and early childhood educators are also 'performing' these discourses, actively participating in the session and reinforcing them by taking on a socially defined, publicly visible role. Taru Leppänen (2011), analysing mother and baby music classes in Finland, uses feminist theory to explore the way that motherhood, socially conceived, becomes embodied in the performance of the class and mediated sonically through the songs and activities (also Faircloth, 2010; Ennis, 2015:1–2). The adults are typically expected to come down to the child's level, to join in, to sing, to play the instruments, to perform the actions – a role, incidentally, that many outside the white, Western middle classes find odd and uncomfortable, as we will see later when I introduce a group of Somali-born mothers (Young, 2017b). The characteristics of childhood are seen as needing to be preserved, protected and carefully nurtured through the type of work that is offered (Moss, 2014). For this reason, it can be difficult to challenge this image of childhood and to point out how it positions very young children, stereotypes them, sentimentalises and infantilises them in ways that are to their disadvantage. As I alluded to in the first chapter, an obstacle to the analysis of early childhood music can be this tendency towards emotion-wrapped, romantic idealisation.

By open-mindedly recognising and analysing the ways in which (musical) babyhoods and early childhoods are socially constructed through discourse, through routine everyday interactions, through portrayals of children in the media, through a marketised model of childhood in consumer goods such as toys and children's music, including little children working as buskers, our view of children can broaden out. This makes room for difference. The Guatemalan twins, shaking their chinchines, balancing outsize straw hats on their heads and smiling shyly for photographs can be included in conceptions of musical childhoods. We can recognise young children as interconnected to the worlds of which they form a part, shaped by economic circumstances and social, cultural environments. Equally, a view of musical childhoods as socially constructed can highlight how young children are narrowly pigeonholed into developmental milestones or steps of progression, how they can be viewed as unformed, 'not yet', as incapable and lacking, or objectified as 'cute', expected to pose and be photographed.

In Westernised societies childhood has evolved with clear demarcations, unlike other societies. There is a clear separation between children's worlds and adult worlds and even between older and younger children. Babies and the very young are kept apart in special spaces and times, and these are made safe (locked up even, 'baby prisons' as someone once quipped to me) and suitable for young children, with special-sized furniture, plastic surfaces, padded corners, play areas and so on. Babies and little children peer out at the world at large from their buggies or car seats. Similarly, we create spaces for music sessions, as in the example of the typical session in the opening vignette. As a result, very separated, 'childish' ways in which young children engage with music and distinct forms of children's music and musical experiences have emerged. Children's music is created and sold, and increasingly performed in special children's concerts. The provision of concerts, theatre pieces with music for early-years children and even opera for babies is a fairly recent phenomenon and reflects contemporary images of early childhood and perceptions of middle-class parenting practices. These musical events take place in arts centres and concert halls, converted into designated child-friendly musical spaces, often bubble-like, protective, softly cushioned – cocoons within the larger spaces (Fletcher-Watson, *et al.*, 2014; Young & Powers, 2009).

There are separate children's musical products, lots of them, including toys, recorded music for young children and children's musical media, created in a commodified image of children's music. I would include the private, purchasable music session with this commodity market of early childhood music. This image is created to be a purchasable product and so certain characteristics are exaggerated and others are either removed or narrowly defined. The commodified version is designed to stimulate adult desires in order to create a market and increase profits. Children are positioned in a marketised, commodified musical world that strongly determines how they can be musical, pushing them into a particular mould. Some see the consumerist musical childhood as harmful and corrupting and consider that children should be shielded from it and only be exposed to 'proper, good' music, typically traditional children's rhymes or classical music (e.g. Palmer, 2016). Many of those who argue for a unique, creative, natural childhood would align with this group (Gray, 2013). Commodity items are not harmful per se – for it is always how things are used, within specific situations, that matters – but the distortion of characteristics for commercial purposes, and why, is what needs to be analysed.

In many Western societies, as a general rule, very small children are not playing or sharing in adult worlds of music-making. Young children's characteristics and requirements are thought to conflict with adult entitlements to child-free spaces. Little children are seen as disturbing, noisy and messy. As I was working on this book I read in some newspaper articles conflicting opinions about adults taking young children to pop and folk festivals, some regarding them as suitably child-friendly spaces, while others were strongly critical. The surprising vehemence with which some journalists complained about the presence of children at music festivals is indicative of the acceptance in our society that young children, particularly babies, are to be barely tolerated in, or even excluded from, public adult-only spaces. There are of course families where adults make live music at home and very young children are able to participate in their own way, and certainly I would say that, without exception, recorded music plays some part in family life. The family home is the primary environment for musical engagement and participation, but in the wider community the division between the music worlds of children and adults is sharply drawn. We will see in later chapters how this separation is in contrast to many societies where children are hanging around the edges of adults' and older children's music-making activities, watching, listening in, imitating, being allowed to sit close by as they rehearse or perform, or being given real jobs to do such as playing chinchines during busking.

So the ways in which early musical childhoods are constructed reflects the specific social, cultural, economic and political societies in which we live. According to this view, there is no absolute, fixed and unchanging childhood, it is always socially and culturally determined (Jenks, 2005). As I will go on to explain later in this chapter, the social constructionist view went too far the other way in arguing that what childhood *is* cannot be pinned down. But first I want to dwell on the social constructionist view, namely, that the things we think we know about childhood are not self-evident truths and neutral facts but always the result of human meaning-making. For example, a model of musical development is not a 'truth' about young children's musical abilities, but a particular way of seeing and understanding their musical activity that has grown out of a particular worldview, or paradigm. The psychology of musical development, or other aspects of development for that matter, does not reflect the musical nature of young children; it is a constructed version, a narrative, a story. These constructed truths and facts about children then become embedded as a set of hidden rules and expectations that define what is considered to be normal or abnormal, or even right or wrong. Expectations of children's musical development then become a kind of artificial reality that is applied to children not only to describe what they might do, as a template for possible actions, but then flips over to become a prescription for what they *ought* to do. From a critical-theory perspective, constructions of childhood and the discourses that maintain them are not a neutral or abstract way of describing, but also convey messages about whose version of reality is accepted as the norm and who gets to decide (MacNaughton, 2005). Therefore, the social constructionist view of childhood pays a lot of attention to norms, values and power relations, all of which are involved not only in the process of constructing normative versions of childhood but also in the process of holding them firmly in place (Thomas, 2004).

In a very real sense, then, children themselves and childhoods are formed and constituted through these forms of discourse. These discourses operate in the common-sense world and are discernible in the ways in which children are represented in everyday talk. So it is important to recognise how they operate if we are to make changes. Viewing musical childhoods from this position – as constructed through forms of discourse – allows us to 'read' the representations and images of young children as musical and the musical experiences shaped for them from a critical viewpoint. We can read the early childhood music session, or musical items, musical performances and so on, as places for the construction of a certain type of musical childhood. It can open up new understandings of the historically shifting, sociocultural way that music in early childhood, in general, operates within society. It is certainly not my aim to critique practitioners or to disparage in any way, far from it, but to assist in the process of understanding the discourses within which we all work and the constraints therein (Young, et al., 2007). Why do we view small children as innocent, vulnerable and in need of protection? Why is there anxiety to preserve the innocence of childhood? What is happening within society at large and within families to make the music session, the purchasable music items, the performances for small children, all these musical provisions we make and the ways we talk, describe act and perform musically with very young children become what they are? And does this advantage or disadvantage children, all or some children, and differently according to class, race, gender and age? As we will see, one of the current prevailing and powerful stories of childhood is that the young child is understood to be malleable, able to be developed and improved and that the 'good parent', or more accurately the good mother, has a responsibility to present the right opportunities and correct forms of support to mould the child. Children thus become a project, to be parented, to be formed, to become rather than just to 'be' (Jones, 2015:48).

With babies and toddlers there is the additional dimension of their very young age, which we need to factor into our understanding of how early childhood is socially constructed. 'Ageism' is a sociological concept that has been adopted in relation to old age, but it can also be applied to very small children to highlight the stereotyping that can lead to forms of prejudice. Alan Prout (2005:10) explains how children have been constituted as the 'cultural other' of adulthood. He presents a framework of meaning that includes opposites that position children as 'other' in relation to adults and lists a set of opposites that includes private/public, nature/culture, irrational/rational, dependent/independent, passive/active, incompetent/competent and play/work. If babies, toddlers and very young children are positioned as just at the very beginning of their pathway towards becoming adults, and this progressive, developmental view of children is deeply embedded in our cultural view of them, then they are the furthest away from adulthood, the least adult and, as a result, all the other oppositions in Prout's list are also calibrated to a maximum. So the youngest children are conceived as the closest to nature, most dependent, most incompetent, most closely associated with play and so on. Babies and the very youngest children are positioned as so 'other' in relation to adults that they can be set apart, marginalised, almost forgotten about, tucked away in private places, looked after by women. I should add, at this point, that this positioning of the youngest children is particularly pronounced in the UK, and that in some other countries the very youngest are treated with more awareness of their rights and entitlements. The point made by Alan Prout, which I take up in this book, is that unless we unsettle these oppositional ways of thinking about children we cannot respond adequately to the contemporary changes that children are experiencing (2005). Unless we recognise how the youngest children are not only positioned as 'other' in relation to adults but also as the 'least' adult in so many ways, the status quo is maintained. We need to move beyond these oppositional conceptions, challenge developmentalism, challenge the constructions of very young children, recognise our own attachments to them and find a conceptual toolkit that can create alternatives (Taylor, 2013). A tall order indeed.

A new paradigm

In the opening chapter I briefly introduced the 'new' sociology of childhood, that important paradigm shift in how children were viewed and understood. As well as explaining how childhood is socially constructed, the change in perspective also called for the recognition of children's agency and their independent rights (James & Prout, 1990). The fields of education, social work and psychology had long been interested in children, but up to that point sociology (and anthropology, for that matter) had paid little attention to children, and certainly not the very youngest (James, *et al.*, 1998). This new paradigm challenged a previously dominant view of childhood that had understood children as incomplete or 'becomings', moving along a pathway towards adulthood, in effect 'adults in training'. They argued that a view of children as 'becoming' places the focus of attention on the endpoints of development and socialisation in adulthood, so that children are seen merely as passive receivers. From this perspective, parents and teachers hand on knowledge, skills and cultural understanding, which the child is expected to internalise and learn. In many traditional accounts of how children learn in music, this view of a one-way, handing-on process of musical acculturation is strongly present. The alternative is to view children as having musical agency, that is, musical aptitudes, proclivities, creativities and competences that they apply and use in their own ways. The children as 'becomings' concept of socialisation paralleled a very similar paradigm in developmental psychology, where children were seen as moving along a linear pathway to becoming adult musicians. These concepts of development and socialisation look solely to the future life of children and thus neglect the importance of their present actions. The consequence, according to Leena Alanen, one of the leading initiators of this changed view of childhood, is that 'the child is negatively defined': not by what 'the child is [in the present], but instead by what she is not, and by what she is subsequently going to be' (Alanen, 1992:81). Another consequence is that the notion of 'becoming' puts the attention and interest onto those who 'do' the becoming; teachers, parents, the media, even politicians and corporations, and not with the children themselves. The 'becoming' perspective, argued Leena Alanen, is therefore biased towards the viewpoints of adults. By contrast, the new sociology of childhood argued that children should be seen as 'beings' in their own right, with an emphasis on their everyday, active, lived experience and what it means for them. The constructions of children as developing and being socialised by adults tend to silence children in the present, as members of society here and now, with views, preferences, ideas and creativities of their own.

As I explained earlier, the 'new paradigm' (Prout & James, 1990) underpinned an evolving interdisciplinary area that came to be known as childhood studies. Childhood studies as a field positioned itself against previous dominant modes in developmental psychology and sociology, and adopted certain key principles of theory, namely, in short, the social construction of childhood, and children and young people as active and as agents (Wells, 2018). A strong stance was necessary in the early days since, as emphasised earlier, developmental psychology occupied such a dominant position with regard to empirical and theoretical accounts of early childhood; and this is certainly true of music in early childhood, where developmental accounts continue to occupy a strong position. Childhood studies prompted wide-ranging research that sought to understand the challenges for contemporary children of growing up in societies where there are changes in the social structure, the economy and in technologies and where patterns of consumption and media are impacting on children's lives in ways we have not encountered before. For this purpose, childhood studies gathered into its fold many disciplinary perspectives, many windows, in order to build up a more complete picture of childhood and, importantly, attempted to create windows that allowed children to reveal their own experiences, on their terms.

However, in very recent years some of the limitations of the original theoretical positions became increasingly apparent. This is not to deny the value and potency of the original positions, and certainly in this book they provide theoretical perspectives that help me to dislodge certain well-entrenched theoretical traditions and ideas within early childhood music education, but there is always a need to revise and debate. More recently, a 'new wave' in childhood studies has emerged which is less trenchant and seeks to reconcile some of what are now seen to be over-strong and unhelpfully oppositional positions presented in the earlier sociology of childhood writings. Later in the chapter I will return to explain the 'new wave' but first I want to pick up the theme of children's agency – children as 'being' – that represents the important theoretical shift introduced by childhood studies.

Children's own experiences and agency

Researchers inspired by the new theoretical perspectives arising from childhood studies wanted to access the meaning and experience of childhood from children's own perspective, through their eyes in other words, rather than through the eyes of the adults around them such as parents and teachers. This initiated an important and very valuable swathe of research that placed children as central and saw them as social actors in their own right. The new perspective on childhood also allowed researchers to demonstrate the many ways in which children are competent and able to exercise agency, that is, their ability to act with intent and awareness. This opened a whole new window on the everyday and ordinary lived experiences of children and has made a major contribution in reframing how we understand childhood. It is this focus on children as they are, in the here and now, rather than how their childhood experiences might influence and shape the adults they may become in the future, that distinguishes the sociology of childhood from other disciplines, particularly developmental psychology.

We can see the impact of this in early childhood music, both in practice – it influenced approaches to practice in which children were given a more independent role in activities that sought to be child-initiated and child-centred – and in research. This shift in the approach to research also called for the adoption of new ways of studying young children and their music that would enable researchers to gain a more child-centred understanding of children and their music-making (Young, 2003a). With very young children, enabling them to be active participants in research has required some inventive and innovative approaches (Clark, 2005). New technologies, particularly lightweight portable video-recording equipment and also video and photographic equipment that children can use themselves, have facilitated participatory research. Collecting examples of children's self-initiated music-play in nursery settings for my research in 1990 involved operating a large, cumbersome video camera and working laboriously through VHS tapes. It is worth remembering that digital recording devices have revolutionised the study of children's own musical activities in everyday, naturalistic situations and this revolution has been very recent. These methods of data collection are providing us with new means by which we can gain insights into young children's music. Bronya Dean equipped children with tiny personal recording devices to capture their singing in sequestered moments of their home life, from which she was able to arrive at a conception of how very young children actively and purposefully use singing to manage their everyday lives (2017). Some creative arts projects involving young children have shown the way in exploring participatory approaches to evaluation where children take photos, video clips and report their experiences using emojis and drawings. Children's musical activity in spontaneous, naturalistic situations can be easily video recorded and then reviewed, with enlightened researchers engaging even quite young children in the recording and reviewing process (Arculus, 2013; Whiteman & Campbell, 2012). The earliest stages of childhood, particularly babyhood, present the most challenges in terms of giving babies an active role in research. But even at this age, there are suggestions as to how the facial expressions, gestures and vocalisations of babies might be interpreted.

However, babies and toddlers have received much less attention in the field of childhood studies than have older children. Their absence is in stark contrast to psychology, where there are volumes of work on infancy. Why? Some have criticised childhood studies for being fixated on confirming that children are competent social actors, not merely passive, and that this has skewed research towards older children. The younger the child, the more dependent they are on others and the less agency and autonomy they are assumed to have. But this assumption of course depends on how agency is conceptualised. Babies are implicitly thought to be passive, which has closed down the possibility of thinking that babies are social beings, that they have culture and could be of interest to childhood studies researchers (cf. Toren, 2004). So the question of agency in relation to babies, and toddlers too, becomes complicated. Do we consider babies to have some agency, albeit limited, or different forms of agency? As everyone who has cared for or worked with babies knows, they are far from passive, but exert agency in ways that only they know best. But at the same time their actions are highly constrained by their lack of physical skills and strength, their small size and their limitations of language and cognitive skills.

Part of the challenge of babies and very young children, of caring for them, playing with them and working musically with them, is understanding how they express their agency and deciding how to interpret it and act upon it. One example of a research study that has explored a notion of babies' own musical culture, thus according them a form of musical agency, is Aruna Correa's study of babies' musicality in Brazil (2013), which draws on a collective body of work around music with babies initiated by Esther Beyer in the 1990s (Pecker, 2014). Babies in the Western world are typically treated as if they are making choices and have preferences from a very early age. Thus, agency in certain culturally defined forms is conceived and attributed by the adults around them. Looking across to other cultures, mothers attribute passivity or agency to their babies in quite different ways. Beng babies in Côte d'Ivoire, for example, are thought to arrive in this world able to understand all languages from the afterlife whence they have come. Mothers talk to them with the assumption that they have full comprehension and engage them constantly in conversation (Gottlieb, 2004). From psychological directions there is a swathe of research that has explored Western babies' modes of communication and provides ample illustration of babies exerting certain forms of agency, but this seems to connect poorly with sociological understandings and suffers from the usual problem with research in psychology in that it pays little attention to social and cultural situations.

Surprisingly little research has been carried out on babies where they actually live and spend their time – at home or in childcare settings with those who care for them – in order to build a picture of the social and cultural musical lives of babies and toddlers. I will come to musical experiences at home later in this book with a view to redressing this balance.

Children's music

Influenced by these shifts in how children are seen and understood, as active and autonomous, there has been a notable rise in the number of studies that look at self-initiated music-making and musical cultures among children who are a little older, usually in some kind of preschool setting, but increasingly, also, in everyday environments of home and community. Until the last ten to fifteen years, research into musical experiences in early childhood, – what little there was of it – had mainly focused on the responses of children in music tests or on adult-led educational experiences within formal settings; there was very little that enquired into the musical play of children when left to their own devices. As a result of this shift in focus, we are gathering much more understanding of how music is part of the expressive and meaning-making activities that are an integral part of children's lives.

Interesting accounts, discoveries and information from research studies exploring children's own musical worlds are accumulating, little by little. Researchers are telling us about children's musically imaginative worlds: their musical solitudes in cots falling asleep and in bedrooms playing alone; their musical relationships with family and peers through songs, singing games and recorded music; their interactions with video games, digital media and consumption of popular culture such as children's CDs, TV shows, videos. We hear about their musical play in free-play areas, at the sand-tray, at breaktimes, mealtimes and when lining up, in cars, supermarkets and trains. We think about their everyday musical play in relation to the larger-scale structures of their lives such as migration (e.g. Marsh, 2008), changing family patterns and institutional structures (e.g. Zur, 2018). This work, more than any other, is demonstrating how the nature of music and musical experience for young children is changing profoundly in relation to the wider social, cultural and technological changes around them. It reinforces the rationale for this book, namely, that music education certainly cannot proceed without positioning itself within these developments and taking account of the richness and variety of children's everyday musical lives.

Here I select a handful of early childhood music education studies that have explicitly adopted a sociology of childhood perspective. Working within the Scandinavian tradition of childhood studies, in which conceptions of childhood at a structural level are an important theoretical focus, both Maria Wassrin and Ingeborg Vestad contribute informative studies. Both reference Nordic language academic texts, thus providing valuable access points into Scandinavian theoretical thinking. Ingeborg Vestad in Norway studied three- to six-year-olds' everyday uses of recorded music such as CDs and .mp files (2010). She states that her intention was to study children 'in their own right', as subjects rather than the 'objects' of her study, to understand their musical 'being' and not 'becoming', and to explore the tensions between competency and vulnerability (2014:259–260). Thus we see how her work complies with the key tenets of childhood studies I outlined earlier. She identifies images of musical childhoods from everyday discourse, which she terms 'only the talented can' and 'everybody is musical', explaining how these create contradictory images of musical childhood. She explains that while young children are acknowledged as having a 'natural capacity' for music in the first years of their lives and that they should have the opportunity to express and engage in music, this form of musical expression and engagement is still given less value than 'being talented' for music, talent being equated with formal performance skills (2014:267). Thus, musically, the young child is placed in a contradictory no-win situation.

Maria Wassrin explored the conceptions of children as musical held by four music educators in a Swedish preschool (2016:109). In the process of analysing her conversations with the music educators she was deliberately looking for discourses of the 'socially constructed child' and arrived at 'four interpretive repertoires': the muse-ical child, the constantly learning child, the child uninscribed in culture and the child in need of support (2016:129). She then carefully plots how these conceptions of the child translate into certain conceptions of music practice that shape the children as musical; they become, as she describes it, 'performed theories' embodying children's needs, learning and development. In my opening vignette and paragraphs I sought to illustrate the implicit performed theory that lies behind the way an early childhood music session is presented.

The next two studies draw on the work of the US sociologist William Corsaro whose theorising, with its specific focus on children in nurseries, has been particularly informative for early childhood music education. Because his work sits a little outside the main directions of UK and Scandinavian sociology of childhood, I need first to give a brief introduction to his work.

Interpretive reproduction

William Corsaro was curious to understand young children's social lives in nursery settings (1997). In keeping with European sociology of childhood, he positioned children as subjects, the actors in their own social worlds. By contrast, his work is less concerned with understanding childhood at the structural level and how childhood is constructed through discourse. He carried out ethnographies of peer interaction among four-year-olds in preschools in Italy and the US in the mid 1970s and 80s and has continued this interest in the social lives of children throughout his career. By simply spending time sitting on the nursery floor, watching and listening, interacting at times, he was able to observe how children actively create their own cultural worlds in communication with their peers. He demonstrated how child culture differs from adult culture, but, at the same time, is not autonomous and separate. It is not a special, unique children's world set apart from the adult world, as others have suggested or, indeed, as adults often frame it. Nor is it simply a reproduction of adult culture that children are internalising, as conventional sociological theory would have it. Instead, William Corsaro demonstrated that children are appropriating and reworking cultural elements (obviously including musical elements) that they draw from all kinds of sources. Children poach from everything and anything around them, from cultural media designed *for* children, from adult culture, from educational materials, and weave them into their own cultures (Corsaro, 1997:18). They actively rework what they take and in this process transform it – a process that he termed 'interpretive reproduction' (Corsaro, 1992).

Kelly Werle, working in Brazil, adopted Corsaro's theory of interpretive reproduction to explore how music plays a part in children's peer cultures in early childhood settings (Werle & Bellochio, 2014). She explored how music that four- to five-year-old children had taken from media sources is incorporated into their role play and describes how, through creative appropriation of media songs, new meanings are given to the songs and they are transformed. She discovered that the process might start with one child and then other children are drawn into the musical play, a sociable process that Corsaro had also noticed and describes in relation to role play. Thus, she emphasises the collective process of musical play and stresses the importance of studying it as a socio-musical process between and among the children.

In the context of Australian preschool centres, Amanda Niland has also been interested in the collective processes by which songs are caught and shared among young children (2009, 2012). In contrast to Kelly Werle, she introduced songs that she had specially composed in response to consultations with the children and these songs became integrated into children's existing musical cultures. She suggested that Corsaro's theoretical approach provides a way of interpreting the social interactions that are central to young children's singing. Through playful singing together, young children are exploring their world and constructing their childhood peer cultures. She tracked the 'life cycles' of six original songs that she introduced to the children and revealed how the children developed relationships with the songs through interaction with influential adults and peers within the environment of the early childhood setting. She described the evolving musical cultures as featuring aspects of the immediate musical culture of children and staff at the centre, expanding to incorporate the musical cultures from family, community and media. Central to Amanda Niland's arguments is the core idea that children need to play with songs and make them their own, rather than simply sing ready-made songs in formal, adult-guided moments. She thus connects strongly with notions of agency and autonomy that are central to childhood studies.

It is interesting to notice that both these last two studies focused on song. The prevalence of songs in contemporary children's lives, the easiness with which children can engage in vocal play and blend it seamlessly into their sociable play, combined with the fact that the adult researchers can presumably identify song sources more readily than movement or music created with sound-makers, are reasons why songs would be the obvious musical medium for their 'music as social action' studies. Those studies that we will meet in the next chapter that were looking for developmental and cognitive markers tended to focus on instrumental play, perhaps because instrumental play is less fleeting and elusive, can be pinned down and is structured, materially, by the instrument itself. This play tends to be individualised and can be recorded and analysed more readily. So children's agentic, sociable, cultural worlds of 'being' may be singing worlds, almost certainly with movements and dance incorporated, particularly within their peer cultures, or are at least easier to discover and identify through singing than through other musical media.

This quartet of studies also neatly illustrates the divide between research and theorising that focus on the children themselves, their direct musical experience and interactions (micro-sociological, actor-based research), and research that focuses on the ideas of childhood (more structural, macro-sociological) and the social production of childhood by an adult-dominated society. There can be a divide between children in real-life action and childhood as a social structure. How the different dimensions or levels relate to one another is not entirely straightforward and represents one of the challenges in studying children and childhood from an interdisciplinary perspective. Maria Wassrin's work, which I introduced earlier, provides one helpful model of how to bring together theoretical ideas from different levels and disciplinary perspectives and find conceptual relationships between them (2016). She relates democratic values at the philosophical and political level, which give rise to concepts of children as citizens of equal status, to equivalent democratic processes in practice between children and their music educators.

'New wave' childhood studies

In its early days the sociology of childhood staked out its ground firmly in opposition to what had gone before, rejecting biological and psychological perspectives on childhood. Whereas this rejection might have been necessary to allow a new view of childhood to emerge, this position became entrenched and too limiting (see Ryan, 2011). Variability explained by social constructionism has an inbuilt flaw for at its crux it is based on the idea that culture begets culture, relying heavily on language, and that there is no material or physiological basis. Clearly, many features of childhood are rooted in the realities of children's bodies and in the realities of the material/technological world in which they are embedded, and cannot be otherwise. The biological and psychological natures of babies and young children are undeniable, even though their individual abilities vary and their experiences are socially and culturally shaped. Babies and very small children have physical needs that are paramount if they are even to survive in the first place and their bodies are growing, maturing and changing rapidly through the years from birth to five. The physicality of young children, the material existence of their bodies, impacts profoundly on how we understand early childhood.

So, more recent thinking in childhood studies has criticised the hard-line social constructionist view adopted by early-day sociology of childhood for overdoing the extent to which childhood was presented as context-dependent and socially constructed through discourse, by language and by the power structures inherent in a society. Childhood studies has moved into a new phase, trying to escape the limitations and rigid divisions that it created through its earlier activity.

In her discussion of childhood studies as an interdisciplinary field, Barrie Thorne spells out the dilemma (2007). The main question is whether the two 'camps' of thinking can converge: whether the sociological and anthropological approaches that make up childhood studies can meet and integrate with the biologically based psychological and most recently neuroscientific and genetic studies of children? This is a vexed question, Thorne explains, that has resulted in many different responses. The divide between social science arguments and the biological/psychological has a long history and is, in essence, the long-standing nature vs nurture or environmental influence vs genetic inheritance dichotomy in a new guise.

One thing is certain: the 'grand narratives', the sweeping theories from sociology and psychology that attempted to offer explanations that can encompass all children and were supposedly universal, have now been abandoned, shot down on many sides by critical arrows from feminists, critical theorists, post-colonialists and more recently by posthumanist and new materialist ideas (Murris, 2016). In their place, however, is something of a theoretical tangle. Within this tangle, there are some commonalities that help us to navigate a way through. Common to all these approaches is a determination not to replace the grand theories with new 'one size fits all', inflexible, determinist theories. In their attempt to shift concepts weighted down with unhelpful, backward-looking connotations, these new directions are looking for conceptual ideas that can lever in new thinking, often turning to philosophy to find these new conceptual languages. These new theoretical directions endeavour to remain fluid and flexible, open to transformation and responsive to what is new and maybe unexpected. And there is a new-found energy and sense of renewal and creativity in this theoretical landscape that I hope will infiltrate into early childhood music education theorising.

At the risk of over-simplifying but to signpost routes, there are two main directions emerging. One uncovers and reveals oppositional thinking – the opposites such as nature/culture, being/becoming, subject/object, child/adult – and then looks for alternative approaches to oppositional thinking in philosophical ideas around blending and integrating. The new sociology of childhood had adopted a critical-theory perspective in looking for the neglected, for the marginalised opposite, and so it had drawn attention to child in contrast to adult, to being in contrast to becoming, to passive in contrast to active and so on. New thinking seeks to avoid pitting contrasts one against another. Nick

Lee (2001), for example, argues that children and adults are both 'being' *and* 'becoming', that it is illogical to position adults as only 'being' and children as only 'becoming' for they are clearly both (also, Uprichard, 2008). What is oppositional may alternatively be seen as complementary or relational. Thus, to apply this thinking to childhood, the child is not seen as a separate entity, positioned separately in contrast to adults, or viewed as belonging to the soft, pure world of nature and not the hard world of technology for example, but intrinsically linked and interdependent with other people and also with things, in certain spaces, places and times.

The other direction looks for interconnecting themes between disciplines that will enable interdisciplinary or multidisciplinary thinking rather than separation and differentiation between the disciplines (Alanen, 2012; Punch, 2016). Staunch sociological positions have been relaxed and theorists have been re-emphasising aspects that were hitherto neglected, such as bringing biological, psychological approaches back into theoretical play, by finding themes that can connect them or by adopting new philosophical and theoretical approaches that emphasise forms of theoretical multiplicity such as networks. New forms of engagement with the biological, with bodies and with things, material and technological, and also, importantly, the development of self and subjectivity, are emerging that offer valuable directions for future work, theorising and thinking around young children (e.g. Taylor, 2013; Murris, 2016). These very different ways of engaging with the biological, social, psychological and material are emerging from early childhood studies that offer fruitful ways of thinking in new and innovative ways about young children and music. We have yet to see where they lead, but they are full of promise.

Both Alan Prout and Nick Lee, like others currently interested specifically in early childhood, turn to the philosophies of Deleuze and Guattari (1987/2004) to find thinking tools that help them to overcome oppositional thinking and to conceptualise multiple and ever-shifting viewpoints. Deleuze and Guattari's ideas are currently filtering through to become influential in general early childhood educational thinking (e.g. Olsson, 2009; Jones & Duncan, 2013; Taylor, 2013), although not yet in early childhood music education thinking (Osgood, *et al.*, 2013 is the one example I know of). A key idea of Deleuze and Guattari's thinking is 'assemblages'. An assemblage brings together very different elements – human, animal, material – that combine to create a kind of stability that may last for a while, but may then morph into something different. There are no fixed ways in which different elements may combine but many incomplete combinations that are continually open to change. In early childhood the idea of 'assemblages' is fruitful in looking at ways in which very young children may play with material items, with one another, in certain spaces, and then transform and transition into new play scenarios (e.g. MacRae, 2017).

Let us imagine a musical 'assemblage'. A child may pick up a small drum, beat on it with one hand, turn to a friend and hold it while she drums on it, run into an outdoor space and jump up and down with the drum, vocalising and moving freely. The musical assemblage is conceptualised as a web of relationships between musical sounds, the children, their bodies and movements, material instruments, the type of space, the location, and the weaving relationships between all these elements. It also expands to the practices and ways of making music, representations and discourses in that particular time and place. So the concept of assemblages is not merely at the immediate level of action, but can expand into wider dimensions. The capacity of assemblages to capture change, transitions, contexts, connections and interactions makes it a flexible concept for early childhood music research and theory. Its value lies in avoiding the limitations of narrower conceptions and in its ability to embrace so many dimensions from human to material, from sonic to affective, to immediate action, to discourse, and keep them all in play. Its value too is in placing children at the centre, in attempting to understand from their perspective. For music, in which the playing body and the sound-maker (whether internal voice or external instrument) are so intrinsically bound together, reciprocally shaping one another, the idea of assemblages is particularly fruitful in avoiding the more disjointed conceptions of the child's cognitive structures in relation to sound patterns that we will come across in the next chapter. All I would add is that its weakness may be that, beyond providing a means to capture, reveal and describe certain play scenarios that are elusive to other theoretical and analytical lenses, particularly among very young, preverbal children, it is difficult to know what further insightful theoretical understandings and practical implications emerge from the descriptions.

Thus, what is being called the 'material' turn is offering some scholars valuable theoretical tools with which to explore the experiences of young children and their play in the world of objects and surfaces that can assist in the process of reconfiguring young childhoods and provide theories that take much more account of the bodily, material and affective/emotional dimensions (e.g. Davies, 2014). It combines with posthumanist theories that propose that human life is imbricated and entangled in the physical world with all its forms of life and matter, not detached from it, and, most importantly, that we human beings are not central but only one part of the whole natural environment (Olsson, 2009; Lenz-Taguchi, 2010). From this decentred and more humble view of human life in relation to the environment comes a care and responsibility for its sustainability. Importantly, this 'material turn' is not about making a reversal, from mind to body, from discourse to physical matter; it is attempting to flatten out oppositions, divisions and the hierarchies that can result. Musical embodiment has always been a strong theme in early childhood music education, from eurhythmics gathering affirmation from Piagetian sensorimotor theory, through to more contemporary theories of embodied musical cognition (Bremmer, 2015). Thus, I think that a shift to embodied, material thinking may be much less of a theoretical jolt for early childhood music than perhaps some other domains, and that the material turn could become a continuation of an existing theoretical strand that can now gain some contemporary theoretical refinements and reinforcements. But for now these mentions of embodiment and physicality bring me neatly to the next chapter and its biological focus.

3 Bone pipes and brain cells
Biological perspectives

Nikolas Rose, in 2013, opened an article with these words: 'We live, according to some, in the century of biology, where we now understand ourselves in radically new ways as insights of genomics and neuroscience have opened up the workings of our bodies and our minds to new kinds of knowledge and intervention.' There have been discoveries in genetics, evolutionary biology and neuroscience that have propelled those areas to the forefront of scientific progress in our time. Let me immediately point out that there have been matching advances in our understanding of cultural influences on child development in recent years, but the breakthroughs of the biological sciences have created an excitement, particularly in popular writings, that has greatly overshadowed discoveries in the social sciences.

If indeed this is the 'century of biology', what do we need to know for our music work with young children and how might we apply that knowledge? And, importantly, how does this biological perspective connect with other perspectives? There can be an assumption that biological processes are focused on internal mechanisms which shape growth and development, but recent thinking is showing how these biological processes are deeply connected and implicated with the social and material environment surrounding young children (Meloni, 2014). Taken together, these new developments mark a radical move away from earlier assumptions of a sharp separation between nature and nurture, between biology and environmental influence. There is a move towards a social view of biological processes, just as the social sciences are beginning to reincorporate notions of the biological body in their research and theories. New directions include firstly a flexible, plastic relationship between genes and environment, secondly a shift in evolutionary thinking away from individualistic and functional views to evolution giving priority to prosocial behaviours, and finally an increased understanding that the brain is clearly not a detached 'organ' but multiply connected and profoundly shaped by social experience. The biological and the social are not separate after all. At all levels, the biological and the social interconnect. We are *biosocial* (Panter-Brick, 2008). Having set out the three themes, I will go on to discuss each in turn. But first another story from my own experience to ground the discussion in a real-world example.

Vignette

At the age of around four, so our family story goes, Michael was able to sit at the piano and play from memory his older sister's beginner piano pieces. He went on to have precocious aural abilities and musical memory. No one could deny that these abilities had some kind of genetic basis. He clearly wasn't born with the ability to play the piano, but had proclivities and aptitudes which enabled him to pick up the skills rapidly (Tan, *et al.*, 2014; Gingras, *et al.*, 2015). His favourable home environment also played a key part (Davidson & Borthwick, 2002). Anthropologists would want to point out that he was fortunate to have enough food, warmth and avoidance of disease as a baby to survive in the first place, then that there was a piano at home and a sister having piano lessons. Genes and environment work together. Our genes do not determine exactly how we turn out. There is a complex pattern of interplay between our genes and environment that determines what expressions of our genes are 'switched on' or 'switched off'. However, from these beginnings Michael went on to practise the piano, to practise for hours and hours over the years and become a professional pianist.

In contrast to Michael, there are a very small handful of people who have considerable difficulty distinguishing different pitches. They experience a kind of aural version of colour-blindness which is termed amusia (Peretz, *et al.*, 2007). Amusia falls into a class of conditions known as agnosias, which are characterised by the lack of knowledge of something, often very specific. These people are a small percentage: a recent very large sample of 20,000 arrived at a figure of 1.5% of the population (Peretz & Vuvian, 2017) – certainly not the larger numbers that popular ideas about tone deafness often suggest. Some people with amusia have said that music sounds just like a din or banging. Isabelle Peretz found families where several members experience amusia and this suggests it has a genetic basis. Interestingly, some of the younger members of the family had received music lessons and appeared to be less badly affected. This suggests that even a profound, rare genetic auditory disadvantage such as amusia may still be flexible to experience, at least to some extent.

These two extremes of aural-musical ability I have just described are bookends of the normal distribution of ability – the spectrum that you would find in any population in any domain, be it learning to read, being good at gymnastics or understanding quantum physics. The spectrum clusters most people around the average, with a few who excel and a few who struggle. Educators are quite clear that any group of children will present a variation in abilities. They will know that all but a tiny percentage of children who have severe learning disabilities will become literate, but that some children will need a lot more support and structured practice than others. Educators also know that providing structured experience designed to teach children can make all the difference. That may seem to be stating the obvious, but in the case of music the belief still persists that only those at the higher ability end of the distribution, the small percentage who excel, can be counted as 'musical' and will benefit from educational experience, rather than all children across the whole range. There is not the same realisation as there is with reading or maths, for instance, that all children (not just those opting for individual instrumental tuition) need to learn in music, and need to be 'taught', through the adoption of specific pedagogical strategies and structured practice, and that those who need more practice before they 'get it' are simply at a different point on the ability spectrum. So beliefs in genetic predisposition and biologically determined musical ability need to be challenged because they are linked to educators' perceptions of the extent to which they can influence a child's progress.

Going back to Michael, his motivation and ability to focus probably contributed as much as any other trait, if not more, to his later success as a pianist. Each individual has a unique genetic profile, this is true, but it does not determine how we turn out; nor is it static, but can unravel and change across our development. The common belief that genetic effects are preprogrammed, stable and permanent is incorrect. So these variations in genetic heritage mean that babies actively contribute to the experiences they have from infancy onwards. Children can shape their own environment. So, for example, a baby that is more easily distracted may seek out lots of novel experiences, but not stay with them for very long. Another who is highly motivated to persist may stay with one experience for much longer. Similarly, the small child who has a disposition for music will sing more, will show excitement and pleasure when music is played in the car, will encourage musical activity from others and will engender a music-rich environment. Michael had access to a piano at home, he was drawn to play it and his piano playing elicited attention and praise. He was taken to piano lessons, supported and encouraged, and being a pianist from a young age became part of the story of who he was and is.

It also, of course, depends on what we mean by being 'musical'. Becoming a kit drummer, sitarist or pianist, someone able to perform expertly in a particular musical tradition, requires hours of specialised practice and instruction and probably traits of persistence, motivation and ability to focus. But acquiring the musical conventions of our own culture and becoming a very competent music listener is no more difficult than becoming a proficient speaker in our native language (Bigand & Poulin-Charronnat, 2006; Corrigall & Trainor 2014). With very few exceptions, such as the tiny percentage of people who have amusia or who have auditory disabilities, everyone enjoys listening to music and has their own collections, preferences and very clear ideas about what they enjoy and why. Primary-age children who have never taken a music lesson can still typically tell which notes are wrong and which are right in music belonging to their familiar traditions, even in a song that they have never heard before. This is because they gather knowledge about music simply from everyday exposure, even without any formal musical training. Given the proliferation of music via digital technologies that is interwoven into contemporary babies' and toddlers' lives, the affluent Western home environment is far richer in music for today's children than it has ever been. This everyday environment must be providing rich learning experiences for young children, even without any kind of formal or more structured educational experience. But generally, everyday musical competence is not recognised or is dismissed, and only those with specialised performance skills are labelled as 'musical' (at least, that is the case in Western cultures). We have, sadly, a formal music education system which educates the majority away from music, creating an elitism around music which makes the majority feel disenfranchised.

10,000 hours

In contrast to the view that musical ability is dependent on genetic inheritance, there are some who have argued that any musical skill can be achieved if you simply work at it hard and long enough. A 1993 study gave rise to the popular idea that we can all practise our way to musical ability if we choose (Ericsson, *et al.*, 1993). The study's authors found that by age twenty highly-skilled young musicians had practised for an average of 10,000 hours and emphasised the view that accomplishment is down to practice not genes – to nurture and environment, therefore, not nature. In the early 1990s, a group of academics similarly argued that motivation and experience are the essential ingredients in developing musical abilities (Howe, *et al.*, 1995). Much of the writing and philosophical argument that has taken place since a ground-breaking article was published entitled 'Is everyone musical?' has sought to dispel the idea that musical ability is a genetic gift bestowed only on a few (Sloboda, *et al.*, 1994). These arguments were important for mainstream music education in the UK at that time because they underpinned justifications for a music curriculum designed for all children, not just a minority. These arguments were also part of the 1990s drift towards explanations that gave priority to cultural processes rather than biological, the same paradigm shift which saw an emphasis on childhood as a social construction.

The conventional idea is to think of genes as not only acting independently of experience – the separation between genes and environment, the 'nature' versus 'nurture' divide – but also to think of them acting early in development as a kind of blueprint that is present initially and sets the pattern for the building of our musical ability. Research into how the environment influences genetic expressions (termed epigenetics and much of which is very new) is revising our understanding of the gene-environment relationship. As psychologist David Moore explains in his book *The Developing Genome* (2015), this field of research reveals that what counts is not what genes we *have* so much as what our genes are *doing*. What our genes are doing is influenced by the ever-changing environment. Factors such as emotions, nutrition and exposure to toxins may all play a role in how genes are expressed – essentially, which genes are switched on or which are switched off. The earlier thinking around the relationship between genes and environment was that we might have some characteristics that are caused primarily by genetic factors and other characteristics that are caused primarily by factors derived from our experiences in certain environments. Unlike this two-sided and static conception of genes and experience, epigenetic research suggests ways in which genes and environments continuously and flexibly interact to affect development at any stage and produce all of our characteristics, what and who we are, throughout a lifetime.

As with any new, emerging scientific ideas, there is much that is tentative in these findings and needs to be read with caution. As we will see with neuroscience, there can be a tendency to jump on the buzzword bandwagon, to exaggerate the significance of small findings and run away with biased claims. But for the moment the value of epigenetic understandings for this book is to dispel ideas of fixed genetic inheritance that are so unhelpful in our attitudes towards learning in music and to reinforce the idea that biological and sociocultural factors reciprocally influence one another and are not separate and distinct.

Evolutionary origins

If our abilities to participate in music have a genetic basis – even if this genetic basis is not determining but calibrated by experience – this suggests that musicality is rooted in our evolutionary past and represents an adaptation that enhanced our survival (Honing, et al., 2015). Interest in the evolutionary origins of music has burgeoned in recent years and many academics are coming up with speculative suggestions. Taking an evolutionary perspective first needs to come with a cautionary word for we obviously cannot observe Palaeolithic woman and her small children. Without hard evidence we have to be wary of falling into 'just so' stories where a suggestion based on slight evidence and supposition is elaborated and made to sound plausible. Propositions for the evolutionary origins of music are arrived at by bringing together archaeological evidence, analyses of musical behaviours in different cultural groups, studies of our closest relatives (that is, other primates) and from fine-grained studies of musical abilities, particularly in babies (also Fitch, 2015). Theories are then assembled from thoughtful processes of deduction spanning many sources of information (see, e.g., Morley, 2014). Speculative they may be, but theories as to music's evolutionary origins are useful because they contribute to our understanding of what proclivities for music may be innate.

First, there is archaeological evidence. Archaeologists have, fascinatingly, found bone pipes and rasps suggesting that people were making music 35,000–40,000 years ago (Morley, 2014). Obviously, bodies and voices making music and sound-makers made out of plant materials are not preserved. Add to this the anthropological evidence that wherever you go in the world, all peoples have some form of music, and it would seem to confirm that music is, at some level, humanly necessary. People worldwide are motivated to make music, especially to enhance sociable and special situations. Young children are motivated to join in, to learn and to practise making the music of their own cultural groups.

Looking at studies of other primates, our nearest genetic neighbours, presents a rather mixed picture, however. Certainly there are no primates who make music, unless the chest drumming of gorillas counts as music? The fact that primates do not have any other form of music-like activity could suggest that music is not necessary for survival but merely a cultural practice among humans that has gradually been elaborated. Research studies would seem to back that idea (reported in McDermott & Hauser, 2007).They show that whereas humans prefer music to silence, monkeys prefer silence, suggesting that they do not find music relaxing and entertaining.

On the positive side, studies have found that infant primates of various species make vocalisations and that these elicit caregiving and attention from adults (Maestripieri & Call, 1996). That baby chimps vocalise gives weight to the idea that evolving infant vocalisation was essential to survival. The primate baby is born helpless; of all primates, human babies are particularly helpless and rely totally on considerable care from adults to survive. They must, therefore, have evolved some strategies to try to elicit care from those around them. There is now widespread evidence to support the theory that human babies entrain their adult carers through music-like vocalisations and gestures in order to survive and thrive (Dissanayake, 2008).

The evidence of adult-infant vocalisations as primate behaviour does give weight to the idea that the evolutionary origins of music lie in these forms of communication (Bower, 2010). Studies of human babies' responses to music show them to be very perceptive listeners, able to notice all kinds of small differences in musical patterning. These sources of evidence, when combined, all suggest that music-like behaviours, vocalisations and rhythmic gestures are somehow wired into our biology, that these behaviours therefore emerged from natural selection and are adaptive because they served some kind of survival purpose. On the other hand, studies of infant caregiving and of music across cultures have shown that there is such cultural variation that this flexibility and the changeability of music over time suggest that music is a product of cultures, transmitted from group to group and generation to generation. In the process of transmission music changes and is elaborated all the while. We saw from Kelly Werle's and Amanda Niland's work studying mini-musical cultures in nursery settings that within social groups music is constantly transforming. What seems to emerge, therefore, is the conclusion that music is both an adaptation, with some core, fundamental evolutionary origins, and a cultural practice that is transmitted, transformed and elaborated.

So babies use music-like behaviours to engage with their caregivers and to elicit the care and attention they need, and this functional purpose of music as a medium for forming and enhancing social relationships appears to continue beyond babyhood. In evolutionary terms there is also a possible survival benefit associated with music in larger social groups because it promotes cooperation.

Sociable music

This idea that music fosters social cohesion, that it enhances cooperation and strengthens feelings of unity, can also be part of an evolutionary rationale for music. As groups expanded in size beyond the immediate family, they needed to cooperate in order to survive. Group singing, dancing and playing instruments are means of maintaining social connections, particularly during important group ceremonies. After all, weddings the world over conclude with shared food, music and dancing. The majority of musical activity in the world is communal, particularly in traditional societies. It is only more recently, in Western societies and with changes in social and family life and the advent of technologies, that music listening has become a more solitary pursuit. The argument is that prosocial behaviours are essential to the human species and there is evidence gathering that musical ability, particularly the ability to synchronise with others rhythmically, encourages those taking part to be sensitive to those around them and to hold shared goals (Huron, 2003).

Rhythm, and to synchronise rhythmically with others, seems to be the essential ingredient to foster feelings of social connection. Some very cleverly devised studies have been carried out with babies and young children to explore the link between rhythmic musical activity and their demonstration of prosocial behaviours. Fourteen-month-olds who were bounced in time with music were then more likely to help the adult experimenter retrieve an object that was out of reach than children who had been bounced out of time with the music (Cirelli, *et al.*, 2014). Studies carried out with four-year-olds seem to show that taking part in shared musical activities – drumming together, in this case – can increase prosocial skills among these children (Kirschner & Tomasello, 2010; also Rabinowitch & Meltzoff, 2017).

So synchronised rhythmic activity is one important route to social bonding and prosocial behaviour among young children. Imitation is another. An important component of musical ability, of being able to join in and catch what is going on musically, is being able to imitate the vocal and bodily actions of others. Young children are particularly good watchers and imitators (Fawcett & Liszkowski, 2012). Interpersonal interaction among adults often involves unconscious imitation of the other; we find ourselves making similar gestures or taking up a similar stance. This is born of our own prosocial, empathic motivations and has a positive effect of feeling more bonded with the person we are imitating. In a music session young children are typically observing and listening very carefully and will strive to produce exact imitations of the adult's actions in order to conform and be like others. In my study with three- and four-year-olds, I and another educator played with young children on a xylophone in ways that imitated, in sequences of turn-taking, the children's spontaneous musical play, and we found that this imitative play generated longer and more varied improvisatory music-play ideas among the children (Young, 2003b). When we experimented by playing in turn, but without imitating the children's actions, instead introducing more of our own musical ideas, the children's motivation to continue quickly diminished and the music-play sessions petered out.

Mother-baby interaction

Returning to mother-baby interactions, the recognition that these interactions have music-like characteristics has generated a great deal of interest in early childhood music, both practice and research. These ideas are frequently called upon both as a rationale to justify the value of work and to suggest models of practice for mother and baby or toddler music groups. Central to these rationales is the belief that music-like interactions enhance mother-baby bonds and, moreover, that forming good bonds are essential for babies' well-being. These ideas draw on 'attachment theory' and the terms 'attachment' and 'bonding' have come to carry enormous significance in early childhood.

A set of concepts broadly known as 'communicative musicality' – the idea that human interaction at all ages, not just babies, has characteristics which are metaphorically musical in the broadest sense – has come to be well known and widely adopted in early childhood music theory (Malloch & Trevarthen, 2010). The theory has a rhythmical dimension: the inter-timing through synchronisation and imitation that I mentioned above. It has a melodic dimension: vocalisations between adults and babies are initially meaningful not through the words or actual semantic meaning, but through the emotional content conveyed via the rise and fall of the voice which is typically specially adapted in baby- or young-child-directed speech patterns (Trevarthen, 2008). Finally, the theory of communicative musicality also draws attention to gestural communications, the way that the body is also intrinsically engaged, multimodally, with the vocal and rhythmic expressions. As with all theories, it had important precedents in the work of many researchers interested in adult-infant interaction; it didn't arise out of the blue, although the theory is often presented without referencing the wider range of literature. To give but one, key example out of many, Mechthild and Hanuš Papoušek very carefully observed their own babies and described the earliest vocalisations as musical (1981).

In the final chapter I will return to communicative musicality and reappraise it from an anthropological perspective. Here I want to look more closely at attachment theory, or bonding as it is often referred to, which has also become closely bound up with these conceptions of musical processes in babyhood.

Attachment

John Bowlby, a psychiatrist/psychotherapist in the UK in the late 1950s and 60s, put forward a set of ideas about the emotional ties between a mother and her baby and the negative effects of separation (1988). Accordingly, the quality of the early primary relationship is considered to be the foundation of personality and certain characteristic patterns of attachment in all future relationships. If a sensitive mother (and the emphasis falls on the mother) fails to establish secure attachment, this is believed to carry serious risks for the future psychological development for her child.

Attachment theory was put forward as universal, positing that *all* mother and baby pairs, no matter what the culture, class or circumstances, not only will but *should* engage in a set of behaviours to foster bonding during the first months of babyhood or risk negative consequences. Having a close, steady warm attachment to close and familiar others is clearly a good thing, but anthropologists, having a sense of the vastness of cultural possibilities, would suggest that babies can grow up to be healthy in mind and body under many different sorts of circumstances. Taking the principles of attachment theory and studying them in a wide range of cultures suggests that there is considerable variation in how babies are mothered; there is not one simple, universal pattern (Keller, 2012, 2014). In households where extended families live, babies can be handed around from lap to lap and may be comfortably attached to many caregivers. They may not even be very attached to their biological mother, but seek out the closeness of older siblings or a grandparent.

At this point in the book I want to introduce an important idea that underpins my arguments at several places in different chapters. In 2010 Joseph Henrich and his colleagues published an article that had a profound impact on social science. They showed how the majority of research is carried out with one narrow group of people, most often university students, who are an easy and accessible group to get hold of for studies. To describe this group they coined the term WEIRD – meaning Western, Educated, Industrialised, Rich and Democratic – and demonstrated how conclusions from research carried out with this one narrow, limited group are then assumed to represent and to be applicable to the whole of humankind. The babies and little children who are brought in to participate in laboratory studies of infant musical behaviours will be those of mothers with time, resources, the interest and motivation to participate. They too will belong to the middle classes; they are likely to be the children of university colleagues and friends. We will see that studies of children's music at home inevitably recruits from the same demographic, often even the researcher's own child. Moreover – and this point is key – Joseph Henrich suggested that WEIRD populations are among the least representative populations, globally speaking, one could find. David Lancy, an anthropologist who has written extensively on childhood, points out that children's upbringing in Western middle-class families is particularly distinctive and unusual in many respects when compared cross-culturally with other social groups (2014a, 2017). Findings from research with this narrow population then feed into fundamental understandings of psychology and behaviour that we take for granted. This is not to diminish the value of these studies, but to recognise their findings as limited to those very specific populations and not automatically applicable to children outside those social groups (also Blum, 2017).

So, to take the implications of this point back into my discussion of attachment theory, the children studied, along with the orientating ideas and values of these studies, reflect a narrow segment of the population and carry an ethnocentric bias. Hence, what is actually a process of 'nurture' that has emerged from a particular culturally defined set of parenting practices is turned into one of 'nature'. The culturally specific models of behaviour found among Western mothers and wider families are assumed to be natural and biological and therefore should be promoted among all mothers, irrespective of the social group they belong to and with no respect for diversity of parenting practices. Incidentally, the same applies to communicative musicality. It is a theoretical idea which emerged originally from a microanalysis of a relatively short recording of interactions between one mother and her six-week-old baby in a laboratory setting in Edinburgh, Scotland. But I will return to this later.

In music therapy the use of music to enhance and increase attachment has a strong theoretical hold (e.g. Edwards, 2011a; Abad & Edwards, 2004) – a hold that has influenced early childhood music work more generally, beyond music therapy. Jane Edwards describes music therapy work as a 'process of developing a relationship with a caregiver/dyad in order to support, develop and extend their skills in using musical and music-like interactions … [and] to create the optimal environment for secure attachment to be fostered' (2011b:7). Adopting the dominant narrative of early childhood, she talks of the attachment and bonding between baby/child and adult as fragile and vulnerable (2011b:2). Jan Macvarish, on the other hand, points out the prevalence of such narratives and suggests that we should celebrate young children's resilience rather than emphasise fragility and vulnerability, and also suggests that bringing up young children is about love, less laboured and instrumental in conception (2016).

Work based on the principles of music therapy with parent and baby pairs has been translated into approaches for larger groups, notably in the Sing&Grow programme in Australia. Jan Nicholson and colleagues carried out a large-scale study of Sing&Grow that included more than 1,000 participants in several sites, comparing measurements across such aspects as parental sensitivity and engagement with their children (Nicholson, *et al.*, 2010). They did find some small improvements across these dimensions. However, the programme was carried out in a number of different places and there were noticeable variations according to place; variations could be attributed to the demographic of the parents who participated, the retention of parents (many dropped out) and the delivery style of the music therapists providing the sessions. This is a clear reminder that it is not necessarily music work per se that is effective as a kind of treatment, but that many other factors linked to the context, the nature of the music work provided and the relationships formed within the group also impact on the work, and that, moreover, isolating any cause-and-effect relationships from all these variables is methodologically extremely difficult. Their very even-handed reporting acknowledges that evaluation of the effectiveness of such programmes in real-world situations is compounded by these many factors. The reality is that assessing the immediate efficacy of the programme is one thing, but to go on and assess the effect of early music experiences in infancy on later outcomes, and draw some conclusions based on attachment theory, is well-nigh impossible. It may well be that the care we receive in babyhood impacts on later life; childhood experiences clearly play a part in forming our behaviour and personalities. But this is not the same as being *determined* by them. The more we understand about the interplay between biological, psychological and social factors in children's upbringing, the more difficult it is to pinpoint any one factor or to suggest that a music programme can make any appreciable difference.

Nevertheless, attachment theory has a strong hold among practitioners and some middle-class mothers who view 'attachment parenting' as an ideal to emulate, supported by a range of popular science writing in parenting books. Much of the popular information about attachment parenting implies that it has its origins in natural or evolutionary prior practices that are rooted in our biology and that it represents a return to intuitive parenting. Many parent and child music classes promote their work on the grounds that it will improve bonding. It may also be included as a rationale for work with certain groups of mothers who are thought to be in need of extra support to increase their ability to bond and make emotionally rich, responsive relationships with their children, as with the Australian Sing&Grow program. There is an obvious paradox here: attached parenting is argued for as a universal, biological and naturally intuitive way to parent, but it is a form of parenting that must be 'taught' to certain groups of mothers, for whom it apparently is not natural, intuitive or biological. The cultural specificity – the 'WEIRDness' – of the ideology of 'attached parenting' is revealed in this paradox. Certainly in the UK, but also in other countries, there are increasing justifications for interventions into family lives to shape parenting practices into normalised models that fit with policy visions and agendas. These interventions and the policies behind them need to be critiqued. What's more, in its search for rationales and justifications, early childhood music education is now turning increasingly to neuroscience.

Neurological magic?

Opening a web page promoting early childhood music classes, I am greeted by an image of the brain, with some areas brightly coloured, as if lighting up, and musical notation flying out from these coloured areas like fireworks. 'Music creates neurological magic', reads the caption, 'lighting up a child's brain'. Such images and claims are common. Infant brain development is talked of in awe and wonder. The young child's growing brain, so it is assumed, benefits from enriched, external stimulation that music can well provide.

A multicoloured image of the brain, totally excised from the rest of the child's body, detached from the child's social, material and cultural context, represents a highly reductionist, pure-science point of view. The child has become merely a biological entity, an organ. From a social constructionist point of view, a focus on 'the brain' results in an extremely impoverished construction of children, in which mechanistic brain function predominates and the subjectivity of the child, the mind of the child as thoughtful, emotional, social and cultural, in a living, breathing body, is completely erased. Neuroscience is characterised by machine metaphors for understanding brain function, many of them drawing on images of computers, information processing and wiring circuits. In this brain-as-machine image, music is also reduced to a simple stimulus that has a direct physical effect, that 'does' things to the brain in a one-directional, causal way. Yet the very young child's brain is also presented as highly vulnerable and in need of careful nurture within, once again, a set of highly deterministic, 'now or never' assumptions (Edwards, et al., 2015). Neuroscience has become blended with the dominant and prevailing images of early childhood.

On another website entitled Music Education Works, an image of the brain is accompanied by the claim that 'a child's brain develops faster with exposure to music education'. These kinds of claims need to be approached with clear-sighted scepticism and tracked back to the academic write-ups of the original study (Habibi, et al., 2016). In the case of this specific claim, reading the original report reveals that children aged six and seven years who learnt the violin for two years were better at distinguishing small pitch changes or small rhythm changes than children in control groups who had taken part in a sports programme or had no special activity. Does it not stand to reason that children who had violin lessons for two years would have improved in musical perception skills? The Music Education Works website then states that auditory processing enhanced by learning the violin will transfer to language and literacy skills. The claim is simple: if children learn an instrument, they will do better in core curriculum learning too. But this claim is based on a leap of assumption. The area of the brain that processes musical sounds is presumed to be also responsible for auditory processing in language, reading skills and so on. They have no firm evidence for this. It is a proposition. I would agree that it is a very logical and likely proposition, but it is guesswork nonetheless.

A careful reading of the original study report shows that the authors make no definite claims at all, but use tentative vocabulary such as 'may indicate' or 'could possibly'. Therefore, the leap to the headline that 'a child's brain develops faster', accompanied, as ever, by a brightly coloured image of the brain, has already firmed up and exaggerated the cautious claims of the researchers. And there are two other things to note here when one reads more carefully. One is that the children in the violin-learning group were opted into the study by parents who were interested. It is likely, therefore, that these children came from families where playing an instrument was already something that was valued, and perhaps the family had an innate disposition towards music and to being diligent and able to focus (also useful for learning to listen carefully) and so on. Another thing to note, as with many of these studies, is that the sample size was small – just thirteen in the music group (Habibi, et al., 2016) – and the children all live in one area of the USA and belong to one social demographic. Therefore, the findings from this one social group cannot be generalised beyond this small sample to all children. Yet, the headline reporting suggests that this one small finding and the claims made on the basis of this finding could be true for all children – could be universal, in other words.

As Hilary and Steven Rose explain, the science behind the claims of neuroscience is a lot more vague, rudimentary and conjectural than the scientists working with these methods would have us believe. So, they say, we have a responsibility to interrogate that vagueness and not be duped into believing the claims without careful scrutiny (Rose & Rose, 2014:254). Besides, the findings rarely, if ever, can apply directly to educational practice; most of the implications for practice that we read involve extrapolation that is heavily value-laden rather than genuinely evidence-based. So we are faced with the task of working out how to respond to the impressive, but also at times troublesome, surge of neuroscientific findings without either celebrating them uncritically or simply condemning them wholesale.

Since the 1970s there has been an explosion of brain science and it is influencing directions in early childhood music, particularly in the UK in terms of targeted early intervention for children deemed to be disadvantaged (see Vandenbroeck, 2017). The promise of social improvement by ensuring optimal development among children at risk – 'transforming lives' is the mantra – is a popular idea in political circles, taken up with enthusiasm in the UK in a number of recent reports. The principle of social justice, the evening-up of inequality in society, it is believed, can be enacted through music projects that bring enrichment. The rationales for these programmes have a progressive, idealistic and moral ring to them, so that they appear to be self-evidently a good thing. As a result of this 'myth-making', David Wastell and Sue White write that it becomes very difficult to respond to and argue with these kinds of idealistic rationales (2017). They point out that scientific claims do not provide a scientifically-neutral evidence base, but have been selectively filtered through the lens of existing political, policy and professional forms of thought (2017:90). With well-crafted arguments they demonstrate how science is used to give a ring of authority to policies which are already considered to be politically right. The scientific findings have not provided the original impetus, but are selected, reduced and repackaged to support policies, arguments and decisions that are already in place, not vice versa. Brain-based music studies seem to hold the promise of pseudo-scientific support for advocacy arguments that will provide the ultimate answer. In the UK certainly, and in other countries most likely, this persuasive power is increasingly being used in the context of constraints on public spending. At a time of economic insecurity many are wanting to demonstrate the power and importance of music to policymakers and to education and arts decision-makers. But the research is highly complex and it is not possible, at least not yet, to make clear links between neuroscience research and what we should do in education (Della Sala & Anderson, 2012). To state it plainly, the neuromyths are misleading.

Towards the end of the 1990s, a decade termed by the US and other governments as the 'decade of the brain', the philosopher of science John Bruer critically reviewed the claims being made about babies' and young children's brains. He identified three mythical statements about the nature of infant neurobiological development, which he said underpinned the 'Myth of the First Three Years' in a book of the same name (1999):

1. There is a period of rapid synaptic growth in the early years which is unmatched in any later period of life.
2. There are 'critical' or 'sensitive' periods for particular aspects of brain development in the early years during which development depends on or expects certain environmental experiences.

3   The brain requires 'enriched environments' or 'stimulation' in the earlier years to develop functionally.

John Bruer traces these three mythical statements back to their origins in research and shows how the original research should lead to much more modest interpretations than the hyped-up claims and recommendations found in much public and popular writing. He warned that the 'myth of the first three years' results in distorted views of children, parents and policy. If the research does not support this view, why then has it come to have such a hold? The reasons, he explains, are sociocultural, ideological and political rather than scientific.

Although Bruer's original book on the 'myth' was published in 1999, in a talk in 2011 at the University of Canterbury Bruer reiterated the same points, saying that the 'new' neuroscience was mostly 'old' neuroscience repackaged. He remarked that since his 1999 book there had not been much advance in the neuroscientific bases for the claims made. He pointed out themes which had persisted throughout this period of time: firstly, the persistence of highly reduced mechanistic explanations of how the brain works; secondly, an affinity for attachment theory and what are purported to be its neural underpinnings; and, finally, the continued selection and citation of the same pieces of neuroscience research which are now outdated. Reflecting on this last point, I looked carefully at a newly published book for the citations of neuroscientific research. Sure enough, most of the cited research was over ten years old and some of it around twenty years old. Given that brain scanning technology was still relatively crude at that time, and that these are often unreplicated studies, Bruer's comments hold true for the music field. John Bruer is a not a lone voice by far. He has been followed by many others, eminent scholars, who share his views and concerns. In 2002 the Brain and Learning project of the Organisation for Economic Co-operation and Development (OECD) drew attention to the many misconceptions around the mind and brain. It was the OECD that defined the term 'neuromyth' as 'a misconception generated by a misunderstanding, a misreading or a misquoting of facts scientifically established (by brain research) to make a case for use of brain research in education and other contexts' (OECD, 2002:111). Neuroscientists themselves have also challenged the exaggerated claims and misrepresentations of neuroscience. In books, articles and other media (Bruer 1999; Legrenzi & Ulmitá 2011; Rose & Abi-Rached, 2013; Wastell & White, 2017) academics provide painstaking analyses to demonstrate why neuromythologies are inaccurate. They are joined by bloggers under such titles as 'Neurocritic', 'Neuroskeptic' and even 'Neurobonkers', who ramp up their efforts to dislodge the myths and misconceptions.

Yet in spite of the scholarly work that has challenged the exaggerated claims arising from neuroscientific research, the neuromyths are highly persistent (see Penn, 2014:90–92; Dekker, et al., 2012). Why is that? Why do the facts not seem to dislodge opinions and beliefs? Various studies have revealed that adding neuroscience to an explanation adds to its appeal and apparent validity, irrespective of how relevant or even accurate the neuroscience is. Knowledgeable students, in one study, were given falsified research reports to read and they described the set of reports that contained brain imagery (completely irrelevant to the explanation) as more reliable and accurate than those without the imagery, even though in both cases the reports were the same (Weisberg, et al., 2008). The study's authors concluded that neuroscientific information provides added value which tends to convert an incorrect or weak explanation into a credible one. Deena Weisberg and her colleagues called this the 'seductive allure' effect. The brain holds a certain mystery, after all, and it may be that the brain images seem to provide something concrete and the promise of high status and scientific proof (McCabe & Castell, 2008). Brain scans with all the trappings of expensive machinery, invisible beams, medical centres and specialised, white-coated scientists seem like highly credible, hard science. Moreover, neuroscience seems to offer an easy and attractive solution to otherwise intractable problems. Adding something which supposedly acts directly on the brain, such as music for little children, promises a simple remedy, a short cut, that avoids the need to grapple with complex social issues such as social disadvantage and poverty. Indeed, it suggests that there can be optimum, scientifically determined conditions in which to care for and educate young children that will result in capable, successful, productive and happy adults. Child welfare advocates and politicians join voices in arguing that social problems such as inequality, poverty and educational underachievement are best addressed through 'early intervention' programmes to enhance the emotional and cognitive aspects of children's brain development (Vandenbroeck, 2017). The worry is that in the field of early childhood music education, unsubstantiated claims about how children's brains can be changed through musical input may lead to the implementation of practices that seem appealing but will have no benefit whatsoever (Goswami, 2006). They may in themselves be fairly harmless but they act as a smokescreen, diverting attention and, more seriously, money, time and effort away from the real issues and away from designing approaches that might properly address those issues.

There is another serious consequence. Interventions targeted at young children and their parents that draw rationales from neuroscience, attachment theory and adult-infant interaction – all the themes that I have been discussing in this chapter – tend to draw attention to what 'parents' – mothers, in other words – may not be doing, implying that they are failing in certain respects. These interventions divert rather than focus effort and resources where they should be targeted: on social and economic problems at the structural level that result in poverty and inequality. Neuromyths, coupled with ideas of attachment and bonding, add to the intensification of early parenting and to conceptions of children and their upbringing in very simplistic biological and instrumental terms (Penn, 2017). Neuroscience (and attachment theory) has, therefore, been annexed for its persuasive and political value, rather than for its ability to provide accurate information or information that has direct and useful application (Vandenbroeck, 2014, 2017).

Neuroscience methods

In these next paragraphs I provide some more information about the methods of neuroscientific research because this will help to reveal its limitations. Steven Rose spells out the two basic problems with neuroscientific research: firstly that the technology for studying brain responses is still very simplistic, and secondly that the tests are so oversimplified that they have no connection with real-life activity. He has spent years involved in brain research, so he speaks with an authority we should heed (2014). It is stating the obvious, but clearly a major difficulty in studying the brain's activity is in getting access to neural processes. There is no doubt that advances in scientific techniques such as magnetic resonance imaging (MRI) and functional magnetic resonance imaging (fMRI) have led to an enormous increase in understandings within the very wide field of neurology, and there is also no doubt that the technology is advancing all the time, but, notwithstanding these advances and gains, the technology is still relatively rudimentary.

Expanding on his two basic problems, Steven Rose explains that what the brain scanners can find out is extremely limited and imprecise. Here is an amusing illustration of just how imprecise findings from the scanners can be. Researchers preparing an fMRI scanner for a set of tests typically place some object in the scanner to calibrate it; a watermelon is a favourite choice. One team placed a dead Atlantic salmon in the scanner for this purpose but were amazed to discover that, far from looking at a blank screen to prepare the equipment, the dead salmon appeared to be 'responding' to the pictures of emotional scenes that they were about to use for their next study (Sanders, 2009). They wrote up this incident to demonstrate how easy it is to get bogus results from such complex technology unless checked very carefully.

The objective of all neuroimaging research is to identify the areas of the brain which selectively become active during a given task. The cerebral areas are composed of a multitude of nerve cells or neurons. Nerve cells depend on oxygen and the more active the cell, the more oxygen it needs. Oxygen is carried in the blood; therefore, measuring how much blood an area needs indicates the level of oxygen and suggests an area of activity. A magnetic resonance scan measures the levels of water in the brain and with a delay of a few seconds. Even such a small delay may be distorting results. True, there are more sophisticated types of scanner being developed all the time and some new equipment can give more instantaneous readings. But many of the studies which are cited and re-cited as evidence of brain responses to musical stimuli are drawn from earlier studies using the earlier, much less precise technologies. The researchers then receive extremely complex mathematical data that they analyse and average out to arrive at the coloured brain 'blobs'. So just knowing which area of the brain 'lights up' when someone is listening to rhythm patterns, for example, tells us only that certain areas of the brain appeared to need more oxygen, and that is all.

Any implications from a response revealed in the patterns of blood flow are an interpretation, intelligent guesswork. Even the assumption that increased blood flow means increased neural activity is not necessarily accurate (Sanders, 2009). Brain science results are correlations. In other words, they find a relationship between a stimulus, usually a very simple stimulus, and patterns of blood flow in the brain. The fact that two things are identified as happening together does not automatically mean that one causes the other. That blood flows in one part of a brain are shown as 'lit up' on an fMRI scan does not mean that the rest of the brain is inactive. Nor is it straightforward to determine what activity in a region of the brain 'means' or 'causes'. The brain is not a fixed machine-like organ, with parts all functioning separately with separate tasks; rather, it is highly plastic and adaptable. One thing, however, does seem to be clear: as the research expands knowledge of brain functioning, plasticity seems to be a predominant feature and uncertainty about functions and whether they are confined to certain areas is increasing rather than decreasing.

Given the practical challenges and ethical concerns around research with babies and very young children, neuroimaging is almost entirely carried out with adults or animals and this is certainly the case with many of the findings for music. More contemporary equipment is a little more adaptable for babies and the very young, but the older equipment certainly was not. As children mature, the research process and purpose can be explained to them, and there are attempts to make the process child-friendly, so there is now a little work carried out with older children. Nevertheless, a majority of the information about how music might be processed or its possible impact on children's brains has been hypothesised from research with adults or animals. Since we know that children's brains, particularly during the early childhood phase, are differently formed from those of adults, it is immediately obvious that these ideas are based on generous translations and guesswork from work with adults. True new developments such as baby seats that can position an inclined baby into a head-scanner (albeit strapped in so that they don't move and then only for very short periods) are allowing for brain scan data of babies to be obtained. Scans can be carried out while babies are asleep, although the brain is in sleep mode then, of course. But as soon as toddlers are up and away, brain research becomes almost impossible for they could not be expected to lie or sit still in a scanner and it would be unethical to strap them in, immobile, at least for any length of time. There are some general findings drawn from scans on children who have required them for medical reasons, but these children are not a typical and therefore representative sample.

Steven Rose's second point is that the tasks have to be highly simplified. Clearly, with tiny babies and very young children the test has to be very carefully designed. The task must be something that can be done while the baby's head is held fixed in a scanner or sitting on a lap with their head covered with a hairnet of electrodes (the hairnet, EEG, measures the brain's electrical activity directly, in contrast to the fMRI, which records changes in blood flow). The baby cannot move or bounce about as freely as babies might typically do in response to music. So the task is reduced to listening, and listening to just very small, isolated elements of music. These elements might be a couple of pitches or a small rhythm pattern. They are hardly music in its genuine form. The brain is very active in many different areas even when apparently focusing on one task. So, to think of imagined instances, the baby may become animated by her parent strapping her into the scanner baby seat or bothered by the pressure of a strap on her forehead. How do we know it is not a continuing reaction to her parent's smile or discomfort that is producing the result? So the experimental design requires a control task that is as close as possible to the task being studied, except for one small change. Researchers who were interested in how a baby music session might then have an impact on children's ability to process language and music had the babies in scanners listen to a 'normal' flow of language and music and then a flow of language and music with a very small disruption to it (Zhao & Kuhl, 2016). If the babies appeared to notice the disruption, the researchers took that as a sign that they were better at processing music and language. Yet does this one small thing, noticing a small musical disruption, translate into the much grander claim that the babies became better at music- and language-processing after receiving a short series of music sessions?

There is another caveat to take into account. The machinery is very expensive and operating costs are high. So only a small number of researchers in very affluent countries, typically the USA and Canada, have access to brain scanning equipment. The costs and length of time it takes to scan means that only a few children usually take part, so the sample sizes are very small. Once again, they are most likely to be drawn from more affluent, educated middle classes; – WEIRD families – and, as I emphasised earlier, taking findings from one very small social group tells us only about that one small group of children, their parenting, their environment and nothing more.

Finally, we should understand that the pressures on university academics to produce positive research outputs, particularly when they have taken up costly laboratory time, tempt them into trumpeting their findings, downplaying the limitations and making claims for their practical usefulness which the findings barely support. We should also recognise the commercial motives of those in early childhood music who are promoting particular approaches and methods and use the 'seductive allure' of brain-boosting messages to seek advantage over competitors in an early childhood music market.

Future promise

However, in spite of these cautions and caveats, the correct response is not to abandon neuroscience altogether. Hopefully we can move beyond the hype, and the need to debunk the hype. It is certain that neuroscientific research has the potential, in the future, to provide valuable information about neural responses to music that will inform music education practice (see Hirsh-Pasek & Bruer, 2007). Collaboration between neuroscience and early childhood music education may bring mutual benefit given the different knowledge bases, experiences and expertise of the two fields. But the emphasis here is on the future and the words *might* and *may*. Currently, there is a gulf between science and direct application to work in music with young children. Realistically, several point out that it will be many years before educators can take advantage of the promise that it offers (e.g. Goswami, 2006). Trying to fill that gulf with guesswork and leaps based on simplistic interpretations is premature and, most seriously of all, it is misleading and distracts from the real issues. There are very many interesting proposals for neuromusical processes emerging from laboratory work, and we do need to listen to them, consider and appraise them. We must better understand what neuroscience can and cannot tell us, and critically examine the ways in which neuroscience findings are being adopted and used in early childhood education. The usual situation is that neuroscientists work in isolation, producing results that educators must then decipher and analyse to decide what the implications might be. In the future there will be, ideally, more interdisciplinary collaboration between educators, psychologists, sociologists, anthropologists and neuroscientists. It is also important to recognise that there are no silver bullets, no quick solutions, no simple remedies to complex social inequalities. Moreover, neuroscience will not replace social, emotional and cultural analyses and understandings of children's participation in music and their musical learning; it will be one integrated contribution to an interdisciplinary network.

Supposed findings from neuroscience are often brought in to add weight to arguments of infant determinism. As Erica Burman writes, 'every claim to the importance of early experience now seems to invoke neuroscience, without really specifying what or how this is relevant' (Burman, 2017:160). Helene Guldberg adds, 'whether based on attachment theory or neurobabble, the claim that human beings are set in stone by the age of three is scientifically unsound' (2013). The myth of infant determinism, however, is all-pervasive (Bruer, 1999; Kagan, 2000).

Determinism

John Bruer suggests that while scientific findings of early children's earliest developments are very helpful to parents and educators in many ways, and that is not in doubt, the belief in infant determinism has been taken too far. Neuroscientific understandings of the sensory system demonstrate the importance of stimulation for the healthy development of sight, hearing and language. But this is *normal* stimulation, that is everywhere around us, just a normal environment. Only children living in the most abnormally, abusive and severely deprived situations such as babies in orphanages kept strapped into bare cots, without human contact and half-starved, might suffer from sensory deprivation (Bruer, 2011). Evidence of the effects of severe deprivation does not then automatically correspond to an argument that enriched environments and attempting to increase stimulation beyond the normal will have any impact on brain development. The 'enriched sensory environments' argument is frequently cited as a rationale for arts and music work designed for babies and toddlers. Indeed, one risk of overinterpreting the importance of experience can be found in the simplistic and possibly harmful proposal of very early and excessive amounts of sensory stimulation during early babyhood. Providing interesting things to play with and experiences to interact with will of course provide valuable experiences for the very young, but their importance and value should not be overstated, nor argued for in terms of brain development or critical periods.

It is known that the brain produces more synapses – that is, neural connections – in the first few years of a child's life. Thereafter is a prolonged period of pruning of synaptic connections (Huttenlocher, 1979). So, interestingly, the process of brain development is not one of continuous growth, nor of increases in capacity, but would seem also to involve reduction in the complexity of neural connections and greater specialisation. But neuroscientists have not yet come up with any clear answers as to the real significance of this initial growth followed by pruning, nor how experience may shape the synaptic connections and shape the pruning process. Indeed, there is no obvious relationship between greater synaptic connections and advanced cognitive ability; this is also a highly simplistic supposition. The pruning process would seem to be equally crucial to brain development but I have yet to find a web page that promotes music sessions on the basis that they assist 'synaptic pruning' or 'brain reduction'.

Conclusion

To bring this chapter to a conclusion, it has focused on biological themes, discussing (epi)genetic, evolutionary and neuroscientific accounts of music's origins and how these ideas combine and work their way into ideas that circulate in discourse. These ideas influence policy, rationales for practice, the marketing of work to parents and play a highly influential role in how practice and music work with very young children is shaped. Attempts to explain young children as musical merely in terms of biology, as brains, genes or evolutionary survival needs, are doomed to failure because they are reductionist, tend to be determinist and erase the cultural, social and political dimensions. It should be obvious that the current enthusiasm for brain imagery and neuroscientific explanations is a cultural turn reflecting culturally inflected values and discourses and powerful images and constructions of childhood that are in circulation. But before we move on to consider social and cultural perspectives, we will look through the lens of psychology.

4 Pathways and pigeonholes
The view from developmental psychology

As I described earlier, developmental psychology came in for harsh criticism in the early days of the 'new' paradigm social studies of childhood. Childhood from the perspective of the sociologists was seen as socially determined and so, it was argued, children cannot be pigeonholed into universal, rigid, predetermined pathways of development, marked out by age-related steps and stages. Psychology was criticised for not recognising the importance of social processes, how the socio-economic, cultural and historical context shapes childhood, and for not recognising children's own agency. The view from developmental psychology, it was argued, creates childhoods that are all supposedly the same, in which children follow pathways of 'natural' growth.

Before continuing, it is useful to set out the two perspectives side by side in a simple comparison. Developmental approaches emphasise the sequential cognitive, behavioural and emotional development from birth through early childhood. Differences between children of different ages are emphasised and development is understood to be a progressive pathway. Developmental models emphasise the similarities and consistencies between children rather than variations among them, sameness rather than difference. Constructionist perspectives, introduced by the sociology of childhood explain children's experiences and actions as the outcomes of complex social and cultural processes. As a result, there is considerable variation and diversity in the childhoods lived by children. Differences between children, rather than similarities, are emphasised. In this view, children's lives are understood as emerging from active processes between adults and children in which there are reciprocal processes shaping behaviour. Children, it is argued, can act; they have agency to understand and act upon their world; they are not 'preprogrammed' by homogenous developmental processes. Children's own perceptions and understanding of their lives are given much more importance and the full breadth of their lives, including everyday aspects, come into the picture.

I explained how, in the early days of childhood studies, these psychological and sociological views of childhood were set in opposition to one another. The recent 'new wave' childhood studies has recognised that oppositional thinking is problematic in itself and has looked for ways in which opposing positions can be brought together. It is widely agreed that psychological and sociological views of childhood are not irreconcilable and that an integration will be more productive. Integration will allow for more multifaceted understandings of young children that take much more account of the complexities and intricacies of their musical lives. Some are suggesting that those who originally set out a manifesto for the new social studies of childhood unfairly characterised developmental psychology in a rather simplistic way in order to sharpen their arguments. They point out that the psychological-developmental views of childhood were much less rigid and fixed – and were becoming increasingly flexible to the sociocultural context – than the early sociology of childhood scholars had implied. Equally, the constructionist perspective does give rise to analyses of childhood that reveal similarities and commonalities between children. So the sociologists' argument that childhoods are endlessly variable is not strictly accurate either. There is value then in understanding what core features of musical maturation may be the same or, at least if not the same, then what might be similar among a majority of children. Moreover, early childhood is clearly a phase of life in which the child is developing rapidly in all aspects. With major changes in physical size, maturity, skills such as language, movement and singing, the range of activities children can participate in, their increasing understanding of the social and material world, developmental psychology, or at least developmental understandings in some form, remain highly relevant in plotting changes through the transitions of early childhood. So theories that can assist us in understanding the transitions, the pathways and progression of changes over time in early childhood are very useful. But, they must also be highly flexible, contingent and adaptable and be incorporated as one part of a teaching toolkit, not dictating practice but standing in the wings, informing. They must also, importantly, be able to incorporate the musical childhoods of the present and of the future. The conceptions of musical development that currently permeate early childhood music education are built on traditional conceptions of music and retrospective musical childhoods.

Early childhood music practice, being conservative in outlook, still tends to be tied to traditional and narrow conceptions of developmental psychology as its primary point of reference. Therefore, I need to make a rapid journey through this chapter. First, I adopt the original position of early-stage childhood studies and draw on their arguments to dislodge developmental psychology, dug-in and holding on to a position of dominance in early childhood music, and then place it in a more balanced position in relation to other theoretical perspectives. I then retrieve a developmental perspective in a re-formed position, and integrate it, newly fashioned, into an interdisciplinary approach. It is one perspective, but only one of several perspectives, from which we can view musical childhoods.

Musical development research and literature is extensive and it is not the aim of this chapter to provide any kind of representative overview. I have been highly selective in making reference to key examples of research and theories where they are useful to illustrate the main points. In keeping with all the chapters, I begin with a real-life illustration to ground and illustrate the discussions that follow.

Vignette

Once a week I used to drive my then three-year-old grandson Ted home at the end of the day – a drive of only ten minutes which became a regular singing time to which we would each contribute songs. For several weeks Ted sang a melody I couldn't place; it was quite unlike our usual repertoire. This song slowly soared and swooped, highly melodic using a full vocal range and long sustained notes. It was clearly an expressive and meaningful song for him, and seemed to have no words, at least no words that I could make out. This song was melodically far away from any of the limited-range children's songs which I was singing for him on our journey home, for, being well versed in children's vocal development, I thought I knew what to expect his three-year-old voice to accomplish. The mystery song persisted for several weeks and it clearly frustrated him that I could not join in, nor knew what it was – until, that is, I spent an afternoon at his home and he requested a favourite Disney DVD of that time, *Finding Dory*. There, as the opening theme music unfolded, I heard his song, richly orchestral with the main melody carried in a wordless choral line. The film tells the story of a baby fish who gets separated from his mother and then reunited, a meaningful, emotional story for any three-year-old who spends daytime with a professional childminder while his parents work.

How Ted was learning to use his voice physically, as a singer, will be common to all children. For the first three years of life children's vocal apparatus (larynx, vocal folds and surrounding support structures) and their lung capacity are maturing rapidly. This biological growth, along with their pitch processing capabilities, imposes certain physical limitations on children's abilities to sing that can be broadly mapped out with the expectation that they are much the same for all children. Vocal development pathways in terms of biological capabilities usefully predict what children at certain ages may be capable of in singing (see Greenhalgh, 2018). Similarly, physical growth and maturation shapes what children are able to do in rhythmic movements and in managing and playing sound-makers. Knowing about children's likely physical road maps of development is informative for practice.

But how would we squash Ted's rendition of the *Finding Dory* song into a singing development pigeonhole? As with all children, he lives in a world that includes his home, extended family, his school, his preschool, the home of his childminder and her family, and a musical culture that includes screen-based, commercialised media for children. Children belong to a gender, class and an ethnic group; they are a particular age; they have particular physical (dis)abilities; and they have a unique set of experiences. Their singing is influenced, therefore, by a myriad of varying social factors. A reduced explanation of singing development that focuses on musical elements and vocal skills, that plots singing from the simple to the complex, from two-pitch falling minor third intervals (as some models suggest), clearly misses out on the whole family, home, media, technology and socio-economic context in which children live, and, I think very importantly, the expressiveness of the emotions attached. Ideas about what is normal in development have been closely linked to ideas that development is driven by natural biological processes of maturing and growth, and that this is a process that takes place within the individual child, that is, largely detached from context, situation, subjectivity and emotion. This has been the major criticism of psychological perspectives on childhood, namely, that they remove contextual factors and thus produce an image of the child who is detached, individualised, focused merely on narrow skills and musical knowledge – an artificial musical child who does not exist.

The example of Ted demonstrates that singing unfolds with others, in sociable situations within which songs are shared. If their singing is received and listened to, joined in with, then it has musical meaning. Children live rich emotional and imaginative lives. Ted's singing of this song resonated with his emotional engagement with the film, its narrative and imagery, a complex dynamic interaction in which development is embedded and requires a much more complex understanding of the multiple ways in which children progress musically. Nor is their learning a smooth, continuous, predictable pathway, but discontinuous and unpredictable. Many are taking from Deleuzian philosophy the concept of a rhizome – endlessly proliferating, connected, interconnected, shooting in unpredictable directions – as a useful alternative to the linear pathway. Nor do little children start with the simple and progress, step by step, to the more complex. The *Finding Dory* song was complex. Children attempt what is meaningful and motivating for them, and will take from experiences around them what they can currently absorb and manage, adapting it musically to their current abilities. At the time I was writing this, a YouTube clip was circulating on social media of two-year-old Khaliyl Iloyi rapping with his father, which provides a powerful example of how children take musically from what is close to them. The little boy performed bodily movements, a slow heavy nodding of the head in rap style, the strong underpinning downbeat felt through the body of his father as he stood between his knees, the rhythmic punching out of syllables and meaningless word-scraps from his own vocabulary reserves. The whole musical event was highly meaningful for the boy, absorbing embodied markers of musical identity within the folds of his father's musical world.

Developmentalism

Developmentalism has had a greater influence on our conceptions, understanding of and approach to children, their education and childhood, their musical activity and experiences than any other disciplinary perspective. Discovering the stages of development and their implications for pedagogy and practice became one of the main aims of twentieth century research, particularly after the cognitive revolution of the 1960s stimulated by Piaget's stages of cognitive development. Notions of children's progression from one developmental stage to the next are deeply entrenched in education practice, but rarely made explicit or carefully examined. Curriculum books and programmes are still largely underpinned by a developmental conception of children. The example of Ted's singing in the car shows just how much has to be taken out and erased from children's musical experiences if the only perspective, the only story, is a developmental one. There are, as I stressed in the first chapter, many alternative perspectives from which to view and interpret the musical activity of young children, many stories to tell. Furthermore, developmentalism defines how children can act musically and be musical according to very specific normative definitions. Did Ted's soaring song, quite outside the normal expectations of singing development for his age and stage, suggest that his singing and his musical development was in some way lacking, that he was unable to control and pitch his voice accurately, or articulate the words, or remember a whole song? By trying to pigeonhole what they do into normative stages, children's music-making can so easily be found wanting, framed negatively, and the positive aspects that do not fit the ready-made mould can be easily overlooked.

The concept of development assumes that children are moving towards an assumed endpoint in adulthood, that they are progressively *becoming* more knowledgeable, skilled, rational and predictable. But this conception has an inevitable downside, for it then positions very young children, just starting out, as the least adult, as unknowing, unskilled, irrational and unreliable. When the social constructionist view of childhood pointed out how views of childhood are constructed, it questioned this deficit model, asking how and why children were positioned and imaged in this way and considered 'lesser than'. Earlier I argued that the youngest children suffer the most from this deficit positioning. Indeed, as I suggested, adults' interests, desires and needs may be being served by positioning and imaging young children in this way, by framing them as innocent and vulnerable. The way we conceive of their dependence and the forms of incompetence we ascribe to them are neither essential nor inevitable, as countless ethnographic accounts of young children around the world have shown. Even babies, since the 1960s, have been shown to be able to exercise agency, to contribute to the relationships of which they are part and to shape their own development. They seek out what they need, what interests them, and ignore what does not. They can communicate in an expressive language of vocalisations, gestures and facial expressions. They manage themselves physically within their increasing movement vocabulary, moulding themselves or resisting, tensing or relaxing; they can look and track and reach for things, batting them and later grasping.

Moreover, developmentalism not only blinkers our view of young children as musical, it also imposes limitations on the pedagogical process, narrowing our role in it. With my music educator hat on, driving Ted back home, I was only offering him simplified songs that I associated with his singing age in developmental terms, not all kinds of expressive, imaginative songs drawn from my real musical life. Did I sing him my favourite Zumba class salsa, or a Fauré song that I have always loved? No, I sang him 'clap your hands' and songs of that ilk, which seem impoverished and slight when I think back.

Developmental models set out to describe typical pathways of progress, what children might be *capable* of, but they then flip over into becoming predictive pathways, setting out what children ought to do, progressively, step by step. In educational practice in many countries, and certainly in the UK, these predetermined ways are marked out strongly in the prime learning areas such as language development and numeracy, that is, in the steps and stages of progress that are given more value and thus attention in early childhood education. Such is the low value generally accorded to music in our education system that children's musical accomplishments and how to support them are not a high priority, nor an issue of concern, particularly given the prevalent beliefs that, as I mentioned earlier, musical ability is a gift of the genes and therefore not susceptible to improvement via structured teaching. However, the consequence of applying strong concepts of developmental progress along narrow, fixed pathways can be seen in the areas such as language development that are given importance. If children do not follow the prescribed pathway of progress, they are considered to be 'delayed' and often quite blatantly described in what are clearly deficit terms. One of the serious consequences in education of over-rigid application of developmental models is the negative categorisation of children.

There are some key issues and questions in relation to musical development that I go on to explore in the next sections. Here, below, I list the issues before going on to expand on each in turn.

- Information gathered systematically from research about children's musicality across the birth to five age phase is in short supply and what we do have does not connect up well. Change across time is not plotted evenly and the methods used to study very young children's musical competences vary from babyhood through to school age.
- There is a quantity of research into the musicality of babies but this has been less interested in what changes across time and what influences change and more concerned with identifying innate competences.
- What information we have has been drawn from small samples and mainly from WEIRD families. We do not have information about musical development across diverse groups.
- Musical competence has many dimensions and varies with musical traditions, so deciding what musical competences count and then how they change is complicated. What counts as musical progress is valued differently by different social groups.
- Changes in musical competence are brought about by environmental experience.

Issues and questions

The first point to hold in mind is that most of the research into musical development has been carried out with children older than five years, mainly in middle childhood during the years of schooling when children are easily accessible and testable. Some research has dipped down to the earliest ages of four and five, perhaps three, when children are attending preschool but this tends to be the exception. For example, one of the most widely known proposed models of musical development, known as the Swanwick and Tillman spiral, is based on data collected from school-age children, with a little data added in later from three- and four-year-old children as an afterthought (1986). The earliest stages of the spiral from birth upwards are based not on data but on theoretical speculation influenced by Keith Swanwick's interest in Piaget's theory of cognitive development. Therefore, although there is a strong belief in the importance of developmentally appropriate practice for early childhood music, in reality research studies that track children's musical development across the birth to five age phase and provide us with reliable information are in very short supply. There are some which follow children for a shorter period of time, but again very few, and they all take very different foci, in different locations, with different age phases and methods of study. Models of singing development, for example, have mostly been arrived at by studying largish, single-age cohorts of children in educational settings and plotting different levels of competence among those children. Stacking the different levels of competence found among one age group does not imply that developing singers, starting at younger ages, will progress along that pathway arrived at from plotting emerging competences in one older age group. The upshot is that we know very little about children's musicality in early childhood, and we certainly know almost nothing about their musical competences and how they progress in the present circumstances of musical childhoods. Donald Pond of the Pillsbury studies may tell us about children's spontaneous music-play in 1930s California (published later in Moorhead & Pond, 1977); Helmut Moog may tell us about children's responses to a set of tests in 1960s Germany (1968); Johanella Tafuri tells us much about children's musical development in 1990s Italy (2008). All of these provide very valuable information about how young children's music changes and progresses in their countries during their times, from their particular perspectives. But even Johanella Tafuri's children, the most recent, were not living in today's touchscreen digitised music worlds.

Undeniably, there has been an expansion of interest in studying the musicality of babies as part of a wider expansion into infant psychology. The 1960s and 70s had seen a change of view from the baby assumed to be a 'blank sheet', incompetent and knowing nothing, to a competent baby depicted as arriving already equipped with, or at least predisposed to acquire, sophisticated skills (Burman, 2017). This expansion has gone hand in hand with the development of novel methods for testing babies' responses and behaviours, and has provided a new basis for understanding how children experience their musical environments after birth. With babies there have been a number of focused studies, mainly carried out in a handful of laboratories, that have looked at responses to very specific music listening and perception tasks (see Trehub, 2015). Overall, our understanding of babies' capacities for perception, cognition, memory, learning, social engagement and communication is now far greater than had been imagined before (LeVine, 1998:111).

The main reason for this attention to babies, however, is that studying babies can suggest the origins of musical abilities that are common to all children and give some pointers for generic theories of musical foundations. The focus of interest is on what musical abilities might be innate, as 'hard-wired' universals of human musicality, and may have some kind of genetic basis therefore (Trehub, 2015). For early childhood music education they are indeed valuable in showing us just how musically competent babies are and for revising our musical expectations of very young children. However, in general, the aim of these researchers is not to plot how these competences might change and progress as children grow, or what factors might influence change.

Two notable Canadian researchers, Sandra Trehub and Laurel Trainor, have founded laboratories where many studies into infant auditory perception, in particular focusing on responses to musical elements, have been carried out. As with neuroscientific studies, the research isolates and explores small, discrete musical elements and is interested in whether babies can detect changes as a sign of perception, discrimination and early musical abilities. They reduce infant musicality to decontextualised, small, isolated skills that may then later link, combine and evolve into more complex skills. The tests are not representative of real-life musical experience. Read any account of the psychology of infant musicality and it presents a long list of studies, each apparently demonstrating one atomistic musical skill. One study may be slightly modified or even refuted by a later study; plotting this incremental field of research can take persistence. Babies as musical – individualised, rationalised, isolated – are framed within the context of the research studies, defined by what is of interest to the adult researchers, and responses are attributed and interpreted by them. Experimental studies of this type take place in a social vacuum, deliberately so, in order to isolate specific skills.

David Peterson recently spent time in three infant study laboratories, making an ethnographic study of the research environment and processes (2016). He pointed out the difficult balancing act involved in producing robust science, with exactly similar procedures carried out with every baby in order to arrive at strong statistical evidence, while at the same time trying to achieve this with babies who at any moment might fall asleep, resist with a tantrum or chew on the research materials. As a result of 'the rarity of infant subjects, the unpredictability and ambiguity of their responses, and the pressures of the academic environment', the 'experimenters are willing to overlook many of the hiccups that occur during experimentation' (Peterson, 2016:4). To compound the overlooking of hiccups in the data collection process, the attrition rates in these studies are also surprisingly high. I will add here that even attrition rates in formal studies among older children may be surprisingly high. For example, a study of singing development with four- and five-year-olds reported only around 50% participation (Welch, *et al.*, 1996). The number of dropouts prompts the question as to how the responses of the babies and children who are not included in the data sets might have influenced the outcomes. Why did they not participate, or why were their responses not included? What might we learn from the non-participants? The message from Peterson's study is that the reliability and comprehensibility of such lab-based studies may not be as robust as the academic reporting may imply. Again, as I said in relation to the neuroscientific studies, this does not mean that the results from such studies should be rejected, but that they should be taken with a dose of caution and an awareness of the realities of this kind of experimentation.

In the 'toddler' years between about twelve months to three years of age there is very little research into musical behaviours and how they progress. There are some obvious, practical reasons for this gap. Toddlers, once they are mobile, are up and away, inquisitive, not very biddable and have limited ability to understand instructions. Depending on the country and its childcare system, many children of this age may still spend much of their time at home, where they are difficult to access, at least in any numbers, to arrive at larger sample sizes. In recent years more children have been entering daycare at younger ages as mothers return to work, and so there are some studies of one- and two-year-olds in settings (e.g. Suthers, 2004), particularly studies that adopt freer observational methods of two-year-olds playing together in peer groups (e.g. Arculus, 2013; Nome, 2016;) rather than expecting children to perform uniform tasks that can then be collated and assessed.

Helga Gudmundsdottir explains something very fundamental to psychological research – and she is referring to research that attempts to collect the results from a test applied consistently to a group of children – namely, that the context and content of the test has a huge influence on the kinds of musical competences that young children can reveal (Gudmundsdottir, 2018). Interested in toddlers' singing, she has focused on one- to three-year-olds in her studies (the tricky age to study). She has collected their singing from two sources: first from carefully designed methods that include playful activities in nursery settings, and second from video clips of toddlers singing posted on YouTube. When little children are filmed singing by family and friends, as in the YouTube clips, they are most at ease, singing in everyday, familiar situations, just as Ted was at the start of this chapter. For a study of young children attending preschools in Reykjavik, Iceland, she adopted a method which aimed to provide a more playful and friendly setting which would elicit the children's positive participation. They ensured the person administering the test was known to the children, invited the children to sing familiar songs rather than repeat an unfamiliar test song, invited them to play games with puppets and so on. This work is ongoing, but Gudmundsdottir is discovering that very young children have singing competences that refute many of the assumptions of limited pitch range and ability to pitch match among toddlers written into traditional developmental models. The systematic underestimation in the research and practice literature of young children's singing abilities that Gudmundsdottir is finding from her work is sure to apply beyond this one domain of musical activity to other domains. I would like to add that these Icelandic children are the first generation to have lived in an immersive, interactive digital musical environment from birth and I wonder how this too is contributing to their apparently advanced singing abilities?

But, in general, this 'toddler gap' means that the research in the birth to five age phase is very patchy and fragmented (Young, 2016a). There are laboratory studies of specific music perceptual and processing abilities in babies carried out by music psychologists, followed by a very small number of recent, mainly observational studies of toddlers in naturalistic play behaviours. These are followed by a larger group of varied studies based on both formal testing and more interpretive methods around the ages of three and four years, but these studies are mainly carried out in the applied fields of education, therapy or performance arts, are driven by interests in the processes of learning, the efficacy of educational and therapeutic strategies and so on, and are less concerned with plotting development.

In the handful of studies that have looked at aspects of musical development among very young children, including toddlers, the researchers' own children are often the focus of individual case study research (e.g. Papoušek & Papoušek, 1981; Forrester, 2010; de Vries, 2005, 2009). Several researchers have also asked parents to keep diaries, or make video and audio recordings of their children's music-making at home, enabling them to collect more information from more children (e.g. Tafuri, 2008; Retra, 2010; Barrett, 2009; Adachi, 2012). While all these studies produce some informative accounts, there are methodological challenges in the objective study of one's own child. Academic researchers may be able to apply more objectivity, but parents collecting data will be tempted to present their child in a good light, thus biasing what they report. More seriously, the children of academics and the children of friends and family, or those attending private music groups, typically belong to this same specific demographic group – the WEIRD families yet again – and therefore, as I have emphasised before, these findings have limited relevance beyond this one demographic. All too often the children who are the subjects of these studies are assumed to stand for a generic 'child', who is genderless, classless, able-bodied, without race or ethnicity, a mythical child constructed by the study procedures and also by how the studies are written and reported to us. This issue and its detrimental consequences were presented very clearly by Beatriz Ilari and her colleagues in a study of musical development among children living in low-income Latino families in Los Angeles (2016).

So, despite a strong belief in the value of developmentally appropriate practice, empirical studies providing evidence on which early childhood practice, birth to five, can draw for information are in very short supply. What studies we have focus on various ages without continuity through the birth to five age phase, tend to draw their conclusions from one very limited population of children or from the different levels of competence revealed by research with groups of older children.

To complicate matters further, Alexandra Lamont asks a very straightforward but fundamental question: is musical development one thing or many

(2016:405)? Musical capability involves many different areas: singing, making music with material sound-producers (objects, instruments, digital technologies), moving rhythmically and dancing, listening, discriminating and responding to music, creating and improvising, and learning to use and read forms of symbolic representation. Then, within each area, there are many different components. Singing consists of many different skill areas, for example. So should one model of musical development attempt to encompass all those different areas, or are there individual pathways of musical development for the separate areas of competence, and even within each separate area a further breakdown of each competence? Some of these aspects, such as being able to produce a singing tone with the voice or coordinate bodily movements in rhythmic actions depend in part on biological maturation of bodily mechanisms, which implies separate learning pathways tied to physical growth and maturation. Equally, learning to pitch the voice accurately also relies on perceptual and aural discrimination skills coupled with vocal technique, and then opportunities to learn and practise depend on the child's experience and environment. Those aspects of musical capability that are more dependent on physical maturation, such as the growth of the body parts involved in learning to sing, would seem more susceptible to similar – and I stress 'similar', not the same – patterns of development. Pre-empting a discussion I will pick up in the final chapter, even apparently biological maturation is very susceptible to cultural variation. Khaliyl, the two-year-old rapper, is learning to use his voice in similar, but stylistically quite different, directions to Ted. He is learning to produce the timbre and verbal articulation typical of rap artists. Aural perception depends on a combination of genetic ability and experience, and so hearing a lot of singing and a wide variety of different songs will help build up aural discrimination abilities. Khaliyl was building up discriminatory skills for the distinctive nuances of rhythm, timbre and phrasing in rap; Ted was building up skills for soaring, melodic Disney tunes.

Other aspects of musical competence require conceptual understandings, that is, a growing ability to think musically. This dimension of musical development encompasses children's capacities to think musically in all the different musical areas, including pitch and tonality, rhythmic structure, timbre, form and style. Then children learn to apply their musical thinking in the different performance domains of singing, using instruments, moving, composing, improvising, reading music and relating sounds to symbols. These performance experiences will take place in different situations where emotions come into play, introducing a dimension that developmental models ignore and which would embrace Ted's aesthetic and emotional connection to the Disney song and the mini-rapper's pleasure and pride in singing with his father. When one starts to unpick all that is involved in musical progress, it is little wonder that it is so complex and that maybe rhizomatic imagery or ideas of assemblages capture it more completely than linear pathways and brief statements of anticipated ability.

Jeanne Bamberger then asks the follow-on questions which complicate things even more (2005). What counts in musical development? What counts as achievement and progress? Scientific methods of testing on which models of development are typically based usually involve controlled experiments. Typically, a group of children are all given the same test or task to perform individually, one that focuses on a small musical element or specific skill such as repeating rhythm patterns, singing back a short phrase of a song or creating a small improvisation on a pentatonic scale. The aim is to try to home in on one aspect of children's musical ability, with other variables removed or at least reduced as far as possible. Their 'scores' in the tests are collected together and analysed numerically. Jeanne Bamberger points out that research into musical development and what changes has tended to focus on musical abilities that are the easiest to study and identify (2005). But these may not be the most important in terms of genuine musicality and musicianship and, moreover, they are invariably drawn from one dominant musical tradition, Western art music. For example, experimental studies may plot the progress of children's ability to recognise small differences in pitch and pitch intervals or to be able to perform pitch or rhythmic units accurately, but are these abilities the most essential to being musical? Would we not consider expressiveness and creativity, too, to be essential qualities of musicianship? Being able to improvise is not a priority in Western art music, but it is the most important skill in many genres of music. Conversely, much importance is placed on the accuracy of being 'in tune' and 'in time' in the performance of Western music and these, in turn, are set as the benchmarks for children's progress. What is valued, musically, in adulthood and in a specific culture becomes a set of anchor-points for musical progress. Now, with the arrival of sophisticated technologies and digitised music, children are acquiring very different sets of musical competences from the earliest ages and, what's more, will need new musical skills for their own futures. What counts as progress in the developmental models that are typically informing music education is drawn from an image of a limited, conventional and retrospective musical child.

In sum then, young children's music-making and how it develops and progresses is clearly much more complex, integrated, creative and expressive than can be captured via simple tests or set out in tick-box models of musical development. But, as ever, I want to give a balanced view and, in spite of these many limitations that I have spelt out, possible pathways of progress that map out measurable skills and competences are certainly valuable to educators in providing templates for learning that guide, without dictating, as part of a well-rounded, wide-reaching music education. There need also to be ways of accommodating and providing for the many other valuable aspects that are then left out. The overall question threading through this chapter is what image of children as musical is created by viewing them through the developmental window; in particular, what does it show us and what does it hide?

This brings us to the next essential question: what is the relationship between development and learning through experience (e.g. Hannon & Trainor, 2007)? The two are clearly not separate, and yet models of musical development often imply a biologically based, inner processing that unfolds irrespective of experience. A consequence of attempting to measure developmental steps separately from any kind of context is that it reinforces the idea that development appears to happen within the child. What children can do musically is deeply interwoven with the kinds of experiences they receive, whether unstructured and just part of everyday participation in musical lives or deliberate and structured in educational practices.

One interesting and valuable exception to the lack of longitudinal research, and one which addressed this question of the relationship between development and experience, is a study by Johanella Tafuri in Bologna, Italy, that tracked developing musical behaviours of a group of babies through their toddler and early childhood years (2008). I briefly introduced it earlier. She recruited a group of mothers with newborns who attended regular music sessions and kept diaries of home musical activities. Focusing on singing development, what Johanella found was that children could achieve the expected milestones of singing development at an earlier age if the environment was 'music rich', that is, full of opportunities both at home and in the sessions designed to promote learning. The study is interesting for demonstrating, if confirmation were necessary and not already self-evident, that development is an interaction between many factors – social, cultural, biological, developmental – and deliberate instruction obviously makes a difference.

Theoretical conceptions of musical development

I move on now, in the following sections, to explain in more detail theoretical conceptions of musical development. I look back briefly to Jean Piaget's general theory of cognitive development because it has had a huge influence on conceptions of development and learning in early childhood. I also look back to older conceptions of how children develop musically because these still lie deep in the conventional 'methods' and so need to be brought to light. I then move forward from Piaget and look at more recent work inspired by social, relational approaches to development, including inspiration from Lev Vygotsky's theorising (1978) and Stephen Malloch and Colwyn Trevarthen's communicative theories of musicality (2010). This has been a rich vein of influence from psychological directions that has connected with a synthesis of insights into music as social process arising from the sociology and anthropology of music. Thus we can see how the psychological theories emphasising relational processes integrate with the sociological and anthropological theorising of music as social action and interaction, making connections back to music in everyday life, its uses and meanings in children's lives. Finally, I introduce some more recent developments from ecological and systems theory which are attempting to conceptualise even more theoretically integrated approaches for the purpose of understanding young children's activity. Throughout these next sections I draw attention to the images and constructions of young children articulated within these shifts of theoretical perspective.

Piaget again!

The ideas of Jean Piaget and Lev Vygotsky, whose main work was carried out in the 1920s, remain the most influential in current developmental psychology. Their theories have to be seen in the context of their time, the scientific knowledge that prevailed, and the images and understandings of children and childhoods that were current. Piaget gave a comprehensive account children's development as a highly deterministic series of discrete stages that move from sensorimotor action in earliest childhood to autonomous logical thinking in later childhood. Each stage is defined in terms of a specific cognitive structure and he described children's development in largely individualistic and egocentric terms. In very earliest childhood (his stage of sensorimotor action), learning through discovery tends to emphasise what children are not yet able to do, taking conventional adult competences as an implicit endpoint of development. Many of these ideas have been subsequently challenged by carefully crafted research studies showing, for example, empathic and sociable (not egocentric) behaviours, even among babies, and forms of logical reasoning among young children (e.g. Gopnik, et al., 2015). It has often been shown, just as we saw with Helga Gudmundsdottir's work with toddlers' singing, that the type of task and the context are crucial in either revealing or obscuring what children are able to do (Gundmundsdottir, 2018). Margaret Donaldson, for example, famously demonstrated that a subtle change in the task so that it made better sense to children could transform their performance in some traditional Piagetian cognitive tests (1978).

There is no doubt that Piaget's age and stage theory has had a profound influence on models of musical development and on conceptions of young children as musical. The strong suggestion from Piagetian theory that children are unable to perform 'concrete operations' until around the age of seven years (Piaget, 1954) and that before that time they are mainly engaged in exploratory, playful, intuitive discovery that lacks any kind of serious purpose or outcome is still surprisingly persistent in mainstream music education thinking. This has led to several theories of musical development that imply children can do little that is worthy of serious attention until they reach the years of middle childhood. John Kratus, for example, focusing on children's development as composers, suggested that prior to the age of nine children are limited to exploring musical ideas rather than repeating ideas leading to more defined, thought-through 'composing' processes (e.g. Kratus, 1989). There are many interesting studies of children younger than nine years creating their own music that clearly refute this suggestion (see Glover, 2000). Yet it is still largely taken for granted, both in research and practice, that young children progress from the simple to the complex, from the concrete to the abstract, from randomness to rationalisation, from embodied experience to cerebral conceptual thinking. The persistence of these kinds of presumptions contribute, in my view, to marginalisation of early childhood among music education academics, to the types of research that tend to predominate, and to the pronouncements in policy and provision that tend to give priority to older children.

On the other hand, there are ways in which Piaget's ideas may have more in common with recent perspectives on childhood than is sometimes acknowledged. His ideas on cognitive development do show a serious concern to try to grasp children's own ways of understanding their world (Thomas, 2004:22), and through very careful observation he tried to conceptualise and explain how children are actively and creatively constructing their own, distinctive ways of understanding. Thus, young children are described as being in a stage of cognitive ability that is qualitatively different from older children and adults. So, while the 'new' sociology of childhood harshly criticised the shortcomings of developmental models as rigid, limiting and imposing prescriptions, we also do need to understand, respect and find ways to work within young children's levels of cognitive development. Developmental psychology can provide some useful concepts for doing so and there are some interesting examples of applied Piagetian theory in early childhood music that show how this can be done. François Delalande and his team in Northern Italy (2015) and Esther Beyer in Brazil (1996; Pecker, 2014) have both adopted Piagetian concepts (concepts of children's cognition rather than the model of development), in particular the concept of assimilation and accommodation, to develop their understanding of first musical encounters of babies and toddlers. Delalande carried out a study of around fifty-five children aged ten to thirty-seven months attending daycare in Northern Italy, individually playing either a zither or cymbals. Piagetian theory provided him and his team with concepts that enabled them to propose ways in which children understand the process of producing sounds from instruments as sound objects and how they extend and organise their sound-making. Esther Beyer in Brazil spent twenty years focusing on music with babies, combining practical sessions with theoretical explorations based on Piagetian theory and methods to explore children's understanding (Pecker, 2014).

Philosophical approaches

In 1920s Switzerland, Valentine and Jean Piaget observed their own small children and kept reflective diaries in the tradition of the child-study movement of that time, and these provided the starting points for Piaget's theories. It is valuable to look back before the rise of experimental methods as a basis for psychological theories of children's development and to recognise that observation and philosophical thinking about children's learning and musical experience in real-world situations had been the primary method for arriving at pronouncements on the aims and ideal methods for educating children, in general, and also in music specifically. Such philosophical approaches have given rise to several methods for teaching music to young children, most prominently the methods known as Orff, Dalcroze and Kodály that I introduced in the first chapter. It is important to recognise that these approaches to music education belong to specific times and places, marked by European politics, the social and cultural milieu of the time, and conceptions of learning, music and childhood. Émile Jaques-Dalcroze, for example, observed the music-learning difficulties of the children and students he worked with at the Conservatoire in Geneva (Jaques-Dalcroze, 1967/1921). He realised that educational strategies needed to enable his students to feel the music in an embodied way and that embodiment could then provide a basis for conceptual understanding. His movement-based approach to music education thus originated not from experimental research but from reflective thinking about his practical teaching experiences. True, there have since been systematic studies that seek to investigate aspects of Dalcroze pedagogy, as there have been with Kodály and Orff pedagogies, often with the aim of testing the efficacy of these particular approaches in comparison with control groups (e.g. Rose, 1995), but the original inception of these methods arose from observation and thinking.

In Dalcroze eurhythmics the original principles of learning music through bodily movement came, in later years, to align closely with Piagetian sensori-motor and preoperational origins of children's cognitive processing. Geneva was the home both of the Institut Jaques-Dalcroze and of Piaget, who worked at the university. So it is no surprise that in my studies at the Institut in the early 1970s close associations were made between the theory of Piaget and his sensorimotor origins of conceptual thought and the philosophies of embodied music-learning of Jaques-Dalcroze.

The child-study approach based on observation, diary-keeping and reflection is also found in the landmark Pillsbury Nursery study. Opened in 1937 and running until around 1948, this nursery in Santa Barbara, California, was set up with funding from the Pillsbury Foundation for 'the intention of studying the principles which govern young children's relationship to music' (Moorhead & Pond, 1977). The nursery environment was designed to foster children's self-initiated music-making and was well equipped with musical instruments, including drums, guitars and gamelan instruments. Donald Pond, a composer, and Gladys Moorhead, a child development expert, observed, listened and collected detailed records of the children's musical play and their documentation is now written up in a series of small pamphlets. These remain to this day a highly valuable account of young children's music-making when left to their own devices in a musically enriched and supportive environment. The work is unique for its tracking of the same group of children over time, for the wide range of ages from toddlers through to school age, and for the detail which was collected. The Pillsbury Nursery study inspired several follow-on studies interested in children's musical play (e.g. Cohen, 1980; Kierstead, 2006; Shelley, 1981).

Donald Pond's accounts of young children's musical activity reveal a particular conception of musical childhood prevalent at that time and which is also to be found underlying the methods, particularly the approaches inspired by Orff and Kodály. The very young child, having received no formal music education, is seen as uninfluenced by adult culture. Philosophically, there are links made between the 'primitive' child and 'primitive' precultural musics (traditional musics and very early music) through what has been called recapitulation theory. There was a belief, deriving from Hall's recapitulation theory of the early twentieth century, that children's development repeated the evolution of music in a compressed and rapid form, beginning with simple chants and then moving to more sophisticated and civilised musical forms (see Cox, 2015). Here is Zoltán Kodály clearly setting out this conception of development in his writing of 1951: 'In the same way as the child's development repeats in brief the evolution of mankind, his forms of music represent a history of music; indeed they afford a glimpse into the prehistoric period of music' (Kodály, 1974:46). Orff Schulwerk, devised in the 1920s, encapsulates recapitulation theory in the idea that the starting points of both music and children's musical development lie in repetitive rhythmic and melodic patterns, drones and ostinati, and move progressively towards more complex tonal structures. The use of special barred instruments derived from Indonesian gamelan and African balafon (xylophones) was also seen by Orff as a natural starting point for children, using the instruments of precultural musics brought to Europe by anthropologists. Quite clearly, African and Indonesian musics should never be thought of as primitive, but such was the thinking of that time. For sure, Orff Schulwerk has evolved its approaches over the years, although in a recent presentation from Austrian colleagues I was interested to hear the founding principles reiterated, namely, that children should be introduced to the fundamental elements of music in creative and improvisatory activities that engage bodies and voices (Kinsky, et al., 2017).

In these conceptions, evident in both Pond's and Kodály's writings and Orff Schulwerk, the child is constructed as musically knowing, as possessing a form of inner, pure musical wisdom, which is intuitive, creative and natural, and needs to be brought to life by sensitive educative strategies. The construction of young children as innocent, but still in touch with a kind of magical underworld of music, primitive and pagan, unsullied by adult, cultural influences, is evident in the conception of musical childhood as recapitulation. This conception of children's musical cultures as special and separate, incidentally, strikes a contrast with William Corsaro's ideas of interpretive reproduction that I introduced earlier. But at the same time, in contradictory fashion, the musical child in recapitulatory versions of development is placed at the start of a pathway that assumes children know nothing of music in its sophisticated cultural forms and must be inducted progressively towards more complex musical forms of Western culture (see Cox, 2015 for a more extended discussion). The concept of a progression of musical simplicity to complexity mapping exactly onto children's musical development in cognitive and psychological terms is still deeply woven into many of these well-known methods and, in my view, contributes to their conservatism.

Yet constructions of the young child as possessing a pure, unsullied musicality are alive and well, resurfacing, albeit couched in different terminology, in more recent emphases on creativity in education and the progressive, child-centred approaches that call for children to be given the freedoms to discover and express their own musicality and musical ideas. The move to child-centred approaches has become closely associated in recent years with theoretical directions that endorse the value of play as a medium through which young children learn musically. In this child-centred turn there is often a strong emphasis on children's creativity and originality. Children are described as unique; their differences and individuality are emphasised, picking up on the sociological directions of the 1990s and beyond that focused on variations among children rather than sameness. This musical creativity was – and is still – often conceptualised as fragile and special and needing to be released, nurtured and preserved by adults who endeavour to attune to children's forms of musicality in order to understand it on their terms. This child-centred turn has found a well-fitting affiliation and affirmation in the pedagogical principles and approaches of the nurseries of Reggio Emilia in Northern Italy, which famously espouse child-led, creative approaches to curriculum development.

My own research studies and much writing have been strongly rooted in what I now recognise to be part of this nexus of theoretical ideas circulating academically in the 1990s: the paradigm of the times. These were, namely, that musicality is possessed by all, that young children possess their own unique forms of children's musicality, and that playful music opportunities enable children to express and develop their own forms of musical thinking. A somewhat idealised image of the playing, musical child was part of a movement at the time to shift the locus of agency in music education from the adult to the child and to argue that children possessed their own musicality, which education should seek to draw out and build on, and that they were not simply 'empty vessels' to be filled via didactic pedagogical strategies. In early childhood the value of play as a source of children's learning in music required strong argumentation – and indeed still does – in the face of dominant traditions of adult-led, 'top-down', skill-based music teaching, even for quite young children. However, those of us writing and working in this 'music as play' turn drew attention to children's musical agency and forms of competence by emphasising the child as nature – the innocent, pure trope of the romantic construction of childhood. I can see that now.

In one sense, these contrasting positions can be simply understood as children's 'being' in playful, self-generated musical activities and children's 'becoming' in adult-guided, sequenced learning activities. The same tension existed for the recapitulationists in the contradiction between children possessing intuitive knowledge of precultural musics but without knowledge of cultural musical forms. The challenge, which we have yet to tackle properly and resolve, lies in finding ways that children can be both 'being and becoming', integrating both constructions of musical childhood across a spectrum of different pedagogical approaches, as I have tried to argue for and illustrate in much of my own writing (e.g. Young, 2003a). All too often the two approaches are pitted against each other as 'either or' – either child-centred or adult-centred, progressive versus traditional – with both sides vehemently sticking to their convictions without seeking out integrations, blends and hybrid approaches.

Thus, in these shifting ideas of how children learn and progress in music and the pedagogical strategies that these give rise to, we uncover the constructions, the changing images of childhood that they implicitly assume. Children, musically, are presented as pure, natural, innocent, creative and unique, with characteristics that need to be understood and preserved. In keeping with Piagetian thinking, we can see images of children as having their own qualitatively distinct forms of musical thinking and cognitive processing, embodied, exploratory and also containing generative forms of musical thinking. In earlier understandings of musical childhoods, they are thought of as blank slates, in need of instruction step by step in structured learning sequences, and fed only 'good' music so that they learn to be musically discriminating adults. These constructions may be rationalised and explained in relation to contemporary theories of children's musical learning, but these images of musical childhood are very persistent. I doubt anyone would write now in the florid language of Dalcroze or Kodály, but contemporary constructions adopt the language of the times and talk of 'the unique child', innate creativity, empowerment and potential. How we image and understand children as musical gives rise to culturally defined notions of educational practice, and by unpicking the constructions and, more importantly, our own personal and often emotion-invested attachments to them, the way they shape educational practice can become apparent. This understanding then provides the opportunity for change.

But for now I need to return to Piagetian theory, the pivot point of this chapter, to pick up another thread of discussion.

From philosophical to scientific approaches

The influence of positivism, the belief that science is best suited to explain not just the natural world but also the world of human behaviour, including children's development, led to a very different approach to studying and thinking about young children, away from the philosophical and reflective approaches. Developmental psychology with its methods of experimental testing came to dominate educational thinking, reaching its height in the 1970s and 80s. So it was obvious that a developmental psychology of music would emerge from this broader theoretical movement. In 1986 David Hargreaves published *The Developmental Psychology of Music*, a landmark text. In the same year the *British Journal of Music Education* published articles presenting a developmental model of singing by Graham Welch (1986) and a generic model of musical development by June Tillman and Keith Swanwick, based on June Tillman's research (1986). These publications marked the heyday of developmental thinking in music education, the height of a belief in the search for general laws of growth in music shared by all children and attempts to explain how and why children think and behave musically in certain ways.

The swathe of research and theorising inspired by developmental psychology has provided many insights. I am concerned to present a balanced view in which we do not tip the baby out with the bathwater, but at the same time keep a clear-sighted view of shortcomings. It is very valuable to go back to research studies from that time and read the reports for the detailed analyses of children's musical thinking and how they might acquire conceptual understanding in music that they contain. In an earlier drafting of this chapter I included explanations of the work by Marilyn Zimmerman (1991) and Jeanne Bamberger (2005), fascinated to go back to their meticulous unpickings of children's musical problem-solving and their thoughts about children's musical concepts and how they develop. But the children they studied were of older ages than the early childhood age phase I focus on in this book, as is the case with almost all research curious about children's musical cognition and development, because the research often required children to understand the task instructions. So I had to accept that their work sits outside the scope of this chapter. However, reading these studies I reflected that in our current era we seem to have lost some of this painstaking analysis of musical cognition, searching for how to conceptualise young children's musical thinking and particularly to understand how it emerges in real-life, practical situations. As two exceptions, José Retra's microanalyses of movement responses among the young participants of Dutch music sessions (2010) and Veronika Cohen's analysis of two children's playful improvisations as gestural structures in the US (1980) – work that Veronika has extended for many years – both arrive, in quite different ways, at embodied theories of how young children construct their musical thinking.

Moving on from the 1980s models of musical development, psychologists themselves were starting to become only too aware of the shortcomings that were so strongly highlighted, if a little oversimplistically, by the new sociology of childhood and were also starting to challenge the tenets of traditional versions of developmental psychology. There were two main shifts. The first shift arrived from critiques within postmodern or critical-theory approaches, coupled with the arguments from sociology of social constructionism, that research, theory and childhood are the products of cultural activity and never stand alone, independent from the discourses through which they are produced. Although this first set of critiques was voiced by the sociologists of childhood, challenges from critical theorists were also arising from within the field of psychology (e.g. Walkerdine, 1993; Burman, 2017). The second shift was a move towards conceptualising child psychological development as a social and cultural process, mainly through the influence of Lev Vygotsky as well as others. Urie Bronfenbrenner, for example, proposed a new theoretical approach to the study of children that he named 'the ecology of human development', in which he conceptualised a dynamic relationship between individual development and sociocultural context (1979). Alexandra Lamont has developed conceptions of musical development that specifically focus on pitch perception from an ecological perspective, suggesting how the social and cultural environment mediates children's musical behaviours at the individual and personal level (Hargreaves & Lamont, 2017:38–39).

Another group of psychological studies focused on cross-cultural comparisons of beliefs about children, children's behaviours and child-rearing practices, rejecting any assumptions of the universal or 'decontextualised' child (e.g. Göncü, 1999; Rogoff, 2003; Kağıtçıbaşı, 2007). I have found this culturally informed set of studies very useful and Beatriz Ilari and I have drawn on Barbara Rogoff's ideas of learning as participation in some of our collaborative writing (Young & Ilari, 2012). Beatriz is Brazilian-born and a champion of a more culturally inflected approach to theorising young children's musical experiences (e.g. 2013a). Clearly, there is an overlap here with anthropological approaches interested in the wider cultural context and how it impacts on children's music, and this I will pick up again later.

Development in a social and cultural context

So while Piaget's theory and the huge wave of theoretical activity that followed his influence held strongly, researchers became increasingly to realise that, quite obviously, children do not develop in a vacuum and turned to the theory of Vygotsky, which offered explanations for development as a process integrated into the social and cultural context. Vygotsky was evolving his ideas in the 1920s and 30s, around the same time as Piaget, but his texts translated from Russian only reached English-reading audiences in the late 1970s (Vygotsky, 1978). Vygotsky and Piaget broadly agree that children are active learners and construct their understanding. However, Vygotsky placed emphasis on the social and cultural aspects whereas Piaget put more emphasis on the biological and individual. Vygotsky's sociocultural approach recognises that children's development is constructed within particular settings and communities. It is much more cautious about proposing any kind of common pattern of development that unfolds 'naturally' from within the child, suggesting instead that this depends on the environments in which children live and the way they are treated. A sociocultural view of development looks much more at the beliefs about childhood and about how children are expected to develop and learn.

While Piaget was interested in identifying the abstract stages of cognitive development and the mental processes involved, Vygotsky explored the relationships between children's social and cognitive development. For Vygotsky, psychological and social skills are acquired from our interactions with others, and so development is as much social and cultural as it is natural. Children have biological and neurological growth which follows a more or less similar pathway, but they interact with those around them and the process of development is thus interactive. There can, therefore, be many developmental pathways determined by the sociocultural context. The environments within which young children participate musically are culturally constructed, shaped by generations of human activity and creativity, mediated by complex belief systems, including beliefs and customs about the proper way for children to develop. The adults around them, with whom they form close relationships, are the most influential aspect of their environment. Learning is enabled through the cognitive 'tools' that are themselves the products of specific cultural environments: the symbolic systems of language and numbers, including music notations, the objects we use such as musical instruments for children and, more recently, digital technologies. These tools powerfully shape the possibilities for learning, offering both potentials and constraints.

Early childhood musical practices and experiences, and the early childhood settings and sessions in which music for young children takes place, are cultural constructions, echoing the start of chapter two where I described a typical early childhood setting and how it constructs a particular image of musical childhoods and a specific set of possibilities for how children can be musical. The types of songs we sing, the instruments and toys we use, the music technologies, the ways we sing with young children, the ways we dance and move, the kinds of activities that are thought appropriate: all these aspects have emerged out of historical and cultural traditions. So children's musical lives and their opportunities to develop musically are profoundly structured by these processes. Viewed from this perspective, children are not seen as learning in individual isolation but through participation in a range of social practices.

Two of Vygotsky's key ideas are internalisation and the zone of proximal development, or ZPD as it is commonly referred to. According to Vygotsky, every function in the child's development appears twice: first on the social level and later on the individual level, first between people (interpsychological) and then inside the child (intrapsychological) (1978:57). He proposed that learners operate on two levels. The first performance level is what the child can do alone, without support. The second, the level of potential development, is what can be achieved with the guidance and support of someone who is more knowledgeable and skilled, usually an adult, but perhaps also a more capable sibling or peer. In singing a song, children may not be able to sing the song completely on their own, but if an adult joins in when they falter, or prompts the next part of the song, they can sing the song with support. So with just the right support at the right moment, children can be a step ahead of where they might be without it. The challenge is for adults to structure and intervene enough to allow the child to accomplish the task or participate in the activity, and to adjust and realign their actions to enhance the child's singing, without doing too little or too much.

Recent research and theorising in early childhood music education has been strongly influenced, and very much enriched, by sociocultural theory (e.g. St John, 2006). I select just two examples. Mayumi Adachi, based in Japan, has long been interested in applying Vygotskian theory (Adachi, 1994). In one study she asked the parents of four children aged two to four years who received two separate periods of ten weekly music sessions to complete daily journals that included a tick-list of possible activities. She found that, outside of the weekly session, the children revisited almost all the songs that had been introduced, often incorporating their mothers into their play but also singing by themselves. She suggested that this illustrated the 'between people' (interpsychological) nature of children's learning and its shift towards an intrapsychological operation as they grow older (Adachi, 2012:145).

84 *Pathways and pigeonholes*

In another interesting application of Vygotskian theory Peter Whiteman followed eight preschoolers aged two to five years during three years of their attendance at an Australian childcare centre and made monthly video recordings of their spontaneous singing during free play (2001, 2009). The 443 songs he collected were transcribed, and each play episode and associated song coded for musical aspects (song type, melodic range, level of temporal organisation) and social aspects (song function, children's social roles). Through detailed 'child-by-child' analysis of the children's singing he was able to plot how individual children transmit and also acquire musical ideas within a ZPD, highlighting the role that peers and other more advanced singers play in supporting and enhancing each child's developing musical abilities (2001). Drawing on this evidence he argues that musical development is an interactive process between individual children and all the experiences they encounter.

Interestingly, while Adachi emphasises the interactive role of adults, both educators and parents, Whiteman focuses on children with other children. These relational theoretical perspectives have been very valuable in enabling us to understand the ways in which communicative interaction helps children to build musical experience. In both these studies the children were learning songs and how to sing through interactive participation with others. Sociocultural perspectives thus help to overcome the limitations of models of musical learning and development that attend only to cognitive and skill-based learning; they can include Ted's *Finding Dory* song and the social contexts of his singing and modes of participation: his singing the song to me and with me in the car and at home along with the DVD.

Coming to the present

So contemporary thinking in childhood studies does not now reject developmental psychology as strongly as its early repudiation, but calls for contemporary versions of development to be incorporated in a multitheoretical framework that recognises its potential contributions alongside open-minded awareness of its potential weaknesses. At the same time, the field of developmental psychology has recently experienced another major shift as it moves towards a concept of development that is dependent on the many different factors of human life and more inclusive of ideas and concepts from biology, culture, environment, society and individual variation, bringing it to an even more interdisciplinary, integrated viewpoint. A group of ideas known as dynamic systems theories emphasise the source of developmental change in the process of two-way interaction among complex environmental and biological/psychological processes (Thelen & Smith, 2007). We are coming full-circle to earlier discussions focusing on biological perspectives which explained how contemporary theoretical positions see biological factors as intrinsically connected with every aspect of the environment, and likewise psychological factors are now understood to be intractably interconnected with environmental factors. The search for one monolithic theory, the grand all-encompassing theories of

Piaget and Vygotsky, has long been abandoned, just as the all-encompassing theories of musical development have largely been put to one side. What we have now is a flexible and diverse theoretical area.

Approaches such as dynamic systems theories view the child as networked within a system or series of systems that are complex, self-stabilising and self-reorganising. A systems theory approach places emphasis on relationships, with both people and things, and understands relationships and processes to be dynamic, continually in flux. Margaret Barrett's extensive and scholarly corpus of work focused on early childhood music adopts a dynamic, ecological approach in its many discussions of young children's musical experiences (e.g. 2011, 2012). Development is neither inner nor outer, neither nature nor nurture, neither genetically nor environmentally conditioned, neither universal nor relative, but emerges through inseparable processes of interaction and mutual influence. So new theories of development aim to incorporate and bridge what were formally considered to be separate and oppositional dimensions. For instance, theories aim to draw on work emerging from genetics, evolution and neuroscience (the topics of the previous chapters). We saw that probabilistic epigenetics considers how children are born with a repertoire of possible developmental pathways and how environmental influences give rise to the expression of some genetic proclivities and not others. Neuroscientific research, similarly, is suggesting reciprocal influences between environmental experience and neuroscientific development, not in a simple causal pattern of stimulus and brain cell growth, but in more subtle incorporations of neuroscience within embodied and enactive situations. Importantly too, new theories incorporate the cultural broadening of the constructs that we adopt in understanding children's musical development, but I will come to that in the final chapter.

Most recently, the counter-moves to developmental psychology in music have started to draw on another set of arguments put forward mainly by a group of scholars working under a social justice banner. Drawing on a critical pedagogy position informed by the cluster of critical-theory perspectives, they point out that developmental research is biased in its findings, first because it is based on limited conceptions of its subject matter, music (namely, Western art music), and second because it draws on studies carried out with socially limited groups of children. We have already seen how by far the majority of studies of musical behaviours among very young children have been drawn from one very narrow demographic, WEIRD children. So, they say, developmental research, accompanied by the educational approaches that are closely tied to it, needs to expand its horizons, both in terms of its content, that is, the subject matter on which it is based, and in terms of the diversity of children and cultural contexts included in its studies.

The social justice call for both developmental perspectives and pedagogical strategies to be considerably expanded in scope ties into the key argument of this book, which is the need to recognise and work within the changing nature of contemporary musical childhoods. New technologies, as I have already emphasised, are transforming the ways in which children engage with and experience music, so that even what counts as musical skill and competence can no longer be regarded as stable or be assumed. New, ubiquitous technologies are providing rich, personalised and interactive environments for learning and must surely be affecting how children learn and progress musically. They bring every style of music and exciting new mixed-media forms directly into the corners of children's lives; the types of musical skills and knowledge children are gaining from everyday participation is changing profoundly and what they need from education is also shifting. But I am starting to pre-empt a discussion that takes place in the next chapter.

With the movement of populations, groups of children and their parents are increasingly diverse. It is rare nowadays for any group of small children to be ethnically homogenous, and so we cannot assume similar musical backgrounds or similar musical goals and directions. It is clearly not possible – nor wise or even ethical, therefore – to arrive at models of musical development that assume all children develop musically in the same way; nor is it possible or wise to assume we know the musical end points that they are moving towards – and most certainly not to position Western art music as the assumed ideal goal for music education.

There are, of course, commonalities between children, particularly in terms of their physicality and growth, their need for play and sociability and their need for attentive care and emotional warmth, and I am concerned to maintain a balanced view that acknowledges similarities and seeks to understand processes of change and how they happen – what facilitates or hinders the change we would want to see (and, indeed, what do we want to see?). As I am trying carefully to point out, I do not reject outright theoretical perspectives that attempt to plot transitional processes, progression and change among children, but wish to see them incorporated into a more generously interdisciplinary and flexible perspective that is more responsive to the variability of present-day childhoods. Educators might then have broad and flexible – 'rhizomatic', to use the Deleuzian term – templates that suggest, but only suggest and do not predict or determine, what children might be capable of musically. And this is certainly not the same as holding tightly to fixed and predictable models and believing them to represent a kind of truth about children's musicality.

5 Karaoke kids and digi-tots

Sociological perspectives

Vignette

In the living room of their home in a rural part of the south-west of England the two older girls in the family, one of whom is five years old and the other nine years, are setting up an interactive karaoke game. Their little brother, two-year-old Zak, looks on, watching intently as they connect a laptop to a large-screen TV and hunt for microphone leads. Zak leaves the room temporarily and then returns, triumphantly carrying his own brightly coloured, plastic toy microphone. The two girls have a problem setting up the equipment and one fetches their mother. Zak leans heavily on his mother's back to look over her shoulder while she sits on the floor to solve the problem, explaining to her daughters how she has reset the equipment. As the karaoke music and video starts up, the girls dance and sing to the song backings. Zak watches, transfixed, from the side of the sitting room. Then he suddenly jumps into the middle of the room, swings his arms sideways, out and in, jumps vigorously on the spot and sings strings of syllables into his toy microphone. The sisters take little notice of him as they continue with their own singing, simply moving aside to give him space, but Zak's mother, who has stayed in the room, watches and responds to his singing and dancing with smiles, claps and words of encouragement. Then she leaves the room and all three of her children continue to sing to the karaoke, with Zak sometimes standing still, watching his sisters or staring at the screen, sometimes leaping into the middle of his room to join in with his own dancing and singing.

Christopher Small, whose work has had a huge impact on music education, demonstrated how music can be understood as a social process (1977). Zak's karaoke singing and dancing is embedded in his home and family life and gathers its meaning from that place and space, with his sisters and mother, and the particular cultural forms of children's popular music brought into their home via the karaoke game. Zak's 'musicking' – to use Small's term – is not only interwoven with social processes at this microsocial level between these children taking part in family musical activities and the fun they have, but also fans outwards into the macrosocial structures including those of class, gender, culture, race (and others). Georgina Born, writing from a sociology of music position, has suggested four levels (she terms them 'planes'), on which music can be understood as social process or as social mediation (2011). At the first level are the small-scale 'microsocialities', the musical interactions of Zak with his family or the micro-level processes in a music session, particularly in terms of the agency accorded to those taking part. Zak was able to participate in this musical activity at home in ways that he was free to decide for himself: to stay in the room, to look on, to find his own microphone, to imitate, to join in, to create a sense of 'we-together' in this family with his sisters through dancing and singing. Equally, his home life provided him with these sets of opportunities. He lives in a small nuclear family, in a warm comfortable living environment equipped with technology and children's popular music to provide indoor entertainment. On Georgina Born's next level, music can bring to life certain imagined forms of community, or identity, so music in families, for instance, engenders a certain way of being musical that, in Zak's family, relied heavily on the shared karaoke singing and children's popular culture as a medium uniting the family. The family told me they had a lot of fun with the karaoke set, the mother often joining in and 'little Zak' taking part on the margins.

Staying with Georgina Born's second plane, families and all kinds of groups use music to signal, to draw together and build an identity, as 'us'. Music in parenting groups, for example, is used to create a sense of 'we' as mothers, reinforcing a certain image of mothering and of the children. I observed a particular mother and baby singing group where the mothers subscribed to a model of attachment parenting. They all breastfed on demand, several breastfeeding their babies intermittently through the session. They carried their babies in slings and the songs, predominantly South African lullabies with Djembe, strongly reinforced their image of intuitive, embodied, natural mothering with connections to mothering practices that are thought to be deeply tied to our evolutionary roots. But we should not overlook the fact that this sense of group identity, by inscribing social distinctions, will also result in some feeling that they do not belong. As I observed this group, I thought that any mother who did not subscribe to attached parenting and was from outside this middle-class circle of mothers would feel out of place.

Returning to Born's levels, at her next level the musical activity reflects wider social identities in society at large, such as the place of mothering in society today, the positioning of very young children in the context of wider society, and the inflections of social class, race and gender that permeate deep into society but are also mediated through a children's karaoke game, both reflecting and reinforcing them. As I watched it, the Disney karaoke game based on a children's musical reinforced racial, gender and heterosexual stereotypes. The main characters were white and the story was a 'girl meets boy' love story. To be fair, one minor character was Latino and another looked to be of mixed race, but they were marginal to the central characters, tokenistic inclusions. So Zak, as a small white boy, found himself and his family reflected back to him in this children's musical, unlike children from other racial groups or with same-sex parents, who would find themselves to be marginal, or even absent.

On Born's fourth and final level music is entangled in the wider structures – institutional, organisational and political – which include the powerful international corporations that make, market and profit from children's music both in the devices and the content. The karaoke set was marketed by an international toy company and the Disney content is global in its reach. Images of contemporary musical childhoods are deeply inscribed in toy and media products for children. Commercial organisations that operate not for social good by striving for equality but for financial gain (Kincheloe, 2002:85) are making huge profits from the global market for goods that create and reinforce these images of musical childhoods (particularly in terms of gender, as we will see later in this chapter).

Importantly, as Born explains, these planes are not separate or discrete but interrelate. There are interrelationships between the macro issues of culture, power and the micro level, the small-scale musical processes of karaoke singing at home, or any other forms of musical participation such as the music session, playground games, singing on a car journey or listening to music from a smartphone in the supermarket queue. What happens at the microsocial level connects with the macrosocial level. The relationships between people and the learning experiences of children are crucially linked to broader societal processes at the level of national and international economics and politics. Michael Apple shows us how (early music childhood) education is not separate from the political, economic and moral realities of broader society, but is deeply embedded in them (2013). Yet, there can be a tendency for early childhood music education to be detached from wider social realities, to think that it need not be concerned with issues of politics and policies, economics, marketing, multinational businesses and so on. Or, if these issues do momentarily impinge, they are usually batted away or grumbled about, with little real engagement. Hence, there is little attention to and concern for how inequality, poverty and discrimination operate at the structural level in society and affect children's and families' lives, infiltrating every aspect of those lives, including their musical aspects. As Miriam Jones writes, sweeping structural statements such as this may seem to have little relevance to a fun, low-stakes weekly music class for toddlers, but, as she carefully elicits through an ethnographic study, the early childhood music class contributes to cultural reproduction, is part of the 'complex relationships between cultural and economic capital' and thereby reinforces social advantage and disadvantage (2015:43).

So the value of taking a sociological perspective, of viewing through this theoretical window, is that it can provide a set of layered viewpoints from which to attain greater sensitivity to social issues, constructs and parameters and to understand their multilevelled interrelationships. Moreover, a sociological perspective supports a critical stance and invites us to consider which social and institutional arrangements might allow certain forms of 'musicking' to flourish and thrive – or not – and who stands to gain or to lose out as a result. As I am consistently arguing throughout this book, the wider macrosocial processes are as relevant to music in early childhood as the microsocial ones that usually take the lion's share of our attention.

Before I continue any further with this chapter, however, I need to pause to explain the place of sociological thinking in music education. The sociology of music education is a relatively new field and as yet not extensive, certainly in comparison with the much more established and dominant areas of psychology (Green, 1999; Wright, 2016). It has focused almost exclusively on mainstream schooling for older children and has barely impinged upon early childhood music education. Interestingly and rather surprisingly, the new directions emerging in the sociology of music education have not intersected with the sociology of childhood. This is a prime example of where early childhood music education sits on the junction between two domains, namely, music education and general early childhood education. The two areas have drawn on quite different themes from sociological theories. Broadly speaking, early childhood education has moved towards sociology of childhood perspectives (certainly in its European work), while the sociology of music education has drawn themes and concepts from the sociology of music and sociology of education. So this chapter has a specific task. It draws out, expands and attempts to give greater weighting to sociological perspectives, to counter-balance the dominance of psychological perspectives, and then, also, incorporates sociology of childhood thinking with music sociology perspectives. Whereas in the previous chapter I was attempting to position psychological perspectives more proportionately in relation to other perspectives, and was highly selective in the research that I called up, for this chapter I have had to hunt for scarcer and scattered pieces of research to inform the chapter. Furthermore, when I draw ideas from the sociology of music education they often need translating to make them relevant to early childhood.

Children's music-making in social contexts

So, to put it concisely, sociology recognises that children's opportunities to be musical and the music they make are shaped and produced by the structures of the present society in which they live. They are shaped by their family life in homes, by their experiences in nurseries and schools, of living in certain communities, and by wider economics and politics. We have seen in earlier chapters how the rise of the sociology of childhood was accompanied by an interest in children's everyday lives and typically occurring everyday (musical) experiences and an interest in the meaning of these experiences from children's perspective. Children, even the youngest children, were recognised as the active participants and experts in their own lives, and interest turned to how they understand and perceive their own experiences rather than relying on what adults observe and report on children's behalf. Research endeavoured to position them as participants in the research process, as active subjects rather than as 'objects' to be studied. In comparison, psychology, in a nutshell, tends to study children objectively and as individuals separated from their social context rather than as members of social groups such as family or peer groups. Moreover, considering them as active agents turned attention to how children, even the very youngest, contribute to shaping their environments and their relationships with their families: the process is reciprocal.

So theoretical shifts from sociology, and also from the anthropology of music, have created a greater interest in music-making that happens in all the spaces and places where children live their lives: in families at home, in outdoor spaces such as playgrounds, in the so-called third spaces (journeys, shopping, restaurants, waiting rooms) and increasingly in the virtual 'spaces' of the media and the Internet. That said, there has been a long-standing strand of interest in children's playground games in the field of folklore studies stretching back into the last century, but folklore studies, certainly in its more original orientations, centres the songs and games as musical objects, rather than centring the children as the players of those games. Besides, playground games are mainly the preserve of older children, so this tranche of work has some, but limited, relevance for early childhood music. This recent and growing interest in musical activities within social contexts is starting to provide fascinating insights into what types of musical activities young children are engaged in across many varied situations. Researchers involved in this type of study argue that the bulk of children's musical activity takes place outside of educational settings, especially with younger children not yet in full-time education and increasingly, I would argue, with the advent of new technologies. Therefore, children's everyday musical activity – the 'everyday' being a blanket term to denote activity outside of educational contexts – deserves careful study in order to gain greater insight into children's musical competences, how they progress musically, how they make meaning, how they engage with other people, with material things and media, and how all these shape their music-making and musical experiences.

The insights that are being gathered up from these everyday-music studies show how children are being musical on their own terms. They suggest ways in which educators might connect with and build on the musical experiences and knowledge that young children, even the youngest babies, bring with them into the music session. They suggest how we might do music education differently. These insights also provide information that allows us to decide what might be absent or, if not absent, then in short supply in children's musical experiences and how we might want to steer the music experiences we provide to make up these discrepancies. For example, the increasing confinement of children to indoors, among family members is shifting the nature of musical activities they can engage with. So nurseries and schools might encourage traditional playground singing games with mixed-age children to compensate for what might be reduced, or more likely non-existent, opportunities to play freely out-of-doors with other children. Equally, this area of research often reveals competences children are acquiring that are not being recognised or given opportunities to flourish in music education, such as the ways they play with music via digital technologies or the diversity of family musical experiences among children from culturally varied backgrounds.

A greater understanding of children's everyday musical lives also enables us to recognise that the value and purpose of music may be enjoyment, pleasure and enrichment of children's lives now and to analyse the relationships between music for 'being', here and now, and music for 'becoming', which is future-focused. This is particularly the case with early childhood music education which, being the lowest point on the educational hierarchy, is often seen only in terms of preparation for what is to follow, as the foundational steps on a fixed developmental pathway and as providing a merely functional purpose in serving children's 'needs' within a deterministic outlook. As we look through the door at music in family life, emotional pleasure, sociability, enjoyment and entertainment are often the primary purposes (Gibson, 2009). I very much doubt that Zak's mother applauded his karaoke singing because she had in mind how much it might benefit his communication or cognitive skills, but because she shared his pleasure. There has been a huge expansion in theatre and music performance occasions for very young children in recent years and, in my view, it is pleasing to see that these are concerned with creating aesthetic experiences that enrich children's lives for the present (Young & Powers, 2009). They may be put in the position of having to rationalise their work for its attendant gains and benefits in order to please funders and promoters, but the primary aim of the actual work is enrichment and enjoyment.

The home, family and parenting

Babies and very young children may spend the majority of their time at home and in families, even though out-of-home care has much increased, and so interest has naturally turned to studying and understanding their home-based everyday musical experiences. Studies of young children in family life must be mindful of the dangers of intrusion and the ethics of studying children in private and intimate times and spaces. Because of the difficulties of access, studies of music at home are typically case studies of one or a very small number of children, often the researcher's own child (e.g. Papoušek & Papoušek, 1981; de Vries, 2005; Forrester, 2010) or the children of friends and family (e.g. Dean, 2017; Gibson, 2009). At the risk of overstating this point, to overcome the limited scope of these studies we need therefore far more studies of children who belong to diverse social groups. At the same time, in my view, we need studies that ask more probing questions about the patterns of contemporary young children's lives, including the parenting values and goals held by the parents taking part in any studies (see, e.g., Ilari, 2005) and how these are closely interrelated with and impact on children's musical experiences. Harking back to the first chapter, I described how in typical contemporary families in the Western world the number of children is small, the children with their mother (or father) lead relatively solitary lives in the family home, children are surrounded by commodified items including digital technologies, and the contemporary middle-class mother is expected to devote individualised attention to her child to promote social and cognitive development. This represents, therefore, a very specific and recently emerging context which is shaping early musical childhoods in certain very defined ways.

In spite of the limitations I mention, a small number of studies have accumulated which provide depth and detail of young children's everyday musical lives. Within the context of contemporary Westernised family life, studies have explored different forms of participation (Custodero, et al., 2003; Barrett, 2009), which include singing (Custodero, 2006), listening to recorded music (Vestad, 2010; Brooks, 2016), playing with karaoke (Young, 2012), using technologies (Marsh, et al., 2017), and also specific parenting routines such as bedtimes (Sole, 2014), nappy changing (Addessi, 2009) and mealtimes (Forrester, 2010). Anna-Rita Addessi and her students studied the musical dimensions of daily routines at home among young children of varied ages (Addessi, 2009). She describes the interaction between biological, environmental and social-musical rhythms, valuably illustrating a theoretical analysis that makes links across those different levels. She also suggests that routines with music embedded enable children to find their place in relationships and the surrounding culture, including the musical culture.

Julia Gillen and Ann Cameron were interested to explore the daily lives of two-year-olds at home, without any predetermined focus, and collected continuous video recordings of a typical day in several different locations across the world (2010). What is interesting about this study, besides its value in visiting children in different corners of the globe, was that it set out with an open-minded curiosity as to what the video recordings might reveal. As the video data started to come in, the quantity and variety of music and musical activities in the children's daily home lives soon became apparent (Young & Gillen, 2010). Music was part of the fabric of home life and was either sounding in the background, as an accompaniment to other activities, or in the foreground for children's listening, dancing and singing. Music played from televisions, radio, CD and video players. Occasionally the parents sang to their children, mainly at times of transition and particularly to assist with emotional regulation. The little girl in Thailand fell off the outdoor swing, and her mother held and rocked her with a quiet song to soothe her. In Italy the little girl was drowsy after her midday nap, and her mother played an improvised lap game with her, rocking and rhyming, to rouse her gently. The use of music to re-energise or soothe is familiar to everyone (DeNora, 2000) and its incorporation as a parenting strategy in the management of children has been noticed and discussed in other studies (e.g. Corbeil, et al., 2016).

Rachel Gibson was broadly interested in how parents create musical environments for their young children and in discovering the factors that shaped musical parenting practices (2009). Her study, which focused on six families with children aged from birth to four living in the US, is particularly interesting because she collected the full range of activities provided by parents for their children at home. The range included singing interactions, musical resources in the home, music gatherings among the families (who lived in a university complex), and child-orientated concerts in the community at large. She was curious about how parents use music, its functions within family life, and also how parents shaped a family musical identity drawing on their own past, personally meaningful musical experiences. She found that social/emotional purposes for music were at the forefront when parents engaged their children musically (also Barrett, 2009), in line with the point about music for enjoyment rather than instrumental benefits that I made earlier.

The solitude of children at home is a particular characteristic of home life in affluent societies and is giving rise to a set of musical practices that may parallel some of the shifts in adult ways of using music, more as an accompaniment to increasingly individualised rather than communal lifestyles. So there is some recent interest in how children use music when alone, as a soundtrack to their own lives (e.g. Gluschankof, 2016). Bronya Dean has collected young children's singing throughout a day of home life using a small digital recording device that slips into a T-shirt pocket. She was particularly interested in children's singing when they are alone, for example playing with their toys in a bedroom or lying in bed awake before a daytime nap. She arrived at a set of ways in which children use private singing to entertain themselves and to self-manage aspects of their day (Dean, 2017).

Solitude continues at bedtime, and young children in minority-world families conventionally sleep alone. A couple of researchers have been interested in children singing to themselves at bedtime (Addessi, 2009; Sole, 2014). Meryl Sole asked parents of nine toddlers to collect audio recordings and to write descriptive notes on the children's spontaneous vocalising after they had been put to bed and left to drop off to sleep (Sole, 2014). She found that all the toddlers sang and, adopting an approach in which she analysed their vocalisations in musical terms, found that they included free-flowing vocalisations, reworking of learned songs and fully improvised songs. Meryl Sole suggests wide-ranging reasons why these toddlers sang: 'to reflect, experiment, learn, express emotion, self-soothe and make sense of their recent experiences' (Sole, 2014:162).

I recently carried out an online survey of over 100 parents asking them about their use of music in bedtime routines and found that many parents combine singing to children with the of use of recorded music digitally produced in smartphones or by commercial 'sleep toys', that is, soft toys that typically play heartbeats and soothing music (also Young, 2008). Again, it is evident that these commodified musical items carry and convey a popularised and dominant image of childhood: soft, sweetly tinkling tunes, a dreamy world of magic and sentimentality. 'New age' dolphin or rainforest sounds associated with relaxation are popular in sleep toys. Parents often described how the recorded music and musical toys might be left to play while they tiptoed out of the room. Thus we can see how the music and use of musical items is closely linked to Western parenting practices, further enabled by commercially produced digital musical devices. So, as I argued earlier, we need to relate these kinds of musical practices with a wider enquiry into general parenting practices and goals. We might reflect on the fact that being put to sleep alone in a quiet room is a particular practice of Western parenting that would be very unfamiliar to the majority of the world's children, and that singing for 'self-soothing' and the use of musical sleep aids may be very unusual practices that apply only to a specific and quite small population of children. We might remark too on the commodification of childhood and on the fact that parents now must purchase copious items and that competent childcare is thought to require this wide range of varied equipment.

Interestingly, in my survey parents often spoke of singing and reading stories first and then putting on the music as they left the calmed child to drop off to sleep. I did not find that technology was displacing live singing at bedtime, as many have claimed, but was adding to it. Others view the use of recorded music negatively, assuming it results in a loss of live lullaby singing (Baker & Mackinlay, 2006; Sulkin & Brodsky, 2013). In their view, an important mode of natural, spontaneous infant-directed interaction has been lost and they express concerns that the 'developmental needs' of babies are not being properly supported. Idit Sulkin and Warren Brodsky (2013) add the suggestion that technological devices should play more child-appropriate songs and music, and this may indeed be a much-needed recommendation (although what would constitute 'child-appropriate' they do not specify). From another viewpoint, we may query the assumption that lullaby singing is a 'natural, spontaneous' activity, that it has a functional purpose in serving 'needs', or indeed that it is being lost just because recorded music is to some extent taking over rather than adding to, as seems to be the case from my survey. Certainly, lullabies are part of the traditional folklore of many societies and the regulation of a babies' emotional and physical state through music is a widespread practice. However, from an anthropological perspective (heralding the next chapter to come), there are equally many societies, perhaps a majority, where babies and small children are not deliberately put to sleep with either lullabies or recorded music by parents, but slip into sleep on their mothers' backs to the rhythm of walking or as they are gently cradled on an adult's lap while the buzz of family social activity goes on around them.

Car journeys are also a particular feature of Westernised family life. Music has an important place in the car, as I am sure many from their own experience would agree, serving to keep children occupied during journeys. Lisa Koops had noticed that music during car journeys is a particular characteristic of family life and asked five families with a total of nine young children, aged ten months to four years, to keep a record of their 'car music' activities (2014). Broadly, she found that car and house-bound musical activities were much the same: the children sang, moved, listened to music, composed and improvised. The car as a place for music, however, has certain key advantages. There are few other distractions (the children are restrained by car seats, after all) and the parents are an active audience and participants, even if driving at the same time (Koops, 2014). Children often share the backseat with a sibling, which results in musical play and interaction between brothers and sisters. Lisa also found that music in the car could be a good opportunity for discussion and reflection between parents and children about their music-making.

Some young children have quite lengthy car journeys, sometimes daily, and so the quantity of 'car music' listening and participation can be substantial. Chee-Hoo Lum has long been interested in the everyday musical experiences of children in his home city of Singapore. As a passenger on a car journey with a Singaporean Malay family, he listened to the younger children singing to music played to entertain them during the journey (Lum, 2012). He noticed that the two-year-old had memorised all the songs on a lengthy DVD that was played regularly in the car and he remarked on this young child's capacity for absorbing and learning from recorded music. For me, his observations on the two-year-old's memorising are interesting because they suggest that the wealth and variety of music in young children's lives now made possible through new technologies are surely expanding their musical experiences and abilities.

Both Lisa Koops and Meryl Sole lead on from their studies of music in different aspects of everyday life by suggesting educative purposes. Lisa Koops suggests that educators might promote activities to parents that could be practised by children in the car (2014). From a developmental perspective and in light of Johanella Tafuri's discoveries that a musically rich environment in which parents take an active educative role will advance children's musical progress, these are valuable suggestions. An Australian study which tracked a large sample of children over time suggested that parents' support of children's musical activities would carry wider benefits, not just in music but more generally in prosocial skills, literacy and more (Williams, et al., 2015). However, viewed from another position, these recommendations turn the interest and aim of children's everyday musical encounters into an instrumental, deferred, future-orientated, educational opportunity, rather than for music enjoyed in the moment, for 'being'. This raises again a query about the purposes of music in different social contexts and asks questions about the images of children as musical held in these recommendations and the parenting goals they assume. Is it wise to turn the home, the car, or even the most intimate time of falling asleep or nappy changing into an educational opportunity? Jerome Kagan points to the child-rearing advice industry that imparts the very pervasive idea that young children need to be constantly monitored and instructed (2000).

I mentioned intensive parenting in the first chapter and return to and expand those ideas now by drawing on Annette Lareau's work. She terms this recent intensive parenting style 'concerted cultivation' (Lareau, 2003; also Ilari, 2013b; Jones, 2015). From her ethnographic study of children's upbringing in families belonging to different class and ethnic groups in the USA she drew a clear distinction between middle-class families who sought actively to nurture and develop their children's social, cognitive, cultural and sporting competencies (the private music session being a clear example) and working-class families who believed that children develop in their own ways, at their own pace. She termed this alternative style 'accomplishment of natural growth'. However, she also found, obviously, that lack of economic resources made it very difficult for working-class families to give their children the same opportunities as middle-class families. All families loved and cared for their children but the different parenting styles, coupled with lesser resources, restrict access to the possibilities of music for working-class children and thereby give middle-class children an advantage. There is a widely circulating view, both in policy and in broader popular discourse, that 'good' parents buy into extracurricular and enriching activities for their children, with the knock-on effect of implying that those parents who cannot afford to do so are somehow less good as parents (Vincent & Maxwell, 2016).

I move on now from real family spaces for music to consider virtual spaces enabled by digital technologies. They are still closely linked to families and family spaces in that they are primarily accessed via the family-owned equipment at home, in the car or, increasingly with portable devices, out and about. Some children may access these digital spaces for music via their daycare, nursery or in music sessions, but access to digital technologies in these kinds of places is limited.

In early childhood our understanding of musical experiences enabled by the most up-to-date technologies is extremely limited. In the section that follows I will introduce what work there is, but I have to rely primarily on research drawn from the general field of early childhood education.

Digitised music, new technologies and media

In the first chapter I introduced a key idea underpinning this book that the relationships between new technologies, new media and children's everyday lives have resulted in a marked change in the nature of contemporary musical experiences in early childhood. Educators are faced with a moving digital landscape that requires them to remain knowledgeable and continuously update their pedagogical approaches. We need to recognise the digital musical experiences and competences that children now possess (Buckingham, 2009) and take advantage of the potentials for enriched musical learning that digital technologies afford. An interest in young children's use of technologies expands from more than just the devices themselves and their content to how they are used by children in interaction with others in everyday happenings, the nature of these musical experiences, and what children are doing and gaining musically.

These topics are still marginal to mainstream early childhood music education research and practice, however. Only a handful of recent studies have explored young children's technology use from a musical angle. It is not an easy area to research, for the devices and media contents advance rapidly and no sooner has a study of specific equipment and software been published than it is already being superseded and in danger of being outdated. Equally, such is the pace of development that children are likely to have more up-to-date and sophisticated technology items at home than those found in early childhood settings. While writing this book I visited a nursery where a chunky, robust educational cassette player was set out for children to use. I doubt most children knew what it was. To avoid this problem of 'out-of-dateness' I will endeavour to identify key themes and issues, rather than giving detailed accounts of the musical items and equipment. These themes and issues can be drawn from theorising emerging from wider fields in childhood studies and education and then translated for their relevance to early childhood music. The majority of research has taken place in education: literacy studies has been particularly active, looking at digital media and the learning implications. Some paediatric work has explored psychological and social impacts (e.g. Radesky, *et al.*, 2015), and within media studies research is recently beginning to analyse the practices, conceptions and implications of digital interfaces and content for younger children (e.g. Nansen, 2015).

Although research within specifically early childhood music may be in short supply, the general studies that have explored young children's digital equipment use (e.g. Chaudron, *et al.*, 2015; Marsh, *et al.*, 2017) reveal several references to music, typically as one element of more holistic and multidimensional practices. This, indeed, is one of the key characteristics of new technologies: they enable forms of fluid, multimodal activity where music is one interwoven component of video, games, cartoons, apps and so on. We might note in passing that this intertextuality of new media is a defining characteristic that upsets conventional ideas of 'music' as a distinct art form. The Technology and Play (TAP) report points to the prevalence of music apps available in online app and play stores as a testament to their popularity (Marsh, *et al.*, 2017). Music apps, they report, enable children to create new compositions and also listen to a wide range of music. This study also found that YouTube played a significant role in children's musical experiences (also Burroughs, 2017). Parents reported searching for rhymes and lullabies for their children to watch and listen to on YouTube. Interestingly, parents say that their children were able to navigate YouTube relatively independently using the 'recommended' system or the history function.

A consistent picture of widespread use of digital technologies and at younger and younger ages is emerging from the most recent surveys taking place outside of music education (e.g. Chaudron, *et al.*, 2015). This recent dramatic change in both the extent of usage and the dip down into very young ages has occurred with the arrival of touchscreen tablets and smartphones (Holloway, *et al.*, 2015), which have become an integral part of people's homes and lives and are interactively accessible to even very young babies (Fletcher-Watson, 2013). The Monitor Preschool Report in the UK from 2016 (reported in Dickson, 2016) shows that under-fives in the UK are increasingly comfortable using tablets and apps, prefer YouTube for on-demand content, and turn to Netflix for subscription-based programs. This report tells us that one in three under-fives and nearly half of all three- and four-year-olds have their own tablet computer. What is most striking is that babies and toddlers are using internet-connected devices. In 2017 a UK-based survey of 715 families reported that 75% of toddlers between six months and three years of age use a touchscreen on a daily basis (Cheung, *et al.*, 2017). These figures are probably indicative of trends in many other countries and show high usage by even the very youngest children.

Furthermore, contrary to what might be expected given the cost of these devices, access to new technologies is not confined to more affluent families. A study focusing particularly on families in the lower-income bracket in the US that included children aged between six months and four years found that there was a TV set in every home, 83% of the families owned a tablet and 77% a smartphone (Kabali, *et al.*, 2015). On average, these preschool children spent two-and-a-half hours per day watching programs, films and videos and their parents, in general, reported being content with this amount of screen time (Dickson, 2016).

Although the surveys provide the robust evidence, we only have to be out and about in public places such as airports, supermarkets, restaurants and waiting rooms to see babies and young children using touchscreen technologies and can observe for ourselves how easily they seem to master the basics. On a recent two-hour coach journey the one-year-old (of Welsh-Indian heritage) sitting on her father's lap next to me spent the majority of the journey playing with an iPad, accessing stored cartoon clips and playing games, the varied soundtrack just audible to me from her pink fluffy headphones. The iPad clearly offered an attractive source of stimulation and entertainment. The use of mobile media to occupy young children during daily routines and journeys and in restaurants and waiting rooms is now a common parenting strategy, becoming what toy producers perhaps somewhat pejoratively call a 'shut-up' toy (Agomuoh, 2015). The activities are interactive and varied, and I saw how my one-year-old coach companion could exercise independent access and choice, aided just now and again by her father. Touchscreen devices are relatively intuitive and although the iPad is fairly weighty, phones in particular are light in weight, small and relatively easy to handle. Moreover, their portability allows for a wide range of use across very many places and spaces. Among older children, the majority of three- and four-year-olds can use touchscreen technologies with independence, switching them on and off, changing the volume, opening their preferred apps and using camera controls.

Young children's lives may be permeated with digital technologies in a way that is unprecedented, yet we still know very little about how they *actually* use them in routine, everyday ways. We certainly know even less from a musical perspective. Most of the information is emerging from larger-scale surveys that provide general trends, rather than specific detail. Even though we have very little knowledge about actual use, the widespread access in this age group, particularly among the youngest children, has however raised serious concerns among parents, educators and policymakers about the potential impact of touchscreen use on young children's learning, behaviour and their cognitive, social and emotional development (see Kucirkova & Zuckerman, 2017 for review). Worries focus on whether technologies displace human interaction and erode traditional patterns of family interactions and other imaginative, embodied, playful activities. It has been pointed out, for example, that typical touchscreen activities do not foster larger body, sensorimotor activity (a somewhat obvious conclusion, I would have thought) and more open-ended creative play (Radesky, *et al.*, 2015). As with the arrival of all new technologies, opinion is sharply divided, with some arguing strongly against, citing potential risks and harm to children, particularly babies, from the use of screen technologies (Ward, 2013; Donnelly, 2017). That technologies hold promise or peril are familiar discourses surrounding young children's technology and new media. Popular coverage around the use of technologies can be heavily opinion-based, using emotive language that taps into fears and anxieties about the possible risks and harms. However, when scrutinised more closely, these opinions are invariably based on lightweight or anecdotal information rather than systematic research. They can then be in conflict with educational experts who suggest that, if used appropriately and interactively, technologies can be an effective tool in supporting learning and development (e.g. Nardo, 2008).

To provide the reliable evidence as to how new technologies are being used that is needed, and to explore the possible impacts, one long-term study in the UK has been recently set up. Thus far, one finding to come out of this study is a *possible* correlation between screen use and an average reduction in sleep time of fifteen minutes for every hour of use – a loss of sleep time that could have detrimental consequences (Cheung, *et al.*, 2017). However, this finding has led to emotive and exaggerated newspaper reports of iPads ruining toddlers' sleep (Donnelly, 2017). Such reports feed the prevailing anxiety that technologies have negative effects, rather than report precise information drawn from the original research study so that readers can come to their own conclusions. Time and again we have seen through this book how research findings are used not to inform a readership accurately, but are cherry-picked and exaggerated to bolster an already existing policy, opinion, belief or prejudice. The survey found only a possible link from analysis of data sets and needs to go further to explore what is happening in real life. Possible reasons proposed by the research team for the loss of sleep could be simply staying up longer to play with screen activities, an effect of the type of light emitted by screens, or increased alertness delaying sleep. The findings are still emerging and the research team have not arrived at any firm conclusions.

The same study that reported possible links between screen use and sleep also found another possible correlation between touchscreen use and more advanced fine motor control (Bedford, *et al.*, 2016). This finding hints at a positive gain from touchscreen technology play but appears not to have hit the headlines because it contradicts the assumptions of negative consequences around technology that the journalists seek to confirm.

Behind the negativity towards technologies lie images of very young children as closer to nature rather than to mechanistic technology, and a felt need to protect and shelter them from the digital world and the feared harms of the popular media they make accessible. The media, it is thought, will take over children's imaginations with commercial culture that is damaging and corrupting. Forms of timeless, traditional childhood are seen to be disappearing and cyborg 'techno-babies' and 'digi-tots' will replace the vulnerable, cuddly babies of our imaginations. Childhood will be swamped by a commercialised culture that is becoming increasingly global, with children the world over familiar with the same saccharine films, toys, games and music. These anxieties can be particularly strong in early childhood music and arts activity where, as we saw in chapter two, the construction of childhood as possessing its own imaginative forms, creative, embodied and free, is contrasted with a sedentary, supposedly mind-stultifying and mechanistic world of new technology. The world of technology as an indoor world, at home, characterised by inactivity, mindlessness and lack of sociability, is set in opposition to the outdoor world of nature, freedom and physical play. The social constructions of different ideals of childhood are quite clear in these discourses, as is an implied moral undertone. Popular writing in newspapers and advice books for parents allude to good parenting in managing children's screen use and giving access to free outdoor play. 'Good parents' are those who impose limits on the amount of screen time and monitor their children's activities.

Those who adopt the opposite view, although not heard as loudly, suggest that the risks are overstated and the fears unfounded. They see a brave new world for media-savvy young children, describing them as 'digital natives' (Prensky, 2001). Mark Deuze (2012) suggests that negative responses to new technologies and media, particularly in the form of advice proposing no 'screen time' for children below two years old (e.g. American Academy of Pediatrics, 2011) is futile because nowadays we do not live *with* media but *in* media. He argues that, due to their all-pervasiveness, media and communication technologies in our lives have become effectively invisible. Thus it is simply not plausible to suggest that children should live in technology-free spaces, or to suggest that, at the very least, their access should be restricted. He suggests that we should strive to find ways to incorporate this new technology-enabled, media life with considered choices and actions, to make use of the possibilities it offers creatively, aesthetically and ethically (see also Nansen, 2015). From his point of view, the technologies, media and music that it enables are woven into children's lives. Following this line of argument, contemporary music educators need to work with children's experiences, understandings and knowledge of new technologies and media, for they are already present in the music session embedded in the children's everyday experiences (Zevenbergen, 2007). Children will have gaps, for sure, aspects of their musical experience and learning that we consider important for young children so that they can develop in a well-rounded way. Expansive embodied musical activity may well be a dimension that is not fostered by new technologies. Although even here we should be wary of jumping to conclusions. One report, for example, reveals that children sing and dance along with children's TV programmes in over 75% of instances, demonstrating a positive, agentic way of engaging with TV that belies the passivity that TV is often blamed for (Marsh, *et.al.*, 2005). It is also important that educators view new technologies as not merely complementing existing educational approaches. The problem with this approach is that it leaves practice relatively untouched and merely tinkers at the edges, rather than substantially rethinking the pedagogical implications. We need creative alternatives that incorporate the advantages and benefits (as well as appraising the disadvantages and gaps) that digital technologies enable for children's musical experiences and learning.

It is also obvious that the way technologies and interactive media are used needs to be understood within everyday social contexts. Technology use in family life, at home and out and about is also closely interwoven with family relationships and lifestyle patterns, routines and leisure times. We saw in my opening example of Zak how the karaoke musical play was mediated by all these other dimensions. Other studies are adopting micro-foci, exploring, for example, the kinds of play afforded by digital technologies, the types of skills that might be acquired, and the innovative and creative thinking that they engender. What is emerging as a key factor to understand is how adults mediate and interact with children and their play with digital media. There are some very interesting first studies that are looking closely at these aspects of use in both domestic and social settings and exploring babies' and toddlers' everyday 'encounters and entanglements' with mobile media and communication technologies (e.g. Nansen & Jayemanne, 2016). Bjorn Nansen identifies the ways in which babies' use combines the touchscreen interfaces, the adults' participation and how the commercial software operates. He has conceptualised the babies' emerging repertoire of techniques as, firstly, accidental or non-purposeful interactions resulting from touching screens inadvertently and thereby activating certain applications; secondly, use that is facilitated by parents who introduce and guide; and finally, automated use enabled by the software itself. He encapsulates this repertoire as 'accidental, assisted and automated' (Nansen, 2015). The technologies therefore offer a combination of musical possibilities and limitations that are further mediated by interactions with more knowledgeable 'others' (whether adults, peers or siblings). We need to understand these processes in order to work out how best to incorporate new music technologies into practice.

Turning now to research that has taken a music focus, there are some apps that have been designed to foster musical engagement and learning, and researchers are starting to explore their application to music educational situations. Suzanne Burton and Aimee Pearsall studied a group of sixteen four-year-olds in the US using twelve different music apps on iPads (2016). They found a number of features that the children preferred such as visual interest, ease of navigation and familiar music, but found that the apps did not elicit variety in musical responses or, in particular, more expansive responses of singing, moving and so on. They found that the more open-ended apps, which would typically encourage more playful creative interaction, were less popular with the children, but suggested that better design of apps would encourage more independent, self-initiated musical activity. Their overall conclusions were that the apps might be better designed to have learning purposes built into them, and that they can complement traditional music-learning activities, or supplement some learning only if they are of high quality. They also proposed that the music incorporated into apps could be stylistically varied, including pop, rock and world musics, and could thus provide a bridge into other musical worlds. There are clear messages here for the design and development of technology-enabled musical activities for very young children. Their study, however, looked at the children's use of apps without adult involvement. In my view, it is the pedagogy contextualising the use of technology rather than the device per se that makes a difference to children's learning and this needs to be the focus of attention. Nansen's analysis of young children's use as 'accidental, assisted and automated' provides a useful frame.

As well as being concerned with social contexts and how music is made within spaces, real and virtual, sociological thinking is particularly concerned with social distinctions and how lines are drawn between groups of people in terms of race, class, age, religion, gender, sexuality and ability. All of these work in combinations; they all intersect. In this next section I consider gender in particular, a dimension which is crucial to all children as they learn to negotiate their lives. Although I pick out this one dimension to focus on here, I stress that gender differentiation is further refracted through all the other social variables.

Pink and blue

The central, long-term debate is whether biology determines the marked differences that begin to emerge in how boys and girls behave, or whether these are socially constructed, that is, they result from the different ways boys and girls are treated (Blaise, 2005). Many would argue they are a combination of an interaction between biological and social factors, but how and in what proportions are contested questions. Whatever their source, gender differences significantly mark how children create their own identities, shape their own behaviours and how they interact with others. Parents create an environment at home from the moment of birth: rooms are painted pink or blue, clothes are bought, toys are chosen and parents have been shown to interact with boys and girls differently, even from the moment of birth. As Phil Jones (2009:81) explains, these are not neutral objects or acts, they are the means by which both adults and children signal and situate themselves in relation to gender. Very young children, babies in particular, have very few ways to exercise choice in relation to the gendered environments created for them. As children age, they may find ways to exercise more agency and undermine some of the gender expectations being imposed on them.

In the 1980s when I studied for a postgraduate degree in education, gender socialisation and the subtle and unwitting ways in which adults, including educators, reinforce traditional sex roles was high on the agenda of that course (e.g. Honig, 1983). Reproduction theory, that is, understanding gender as culturally defined and reproduced, not biologically determined, was central to those explanations. The process of gender reproduction was thought to take place through modelling and the differential treatment of boys and girls. In the 1990s there was a short-lived period of academic and practice-based activity in gender and music education with accompanying publications (e.g. Green, 1997). Since that short spate of activity, gender in music education seems to have slipped into a back seat. With the rampant 'pinkification' and blue of children's toys, clothes and every item associated, it would seem, as a society, that we have turned back to essentialist notions of gender (Paoletti, 2012). The recent emergence of postfeminism, after the 1990s, has contributed to gender issues being overshadowed in early childhood education (Osgood & Robinson, 2017). 'Postfeminist', Jayne Osgood explains, is a term that is applied to young women who have benefited from the feminist movement in their access to education, employment and more flexible family arrangements, but do not push for further political change (2017). Educators and parents too, reflecting current broader sociocultural attitudes and perceptions around gender, generally believe that children 'naturally' gravitate to play styles, toys and clothing associated with their gender. There appears to be a much greater acceptance, endorsement even, of gendering processes in education. Even the very youngest toddlers attending a music session will be absorbing subtle messages of gender socialisation, and the perpetuation of sex role inequalities in how they are handled, what items they are given, the songs that are sung, how they are addressed and how they are expected to participate (cf. Roulston & Misawa, 2011).

More recent sociological understandings of how young children make sense of themselves as a boy or a girl are drawing on theories of cultural discourses. As with the earlier reproduction theories, the idea of cultural discourses emphasises the differential ways in which men and women behave, both in children's everyday lives and those they see in media, stories, songs and TV programmes. From a cultural-discourse perspective, ways of behaving musically as boys or girls are made available to young children across the whole range of their social contexts: their family home, daycare, nursery, the community around them and, in particular, through the media. The powerful commercial enterprises provide a set of images that parents and other adults introduce into children's worlds, and music, songs and theme tunes are deeply woven into these images and items. As it happens, Zak saw both boy and girl characters singing and dancing in the karaoke video, but differentiated representations of gender and stereotypical gender-defined behaviours are so commonplace in children's popular media as to be almost the norm.

Research has shown that adults, parents and educators may be more relaxed in response to girls' selection of activities or items that are seen as not conforming to gender, but may be less so in response to boys' selection (Kane, 2006). Dominant masculinity is defined in our society by an avoidance of all things feminine. Maleness is thus a narrower path that is more strictly policed both by adults and by boys themselves in their peer groups, even at young ages. When adults discourage anything that is non-stereotypical in terms of gender, however subtly and unwittingly, they are restricting the child's development and self-expression. Thus children do not unfold along a 'natural' pathway of gender-defined musical activities, but are in fact channelled and curtailed by adults and increasingly, as they age, by other children. In my study of children's karaoke singing I discovered that it was almost exclusively a girls' activity, but as yet, within his family life, Zak is immune to any messages that singing and dancing may be less of an activity for boys (Warzecha, 2013). Certainly, he received his mother's praise and encouragement for singing; she did not subtly close it down as some parents might have done.

From a childhood studies viewpoint, children are seen as active agents in the construction of their own identities and are not passively socialised into gender roles (Minks, 2008). They are drawing on the cultural discourses available to them, gender included, and responding actively to the ways in which gender identities are monitored and regulated (e.g. Cannella, 1997). There are interesting research studies that show how children, even at quite young ages, negotiate the cultural narratives in which they are immersed, resisting them or complying with them, very aware of what is considered appropriate and correct for a boy, or a girl (see Skelton & Francis, 2003 for overview).

Studies of gender in general early childhood education have repeatedly demonstrated how gender stereotypes are being perpetuated and reinforced through educational processes. Music education is certainly not exempt from these gendering processes (Dansereau, 2014). Gender stereotypes are deeply woven into musical practices: just think of the gendering of certain instruments that are associated more with male or female performers. Cross-culturally, there are many instances of instruments and performance practices being the preserve only of men, or of women. If education inadvertently perpetuates these, we are seriously limiting the musical opportunities available to both boys and girls. This requires the music educator to be sensitive to gendered music practices, including the content of sessions, how we interact with girls and boys, and the expectations for girls and boys that we subtly convey, particularly around musical behaviours such as singing, moving/dancing or instrument choice and styles of playing. I often observe early childhood music sessions in a consultancy or research role, and sometimes, out of interest, will simply count the number of times that the lead adult addresses boys in comparison with girls. Invariably, a much higher proportion of attention and verbal interaction is given to boys than girls. In particular, those boys considered to be 'lively' are more likely to be responded to and given first opportunities when children are being picked for an activity. What messages are we conveying to both girls and boys through these unconscious acts of differentiation?

Singing, in particular, is often identified as a feminine activity. Boys' avoidance of feminine behaviours can include a reluctance to sing. Adults may not respond to boys' singing in encouraging ways, as Zak's mother did, already reinforcing even with quite young children the idea that singing is not for them. As a result, by the time young children are school-age there may well be marked differences in how successfully boys and girls are learning to sing. Beatriz Ilari and Assal Habibi (2015), for example, studied Brazilian children in Brazil and Latino children in the US and found that in both groups of six- to seven-year-old children girls outperformed boys in singing. We therefore have some clear evidence that gender impacts markedly on children's progress as singers.

There are, however, some approaches that can remedy this situation. Clare Hall (2005) investigated the singing behaviour of a group of Australian five-year-old boys at the start of their schooling and found, as we might anticipate, that they already showed a reluctance to sing. She then introduced these boys to older boy singers aged nine and seventeen and found that peer modelling was an effective strategy to motivate and support young boys' success in singing. With singing and also with instruments researchers have found that children are influenced by the gender of the person playing (or singing) and that peer role modellers, within a small local situation such as a school or community music group, may be a very effective source of positive influence.

What Clare Hall's work very usefully shows is that at the level of actual practice, the first level that Georgina Born identifies, interventions that challenge dominant stereotyping discourses can influence children's musical behaviours. Music provision for young children should not merely subscribe to the gendered musical role models in society at large and the limitations that they contain, but seek to challenge them and thereby extend children's musical options and opportunities and expand their musical childhoods.

Although I focus here on gender, the same applies to all standardised and stereotyped musical behaviours drawn along lines of social distinction. The content and resources provided for a session should endeavour to avoid reinforcing stereotypes. Many song words emphasise sex role differences, or indeed inadvertently carry racial connotations, and a quick flip of the words to avoid stereotypes can be easily achieved (Dansereau, 2014). Props, pictures, stories or topics can also reinforce stereotyping. When, for example, even very young boys dart forward and choose the large noisy drum and girls hold back, there is an instant decision to be made on the part of the educator whether to intervene, to give out instruments deliberately according to non-gender stereotypes, or to just leave it be. Do we insist that girls take the drum, that boys have a pink scarf and girls the blue, do we insist that all the children hold hands to make a circle if some show reluctance? It can be tiring and frustrating to continually challenge the children's gender role expectations; each small incident may seem trivial and harmless but, in my view, the continual drip-feed of small positive interventions can accumulatively carry big messages.

But as anthropologists remind us, reading Alma Gottlieb (2004) and David Lancy (2014a), the majority of the world's children do not have new technological devices or pink and blue toys, do not sleep alone, do not ride in cars or wear nappies, and often live in extended families of siblings, aunties and grandparents. Therefore, hygiene, bedtime, mealtime routines and solitary play with toys in indoor spaces are culturally specific forms of activity, and the musical dimensions of those activities therefore are also culturally determined. This is not to detract from what we can valuably learn from looking closely at young children's humdrum and everyday musical lives, but taking a wider cultural view sheds a light on what might be being taken for granted and assumed and suggests ways in which young children's musicality might be differently conceptualised. From a childhood studies, anthropological perspective, we ask how children and their practices are being culturally constructed in these analyses and conclusions, and how cultural values underpin the theoretical concepts and the interpretations arising from those studies. Most importantly, it ensures that they are recognised as being very specific to one type of child-rearing and set of parenting practices, culturally defined and constructed, not shared by all as universals, and that we do not transfer these concepts and ideas too lightly onto children belonging to different social classes and ethnic groups. These thoughts bring me to the next chapter.

6 Paper sheep and camels
The view from other places

> what counts as strange depends on what counts as familiar
> Biesta, 2006:59

As it happens, neither anthropology nor ethnomusicology has been much interested in the activities of very small children, least of all babies (Hirschfeld, 2002). Anthropologists and ethnomusicologists travelled often long distances to explore and bring back stories of the cultural activities and music of adults. Small children might have been on the edge of their sightlines; babies certainly were not, tucked away in baskets or the folds of their mother's clothing. But most recently this has changed and a small but very informative area of anthropology of early childhood and ethnomusicology of young children's music is emerging that is shifting much of what we understand about early childhood. Studying babies and toddlers from an anthropological perspective brings biology and culture face to face. If we take the conventional developmental milestones for babyhood and on into the first years found in any health, welfare or educational materials, they may tell us that babies can do this or that by a certain age. For example, babies are likely to be able to crawl at a certain age and we are led to believe that this is normal and biologically determined. But if the forest floor is infested with dangerous, biting insects, crawling is discouraged, deliberately delayed, and toddlers are confined to baskets and hammocks. If crawling and then on to walk is a prized achievement for babies that you delight in showing off to your family and friends, then babies are encouraged to crawl, to practise and crawl surprisingly early. This is where culture and environment become relevant and babies and young children are not merely biological, developmental beings; they are both biological and cultural.

Vignette

The small group of Somali-born mothers I came to know well, who had fled the war in Somalia and now live in an English city, shook their heads and looked at one another in disbelief when I told them that the majority of English mothers do not bring their babies or toddlers to sleep with them in the same bed at night. 'Do they not love their babies?' they asked, incredulous at such neglect, as they saw it, in leaving babies quite alone to sleep in the dark without any bodily contact, comfort or protection. Yet, when I observed these same mothers during a music session with a visiting community musician, they sat passively with their babies and toddlers placed still and quiet beside them on the floor, silently watching but barely participating. This was not due to any concerns about the musical content; these were more liberal-minded Muslims than those who have adopted a fundamentalist religious position where music is forbidden. No, participating with your baby in a playful interactive way was just not what they did. 'Are they not interested in their babies?' asked the centre workers who, surprised at seeing their non-participation in the session, interpreted this as a lack of parenting skills, as disinterest in the educational advancement of their toddlers that would herald problems to come, and disinterest that bordered on impoliteness to the visiting community musician.

This vignette illustrates the idea that is central to this chapter. We may know for a fact that different people hold different ideas about themselves and the world, about how to bring up children, about music and the part music plays in their lives, and about how children learn in music and ought to be taught. But we rarely think that these different ideas make a substantial and deeply rooted difference until there is an incident, a moment of contact when two different sets of cultural values bump up against one another. Such moments of contact are revealed in surprise, momentary confusion and sometimes even stronger emotions such as shock and disapproval. There was surprise in the voices of the children's centre workers at the passiveness of the Somali mothers with their babies in the music session, tinged with an edge of disapproval. There was surprise among the mothers that British parenting practices do not include co-sleeping. Each one of us, brought up immersed in our own culture, arrives with the conviction that our own ways of doing things, our own ideas and practices are, obviously, the only way and the right and best way. Moving among our own social groups for all or at least most of the time, we rarely experience any moments of surprise, confusion or even shock. For babies to separate when they sleep alone, if not as very small babies then as soon as possible, is taken to be appropriate in Western parenting practice. The Somali mothers appeared bewildered by the music session and bemused by the antics of those mothers who did join in with their toddlers. To engage babies and very young children in animated, playful activities involving songs and language is thought in many social groups, particularly Western middle-class parents, to be important to stimulate their early learning (also LeVine, 1998:118). In the Somali way of life, as indeed in many, perhaps a majority, of societies, for babies to be calm, passive and conforming is the aim (Young, 2016b). So mothers keep them quiet, do not engage them in animated play and soothe them with breastfeeding and close bodily contact (cf. Gantley, 1994).

Every mother wants to do her very best for her baby and every educator wants to do the very best for the children they work with, but how that is enacted can differ widely according to the child-rearing and pedagogical practices, the parenting, upbringing and educational goals and values within different social groups. Seen through the eyes of non-Western parents, as David Lancy remarks, many 'normal' Western childcare practices are seen as very strange, and possibly harmful to children (2017). Placing children to sleep in rooms alone, not feeding them on demand, letting them cry rather than immediately attending to them, not strapping them to your body to carry, talking to them as if they are conversational partners and (over)exciting them with playful (musical) activities are viewed negatively in many societies. From my conversations with the Somali-born mothers I learned that they were concerned that English mothers must not know how to look after babies and small children properly, issuing stern rebukes, and were keen to instruct them in what for them were incontrovertibly the right ways (Young, 2016b).

Most people fail to recognise or appreciate how much of their lives are governed by habits, values and expectations that are largely the product of history and culture (Lancy, 2016). We may know that what we hold to be good practice in caring, bringing up and educating young children has changed since the times of our parents or is different in other cultural groups, but nevertheless we are pretty much convinced that what we do *now* and what we believe *now* is right. Behind the disbelief or disapproval when things are done differently from the generation of our parents or those of other social groups, there is a slight air of 'we know best', a moral overtone. Same too with our ideas about how music might be integrated into upbringing, parenting, family life and how we work and educate children in music. We believe that our ideas about how children make sense of themselves musically, how they participate in music, how we should use music in our work, what is important to teach them and what it is to be musical are the right ones.

This certainty born of being centred in one particular culture, further articulated through social class, race and gender, can have enormous consequences. The children's centre workers observing the music session expressed a negative framing of the Somali-born mothers' non-participation and wanted to intervene (Young, 2017b). They too were keen to instruct the mothers in how to bring up their children 'properly'; they too issued censorious comments about the mothers' parenting. Importantly, anthropology can reveal bias, that is, the assumption, witting or unwitting, that the way things are done in one's own social group is universal, 'normal' or, more dangerously, that behaviour that deviates from that norm is inferior, problematic and, at worst, needs to be remedied. Anthropologists believe that cultural differences should be respected, that we should avoid imposing outside ideas onto people with very different understandings of the world and making value judgements on other people's ways of bringing up their children.

However, there is another perspective to bring in here. Viewed from the practitioners' position, working within the structures of the English education system, their concerns over the mothers' non-participation are understandable and may have some justification. They knew that the small children of the Somali mothers would soon enter the preschool system, where English is the mainstream language. Therefore, the children should start to hear and speak English via songs and activities, to play with toys designed to foster cognitive development and be encouraged to look at picture books as a precursor to reading. These are the traditions and emphases of upbringing and early education in English society. This small example illustrates the very difficult balance between understanding and then respecting ethnic and racial diversity and allowing for variation in participation and, at the same time, bringing all children and families together within a national society and its collective systems of education. It is not clear in discussions of best practice in multicultural contexts whose culture(s) are to be respected or how to incorporate all, particularly when the groups of children educators work with may increasingly include children from many different ethnic backgrounds. With the recent influx of families from many different parts of the world into European society, this difficult balance has become an urgent topic of research and discussion in the general field of early childhood education across Europe (e.g. Bernard, 2016). Although respect for diversity and mantras of enrichment through cultural variation are held clearly in early childhood policies, the reality of enacting these ideals often results in tokenistic practices such as dual language greetings written on entrance doors or songs from 'other' cultures, but little truly integrated diverse practices. The ideal aim is to go deeper than such tokenistic pedagogical approaches. With increasing movement of populations, finding ways to work positively with and accommodate diversity are becoming more urgent. Sandra found a way to work with Somali-born mothers that was truly integrated: through story-telling and songs acted out with paper sheep and camels. But you must wait until the end of the chapter for that tale.

Anthropological perspectives

Joe Tobin, an educational anthropologist, has carried out a series of very interesting cross-cultural studies focusing on general early childhood education taking place in preschools in different countries (Tobin, *et al.*, 1989). He gives three concise reasons to look across cultures: to question taken-for-granted assumptions, to draw attention to the overlooked, and to expand the repertoire of the possible. As I aimed to illustrate with my story of the Somali-born mothers, anthropology can help to unseat the familiar and reveal what until now has been hidden to us. It can give a quite different perspective on things that may otherwise lie dormant and taken for granted and help us to see dominant, Westernised concepts from a new angle. An anthropological perspective can contribute to a critical standpoint therefore. Yet, despite the potential advantages of viewing through an anthropological window, its research and theories have had relatively little influence on early childhood music education practice.

Cross-cultural studies

That is not to say that there has been no interest in looking across cultures in music education research among young children. There are some studies that have endeavoured to take a wider perspective by exploring children's responses and activities in different locations and cultures. However, many of these studies have not adopted a genuinely anthropological approach but have continued to adopt the methods of psychology. The usual approach is to design a common task, for example singing a short song containing some distinctive pitch intervals, which is then tested in several different cultural contexts to understand how culture may impact on how children could complete the test. When researchers started to carry out cross-cultural comparative studies in developmental psychology, taking, for example, the concepts of Piagetian theory, they soon found that these pathways and models of development are closely tied to assumptions and images of childhood in the countries where the original research had been carried out. Alternative understandings of development started to emerge that took account of the kinds of situations encountered by children in different cultural contexts. Barbara Rogoff, for example, from her studies of Guatemalan Mayan children, has arrived at some very informative reconceptualisations of learning and development based on the children's much closer participation in adult everyday life in these communities (e.g. Rogoff, et al., 2007).

In music education there have been a handful of cross-cultural studies of aspects of musical experience and learning among young children since the late 1990s. These have mainly focused on singing, have studied aspects of pitch- and rhythm-processing through formal measures and tests that are applied to children living in different countries, and have mostly focused on children in their first year of schooling, typically around six years old. Joanne Rutkowski has carried out cross-cultural studies with colleagues in Hong Kong (Rutkowski & Chen-Hafteck, 2001) and Israel (Rutkowski, et al., 2002), using her Singing Voice Development Measure, a tool to assess a child's use of her singing voice. Others have taken this measure and made adaptations to make it more applicable for use in Taiwan, Lithuania and Latvia (Raju & Ross, 2012; Rauduvaite, et al., 2017). This kind of cross-cultural study of singing continues. The large-scale study of singing entitled 'Advancing Interdisciplinary Research in Singing' (AIRS) (Cohen, et al., 2009; Gudmundsdottir & Cohen, 2015) has evolved a protocol, the AIRS Test Battery of Singing Skills (ATBSS). This is a comprehensive set of tests that was designed for cross-cultural research on the acquisition of singing from varied age, cultural and ethnic groups and is resulting in collections of children's singing and findings from a number of smaller contributory studies.

The singing tests that are taken out and about tend to be based on skills of voice production and accuracy that are considered to be fundamental to singing in Western art music. Anthropological studies of singing, as we might expect, challenge these presumptions. Many, drawing on studies of children's singing in varied cultures, have suggested that singing in the young child's world – both music for children in the form of lullabies and children's songs and children's self-made music – occupies a kind of 'border zone' between speech and song (Chen-Hafteck, 2000; Mang, 2001; Minks, 2002; Stadler Elmer, 2012). This suggests, therefore, that we should not define certain types of vocal activity in this 'border zone' as 'not yet singing' – that is, in deficit terms, as developmental models of singing development would pigeonhole them – but should describe young children's vocalisations across a spectrum of different modes of vocalisation and voice use, with equal interest, value and attention to each (Young, 2006). Here is another example. The cultural definition of what counts as a song cannot be assumed. Raju explains how the Estonian word for a song, *laul*, can refer to a melody sung or played on instruments, the lyrics as in the poem on which the song is based, and the melody and lyrics combined. She next queries whether a song with the melody intact and the words only sketched still counts as a song, for in Estonian musical culture the poem, the lyrics are given great importance. Yet, evaluations of children's singing typically prioritise correct melodic reproduction over lyrics (Raju, 2015:15). Lily Chen-Hafteck adds another example that further destabilises definitions of song (2000). She suggests that South African children may not have a notion of a fixed song that never changes because for them a song may always be something partly or wholly improvised.

Where cross-cultural studies adopt a test that reflects the home musical cultures of both groups of babies or children, the dominance of one musical culture over others may be removed. In this next example Gaye Soley and Erin Hannon explored Turkish and American babies' preference for either Balkan or Western metre patterns (2010). Their study was based on a defined experimental study in the traditions of music psychology research, but their test incorporated both musical styles. They found that American babies preferred Western metres to Balkan, whereas Turkish infants brought up bimusically, with both Western and Balkan music, showed no preference. Their findings suggest that the family and home musical environment would therefore appear to influence preference for rhythms as early as four months old.

It is worth pausing to remind ourselves from studies such as this, and the large corpus of work that has revealed the detail of infant musicality, that babies are sensitive to and fascinated by music and able to detect fine variations in pitch and rhythm. They are interested and attracted to music and remember it well. It suggests we lose some of this sensitivity and open-earedness as we become enculturated into one musical style. That a preference for a culturally defined rhythmic style can emerge in the earliest months of babyhood holds very clear implications for practice and for how we develop pedagogical approaches that foster diversity of musical experience among babies and toddlers. It suggests that hearing a wide range of musical styles in early babyhood familiarises children with varied musical characteristics.

Insights into children's music from other places

Anthropologists and ethnomusicologists have come to the study of young children's music and their musical lives and experiences much later than psychology, as Andrea Emberly has pointed out (2014; also Gottlieb, 2000). To the ethnomusicologist small children and their music were of no interest, nor, for that matter, the music of motherhood, as Elizabeth Mackinlay adds in her interesting work on music in mothering (2010, 2012). These were trivial, everyday domestic practices that could be ignored (Juvančič, 2010). Of the little work there is, most is recent (e.g. Young & Gillen, 2010; Pieridou Skoutella, 2015) and the majority of work sits outside the early childhood age phase, focusing on children in the middle years of childhood. Sometimes in studies among older children, just as with studies of adults' music, we get glimpses of younger children taking part from which we can glean some information. Likewise, the very few broad anthropologies that take a general interest in babies and very small children might contain some brief instances of musical activity. Alma Gottlieb's ground-breaking anthropological study of babies among the Beng in Côte d'Ivoire has an associated website with video clips that show toddlers playing rhythmically with sounds made by tapping found objects (Gottlieb, undated). The Beng video clips also offer some glimpses of parenting practices, including a mother gripping her one-month-old beneath her armpits and swinging her from side to side in a playful, rhythmic activity to entertain her that, to my eyes, looks surprisingly vigorous and rapid for such a young baby. Here again is the surprise when confronted with cultural differences in how babies should be held, handled and rhythmically moved that point to deeper beliefs about the fragility or robustness of newborns.

Before going further, however, I should point out some drawbacks of anthropological studies that should be held in mind. Anthropology and ethnomusicology offer rich, in-depth studies of small groups of children – sometimes just one or two children, with parents or families – in one place and at one time, and offer detailed descriptions of their musical activities: what anthropology calls 'thick descriptions' (e.g. Tudge, 2008). Being so specific to one small group and place, the findings are not easily transferred across to tell us anything about children beyond this one group. Throughout this book I have been pointing out that, in the same way, studies of just one or two children or small groups living in Europe, Australia or North America should, likewise, not be considered as representative of anything more than that one family, or one social group, in that locality and its culture of child upbringing. To claim, as minority-world, WEIRD family studies do, that findings pertain widely to all children is presumptuous, ethnocentric, arrogant even. On the other hand, these rich descriptions that take careful account of context and social situations in diverse locations can complement traditional laboratory research and its specific, reductionist testing, generating richer conceptions of children's musicality than those currently available. Anthropologists may propose some implications from their findings that could be taken up and studied further through more focused studies in the methodological traditions of biology, psychology or sociology. They often suggest that their findings challenge some taken-for-granted aspects of existing theories, as I have already mentioned: for instance, that developmental models may not be as universal and fixed as imagined, or that children make music in very idiosyncratic ways and that these ways are tied in to characteristics of the surrounding culture. But beyond this general recommendation that all children are unique and following individual pathways and that we should always take account of context and culture, it may be difficult to pull out more specific findings that may be transferable and applicable to wider groups of children or may suggest applications in practice. What can happen, however, is that several studies find similarities that start to connect and suggest some broader themes. The propositions are then strengthened by being built on more than one study, on accumulated studies. With these provisos in mind, the value of ethnomusicological and anthropological studies of small numbers of children lies also in the ways they unsettle our certainties and open up our thinking to wider possibilities, harking back to the list of three advantages spelled out by Joe Tobin.

So, what follow in this next section are some broader themes that emerge when looking across the ethnomusicological literature – such as we have – that has been interested in young children's musical experiences and activities. Ethnomusicological studies of the ways in which children participate in musical events, whether traditional art-music events, music-making in their locality or their self-generated musical play, can reveal the interesting and varied ways in which children do music, engage in music and learn musically.

What counts as children's music?

So, as we saw from the queries that already started to surface in relation to the cross-cultural studies of young children's singing – what exactly counts as singing or what counts as a song? – ethnomusicology unsettles our definitions of music and musical practices. Importantly, the anthropological perspective asks us to put ourselves in the shoes of the other, to ask what does music mean for this child or these children, what is singing or a song to them, what is musical experience on their terms. Shifting our point of view to the other – be it a baby, small child or Somali mother – shifts our conceptions of music and musical process. These revised conceptions can then provide templates that help us to recognise and embrace musical processes among young children and that illuminate different angles and aspects. Ethnomusicology can be a source of progressive musical thought that can open up alternative ways of understanding musical processes that are often much closer, in my view, to the ways in which young children engage in and make their own music when given more creative freedoms. They may suggest alternative ways of doing music, learning and teaching, or validate tentative ways that are already starting to emerge. In the next paragraphs I provide some examples of how ethnomusicology can provide conceptions of music that offer, in my view, conceptions of musical process that are more inclusive of children's ways of making and participating in music. Thus, we can expand their musical options and avoid the limiting conceptions drawn only from Western art music or shaped by commodified and stereotypical musical activities, by narrow developmental models or by parenting values and norms.

As with the sociology of music that I introduced in the previous chapter, ethnomusicology is interested in music as social practice. A conception of music as social practice, of music as made between people, always emerging, in flow, never fixed, can move us away from understandings of music as objectified sound towards a more contextualised, holistic, embodied conception of music as interaction (Blacking, 1995). It is Western musicology with its traditions of notation and analysis and its elevation of the musical work that has resulted in conceptions of music as object and the need to teach the objective elements of music (see Stevens, 2012). The alternative conception places importance on children learning how to participate in performance occasions, with others, as a sociable, embodied and interactive process (Small, 1977). The musical child of Western European musicology and the educational traditions it has given rise to must learn a set of formal skills that give primacy to accurate performance, such as being able to sing in tune, perform rhythmic structures accurately and so on. These pedagogical assumptions, and their construction of the child as musical, creep right down to the earliest years with activities based on very simple (and, frankly, often very dull and musically impoverished) rhythm and pitch elements. Ethnomusicology opens up alternative versions of children being musical.

Traditional European definitions separate music from other art forms, but this is not the case in all cultural practices. In traditional Japanese (Fujita, 2006:87) and several African (see Trehub, et al., 2015) cultures, for example, there is no original term for 'music'. Music is interwoven with drama, dance and song, and hence is not designated by a specific term. Fumiko Fujita found that the playful musical expressions of young Japanese children are closely bound up with patterns of speech, bodily movement, interactive play (with things and other people) and – interestingly – with synchronised breathing (2006). In this way, she suggests, music is not separate but interwoven with multimodal expressions and closer to traditional Japanese cultural practices. Expressive time-based activity that is multimodal and not narrowly musical is a description of children's activity that I have also frequently offered, drawing on my observations of children in English nursery settings (Young, 2003a). Similarly, Amanda Minks studied children's music and language play in Nicaragua, identifying the communicative resources adopted by children and the ways in which they intertwined speech, movement and song (2013). If we lived within a musical tradition where music, movement, dance and visual art are inseparable and music is social, dynamic and interpersonal (Stevens, 2012; also Blacking, 1995), we would surely have arrived at a time-based arts tradition of social participation as the basis of our educational practices and avoided many of the limitations arising from a bias towards Western art music and its reduction to a sound-only art form. It is noticeable, and very positive in my view, that many of the artist-cultural workers developing work for very young children draw on the integration of art forms in developing their performance art events, as if consciously or implicitly aware that the 'music only' separation is an artificial one and not in keeping with young children's expressive, creative engagement. There is a similarity here with the merging and blending of music into the many different forms of media enabled by digital technologies that I mentioned in the previous chapter. New technologies and the new art forms they enable, combining sound, visuals, virtual realities and responsiveness to movements surely offer exciting, creative possibilities for multimodal, multimedia experiences for the very young, releasing us from the narrowness of music as sound-object pedagogies. Again, many of the most innovative performance pedagogies for young children are capitalising on these possibilities.

In the same way, indigenous learning and teaching processes, those found in many musical traditions, are very often multimodal and inseparable from dance, movement, language and dramatic play. As a quite specific example, Sonja Downing (2008) studied children learning gamelan in Bali: a more formal, structured pedagogy designed for learning the skills of gamelan playing. While only the youngest children in her study, at around six or seven years, could be considered 'early childhood', the embodied strategies that she noticed in how the children are taught are interesting. The children observe modelled playing and then practise the movements, but they were also taught via embodied strategies that included ways in which the teacher may physically touch, hold and mould a child's body. She also noticed that children's observation of modelled gamelan playing may appear to be still and passive, but also has an empathetically embodied, kinaesthetic quality to it, something that Melissa Bremmer also noticed, incidentally, in her analysis of Dutch early childhood music education sessions (2015).

In chapter two I drew attention to the age segregation of young children from older children's and adults' worlds in our society, pointing out that, as a result, adults have increasingly provided very distinctive and separate forms of music and musical practices for young children. These separated forms include the music education practices, but extend into musical parenting practices and the toys, media items, recorded music or music performances provided by parents and how they use these and incorporate them into their children's lives. I explained how, in this way, a very distinctive, separated image of early musical childhood, 'childish music', is created. When we look across cultures we can discover societies where this sharp division does not occur and there are continuous lines of contact between adults' music and children's.

In a fascinating ethnomusicological study of children learning musical traditions in different parts of the world (Mali, North India, Rajasthan, Azerbaijan, Cuba and Venezuela), which tracked the same children over two-and-a-half years and captured them on film (Duran, undated, 2015), we see examples of young children immersed in family and community music processes. So interesting is this study that I reproduce its introductory paragraph here:

> *Children who grow up in oral musical contexts such as the families of hereditary musical specialists commonly learn the body-language of music before they learn music itself. Throughout infancy and childhood they absorb the mannerisms of performance practice and the physical and social graces befitting of musicians. Learning music is accomplished largely by osmosis and imitation, often without a great deal of conscious intent. Children develop an unselfconscious musical confidence born of deeply-nurtured authority.*

Lucy Duran adds, affirming my comments earlier in the chapter, that very little has been written about the processes of childhood music acquisition in the oral traditions of non-European cultures. Although the film is mostly about older children, younger children are captured, strapped to their dancing mothers' backs, cradled between the arms of their sarangi playing fathers or parked on the margins to play with a talking drum (that I would call a *dondo*, but it has other regional names). The families live mainly in warm climate places where home life spills out into the street, village or family compound to mingle with neighbours and extended family. Among the griots (hereditary musical families) of Mali, children begin drumming at an early age, as young as two years old (Tang, 2006:109), mimicking adult drumming activities that they observe. In many communities, as Lisa Koops points out from her studies of children's musical play in The Gambia, children enjoy a rich musical environment which is combined with a positive expectation to be musical (2010a). Rather than believing that music is an ability possessed by only a few, and that live music-making is reserved for a minority who have acquired very specialised skills, music-making is perceived to be an everyday activity that simply all take part in, and the communal and social qualities of musical participation are valued above all.

By far the largest group of ethnomusicological studies of children's own music has focused on playground games. These studies typically look primarily to the expert players, who will be the oldest in a group, usually children in the middle years of childhood. The youngest children, where we can find them mentioned or captured in photos, are 'hangers-on' and 'lookers-on': active observers learning through attentive listening and imitation (e.g. Dzansi, 2004; Miya, 2007; Marsh, 2008). Amanda Minks, mentioned briefly a little earlier, studied Miskitu children's speech and song on the Atlantic Coast of Nicaragua and describes the scaffolding or guiding of younger children's participation (Minks, 2013: 90). She adds that the older children might decide to leave out the youngest and inexperienced in a more complex singing game. But, even if excluded, the youngest children still looked on, sometimes singing under their breath. One photo in her book shows a toddler being lugged around on the hip of an older girl during a singing game, gathering in a direct, embodied experience of the game-playing. Presumably the older girl has to take care of a younger sibling – childcare practices that are commonplace in many parts of the majority world, but not in the minority. Obviously, these musical experiences take us back to questions of how much opportunity children have to play outdoors, unsupervised, in mixed-age groups and invite a contrast with minority-world children who are increasingly confined to indoors and nuclear family life.

The emphasis on 'observational learning' from many ethnomusicological studies of children's music-making is particularly interesting as it mirrors the work of Ruth Paradise and Barbara Rogoff (Paradise & Rogoff, 2009), who have long been interested in indigenous learning processes (for learning in general) through their research into the ways in which Mayan children learn in traditional communities of South America. They have drawn attention to how children learn by observation, and what Rogoff and her colleagues term 'intent community participation' (Rogoff, et al., 2007). Barbara Rogoff describes cultural practices and traditions of learning that support informal learning as children observe and join in as they can with everyday activities that are integrated into family and community life. She suggests that this goes against the common assumption that observation is passive and that children must be actively doing in order to learn.

In a similar vein to Barbara Rogoff, David Lancy points out that, broadly speaking, anthropological studies reveal learning that is contextually embedded in everyday life (Lancy, et al., 2010). Likewise, Melissa Cain and her colleagues refer to the fact that the traditional way to become proficient in many world musical traditions is to learn through 'encounter' rather than structured didactic processes (2013). Embedded learning, or learning through encounter, contrasts with formal school-type learning which is detached from everyday life. Ethnographies of learning portray the development of skills and knowledge as largely a bottom-up process where the 'self-initiating learner' takes advantage of social learning opportunities to replicate (often initially in and through play) the skills and behaviours they observe around them practised by members of their family and community (Lancy, et al., 2010). In the conventional music education model the learning and development process is dominated by top-down transfer of knowledge as teaching from experts/teachers to children.

Many have pointed to children's autonomous motivation that drives them to participate in everyday musical activities which have family, social and cultural value. Lisa Koops concluded that the children she studied in The Gambia 'seemed to teach themselves' and also, interestingly, that play and laughter, the affective dimension, are part of the experience, heightening pleasure and increasing motivation (2010a). The anthropologist Dorothy Lee (1961) wrote about 'autonomous motivation' in a way that helps make sense of the 'social groundedness' of this kind of intrinsic motivation to learn the activities that are recognised as central to everyday life in one's community. She added that a basic feature of human motivation (a core biological feature therefore) is a strong need for collaboration and involvement with family and friends, returning us to the proposed prosocial origins of music as rooted in our evolutionary past that I wrote about earlier.

In relation to motivation, Ruth Paradise and Barbara Rogoff, from their studies of Mayan children's learning, make an interesting observation. Because learning in schools or in the early childhood session is typically detached and isolated from family and community music, motivation is not intrinsic, not autonomous, and so educators have to use extrinsic motivation that has no inherent relation to what is being learned. They write how 'attractive materials and colours, play, 'having fun', eye-catching devices, rewards (stars, grades, praise) … are all used to ensure children's engagement' (Paradise & Rogoff, 2009:125). On a social media page for early childhood music specialists it is noticeable that there is much sharing of tips and strategies to ensure the engagement and participation of children via these kinds of extrinsic motivational strategies.

Ethnographic studies also offer a window onto some examples of formal education in traditional societies where there is a distinct 'master' and 'novice' role and a body of knowledge and skill that cannot easily be learned without some form of instruction, a kind of apprenticeship. In Hindustani music, the art music of North India, which has a complex musical system, a great deal of material must be explicitly taught, but there is also a strong immersive element from a very young age, with children largely following family traditions within hereditary musician families (e.g. Duran, 2015). Learning to play an instrument in Western classical style falls into this model. Starting young with formal learning through the Suzuki method, for example, the mother takes a strong role in assisting with the drill and rote repetitions that proficiency on an instrument requires. Many of these 'master and novice' approaches share an emphasis on modelling by the teacher. The learner observes and listens intently (Campbell, 2003:93). The learning relies on a high level of oral/aural process, followed by exact imitation and repetition by the learner of short musical fragments. There may be a system of mnemonics to assist the aural process, but typically in many world-music traditions no formal notation process as found in the Western classical tradition. It is usually a formalised arrangement between expert and learner in a special place, not the family or everyday community settings described above. The roles and form of learning is generally prescribed. Thus, in master and novice pedagogies the child is definitely on a pathway to 'becoming', with the clear endpoint being adult musical practices which are specialised and performed by only a few expert and highly skilled musicians. In family and community settings there is flexible interaction, collective organisation, learning haphazardly, much less prescription and more emphasis on 'being' musical in the here and now.

There may be elements of formal education systems that we consider undesirable, harmful, abusive even. I remember, in my student days (many years ago now), attending a performance and discussion given by a Burundi drumming group. Someone enquired how the young children learned to drum and the answer, still etched in my memory because of the surprise, was that they must watch, copy and were beaten if they made mistakes. A simple behavioural method of reward or punishment is an accepted educational method in many parts of the world (Lancy, 2017:103), as indeed it was historically in European countries. The formal learning of some musical traditions that start at a very young age might require children to practise uncomfortable, even painful movements for long periods. In a newspaper article Greenstreet reports how the highly successful Chinese pianist Lang Lang was put under tremendous pressure at a very young age to practise long hours by his incredibly ambitious father (2011). Highly rigid, instrument-learning schemes may afford children little musical agency and expect high levels of disciplined conformity, relying on coercion and even punishments, rather than autonomous motivation.

These kinds of indigenous learning processes, particularly the informal, observational and collaborative processes in families and communal settings, may be more prevalent in certain types of traditional society. But in all social groups children absorb their musical understanding, embody the musical style, take on a musical identity and become a certain kind of musical child from birth simply by being immersed in musical environments and learn through many of the musical practices that take place in families, as we saw in the previous chapter. The point here is not that these indigenous processes of learning that occur outside of formal educational settings are somehow in opposition to or 'better than' (or lesser than) what takes place in more formal educational settings. My aim is to show that there is a very wide range of varied learning processes in which children can participate and to embrace them all within a broad and inclusive model of musical learning. The particular strengths of alternative ways, particularly processes based on observation and participation in family and community settings, on multimodal and embodied processes, can be identified, validated and incorporated when possible, to complement and expand what can otherwise remain narrow, conservative 'schoolified' ways of organising early childhood music learning (e.g. Cain, et al., 2013).

And while I talk of immersion in family and community musical cultures, we should pause and reflect that some children learn that they have little place in a musical world around them, or that there are strict limitations on their personal musical agency, as we saw in the previous chapter in the discussion on gendered musical practices. In some contexts young children's first efforts to sing might be at best ignored or at worst mocked. Aya's own singing in the nursery that I imagined at the start of this book had no place in an education system that prioritises core literacy and numeracy skills. From interviews with Muslim mothers in exploring how to design interculturally sensitive approaches to creative music with these families, we found some ultrareligious mothers who were denying access to singing and dancing for their children on the grounds that it is prohibited by their religion (Young & Street, 2009).

Ethnomusicologies of music for children, lullabies in particular

Only a handful of studies have explored musical practices initiated and led by adults in their cultural contexts that are specifically child-directed, and almost all of these are studies of lullabies and lullaby singing. They range from the collection and study of lullabies as musical and verbal texts, mainly by folklorists, to the ways in which lullabies are used within real-world, sociocultural situations. Lullabies represent a very particular type of song with a specific purpose for very young children.

Music psychologists have broadly claimed that lullaby singing is ubiquitous in caregiving and have analysed the musical characteristics, suggesting that lullabies have universal, fundamental musical characteristics (Trehub & Trainor, 1998). They are simple in their musical features – melodically, rhythmically and lyrically – and sung slowly, quietly with a warm voice tone. Anthropology has taught me to be sceptical about broad statements of universality, particularly given the shortage of studies of lullaby singing from outside the Western context. I challenge the idea that lullaby singing is universal and I would suggest that it is primarily in cultures where babies are deliberately put to sleep, and separated bodily, often in 'baby containers' that can be swayed, that lullaby singing is a strong tradition. Recalling my discussion of bedtime routines in the chapter before, when babies simply fall asleep strapped to mothers' bodies or drop off nestled on laps, they do not need to be 'put' to sleep. In support of my scepticism, the ethnomusicologist Alan Merriam, an expert on the music of North American Indians, wrote that there is no mention of lullabies in the literature on their music (1967/2017). As for the musical characteristics being universal, there may well be a high degree of similarity across typical lullabies, but it did not take a long search to discover examples of lullaby singing that do not conform to this model. The BaYaka Pygmies of Central Africa have evolved a distinctive style of singing akin to yodelling, and it is said that the more the baby cries, the louder the mothers yodel (Lewis, 2013). As another example, Dale Olsen collected lullabies from the Warao in Venezuela, whom he calls song people of the rainforest, but found that these lullabies were sung in a way that was harsh, loud and quite fast-paced in comparison with what he referred to as 'conventional expectations' (1996). He suggests that the baby is reassured and soothed more by the presence of a familiar person (mother, father, brother, sister, grandparent, etc.) and familiar voice than by the singing itself. He concluded that these lullabies also served a dual purpose to educate other older children hearing the songs in the same communal hut about important aspects of Warao life. Thus the Warao lullabies are part of extended family life and cannot be assumed to be sung only intimately between a mother and baby. So while the majority of lullabies may share very similar characteristics, I am sceptical that these musical characteristics are necessarily universal, and they are certainly culturally varied within quite wide margins.

Lullabies are typically performed with rhythmic movement such as rocking, jiggling and certain forms of touch, but these too are culturally varied. The ways in which crying babies are soothed differ substantially across cultures. In many non-Western communities babies will be instantly offered the breast and cry very little, as with the Somali-born mothers I introduced earlier in this chapter (Young, 2016b). Andrew Pettit, whose study I introduce in more detail below, found that the urban Indian parents he studied typically laid babies across a broad lap, gently bouncing and patting them (2014). These methods rarely include the Western pattern of extensive verbal soothing, singing to them, carrying the baby while walking up and down or, with slightly older babies, attempts to distract them by offering something interesting and absorbing to look at (Lancy, 2017). These examples may be small and scattered but what I am emphasising here, in keeping with a dominant theme of this chapter, is the importance of not assuming that patterns of musical parenting and upbringing are universal when, in reality, they belong only to specific cultural groups.

Andrew Pettit (2014) carried out his interesting study of infant-directed music from an anthropological viewpoint in an Indian urban environment. While he found that parents and caregivers still sing to young children, he also found that many songs, ways of holding and rhythmically soothing children and other ways of relating to them within extended families were disappearing as India's population becomes more urbanised, adopts new technologies and listens to music from popular media. He found that commercial lullabies and those composed for India's vast film industry have increasingly come to dominate the child-directed song repertoire (Pettit, 2014:3; also Brooks, 2016). He also discovered, harking back to my own interest in digitised-music sleep aids, that the practice of singing to children is slowly being supplanted by playing recordings on CDs, smartphones or recordings built into infant swings, cribs and toys. He proposes that these changes not only signal the disappearance of certain song traditions and changing practices of singing to children, but also mark a shift in societal beliefs about the nature of childhood within changing family structures and gender roles (Pettit, 2014). His conclusions find interrelationships between the changing music practices he observed and the changes in family structure, parenting practices and conceptions of childhood, making those links between music, musical practices, popular music cultures, new technologies and the wider social and cultural constructions of childhood that represent the dominant theme running through this book.

The loss of live lullaby singing and the traditional repertoire associated with it (many parents report singing pop songs from their own favourite repertoire instead of traditional lullabies) has been noted by other scholars in other locations and framed negatively (e.g. Baker & Mackinlay, 2006). From one point of view, a negative response to the changing repertoire can be associated with a sentimentalised, idealised conception of folk repertoire that is placed in direct contrast to contemporary 'popular' repertoire. It is a narrative of loss that we have seen is commonly applied to contemporary changes in early childhood and that is imbued with a nostalgia for 'natural' forms of singing based on ancient repertoire in which images of simplicity, harmony, timelessness and purity pertaining both to music and small children are merged. The musical choices clearly embody and reinforce an image of babyhood and early childhood that some feel is lost with the shift in repertoire (see, e.g., Daily Mail, 2013) or, at worst, not even provided by the human voice but via technologies. Wendy Brooks (2016) studied commercially produced, recorded lullabies on YouTube, apps and television and she, too, points to their increasing use within the Australian families who participated in her research. She expresses the view that commercialism pushes aside concern for the 'social and developmental needs' of young children, adopting an argument from a different angle, based on developmental psychology and framing young children as having specific 'needs'. As with the technology discussion in the previous chapter, it is not a question of whether some songs are intrinsically better or worse than others, or whether live or recorded singing is preferable, but *how* the songs or lullaby musics are used within family relationships. Yet again, it points clearly to the need for more research and thinking around how the use of music in contemporary parenting culture is being modified by the arrival of the technologies and digitised popular media that are now so embedded in everyday life.

Authenticity

A focus on ethnomusicology draws attention to one additional, important issue. I will introduce this issue by recounting a story told some years ago in a conference discussion on how a Maori song that was included in a well-known scheme of work for kindergarten children was originally intended to be sung during Maori celebrations marking the transition of young men from boyhood to manhood. The scheme's authors had almost certainly selected the song for its objective musical characteristics, in music developmental terms, as being suitable for young children. It was a short, rhythmic song of limited pitch range with apparently simple, repetitive Maori language words. No thought had been given to the song as a cultural artefact, its origins and ownership, the meaning of the words, or its social and functional role within Maori society. Obviously, in social and cultural terms the song was completely inappropriate and unsuitable for singing by non-Maori, kindergarten-age children, and it was highly disrespectful for the scheme's authors to have given no regard to its origins.

Adding to this discussion of taking songs from beyond our own cultural familiarity to use in practice and on the basis of what criteria songs are selected, Lisa Koops (2010b) describes the practice of adapting songs to make them easier for young children. She cited the case of a workshop in which teachers suggested changing the Mandinkan language lyrics of Gambian children's games to a made-up English version. She asks whether we do more harm than good when musical material is used superficially or with alterations and 'how much accuracy and cultural context' is necessary, particularly balanced against all the other demands on educators. As Koops stresses, it 'risks misrepresenting the musical practices being studied' and 'fails to take advantage of the benefits of culturally infused music teaching' (2010b:10). Authenticity and respect for musical origins are therefore important issues to consider when selecting songs and other musical materials from diverse cultural sources for use in music sessions.

Communicative musicality: an anthropological perspective

In the previous paragraphs I have been discussing anthropological perspectives on children's ways of participating and engaging in music within their cultural contexts, contributing to the thread running through the whole book that has explored and opened out constructions of musical childhoods. Also running through the book has been a secondary theme, an undercurrent, that of contemporary parenting culture – musical parenthoods, if you like – and how they shape musical childhoods. My vignette for this chapter aimed to provide a real-world illustration of a particular cultural niche for bringing up children that revealed how the parenting culture of the Somali mothers is already determining the musical experiences of their babies and toddlers, framing how they can 'be' and 'become' musical, to reiterate that idea.

One of the most influential theories in early childhood music education in recent years, which I have already introduced in previous chapters, has been the theoretical concept termed 'communicative musicality'. In this next section I want to show how this theoretical concept has arisen from, is determined by, and how its adoption is reinforced by a very particular model of parenting practice. Identified by Stephen Malloch and Colwyn Trevarthen from microanalyses of the vocal exchanges between a mother talking with her six-week-old baby sitting opposite her in a plastic baby seat (in itself a cultural artefact of a particular type of distal parenting practice), this analysis revealed rhythmic regularities and prosodic phrasing in the turn-taking of vocalisations that they described as musical in nature (1999, 2010). Their theory then expanded to propose that one of the roots, if not *the* biological root, of musicality lies in the communication between mothers and infants and that musicality is generated by the human need to be sociable. Babies indeed need to engage the adults around them in order to survive and, in the terms of biological anthropology, they are adaptively primed to have ways of increasing their survival chances. I discussed these ideas earlier in relation to biological perspectives. The important point is that babies possess a wide and flexible repertoire for engaging with adults that varies culturally and is not fixed.

When Alison Street (2006) collected examples of mothers interacting with and singing to their babies in the privacy of their own homes, one of the most interesting aspects of her study was how differently the mothers used singing to engage with their babies. Yes, they all had a repertoire of ditties that were very personal to them, and times and occasions when they typically sang, but, apart from some broad generalities which Alison could draw from across these mothers, what struck us was the variation. As in another study asking mothers about their musical activities with their babies, all kinds of individualised and very personal stories emerged (Young, *et al.*, 2007). Mothers clearly don't use music with their babies according to a formula, following recommended guidelines to ensure turn-taking, or crooning in a quiet voice and making sure their lullabies have sufficiently simple melody lines, as models of lullaby singing suggest; they do just what comes to them at that moment: a snatch of a current pop song, a string of nonsense words matching what they are doing, or a surfacing memory of a song from their own childhood. They do it because they love their babies; they do it to relate warmly and affectionately, in idiosyncratic and highly personal ways just between them and their baby, to create an emotional climate in which both they and their baby can thrive, not because they know it will make synapses connect up, or provide the foundations for language, or whatever else. To '*be*' a parent is a relationship. Whenever did parenting become a verb, as in something to be done, a chore, to be worked at?

The theory of communicative musicality has been widely used to explain aspects of early childhood musical behaviours and to provide a rationale for educational activity which seeks to promote the foundations of communication and bonding between mothers and infants, or to promote prosocial behaviour in young children. Indeed, I adopted the theory to explain interactive play on musical instruments between three- and four-year-olds and an adult play partner in which child and adult turn take (Young, 2003b). I had found that if the adult joins in, children often fall into offering short-phrased ideas on a xylophone or bongo drums in order to generate a kind of improvised conversation which has musical structures of regular phrasing and cohesive rhythmic ideas. Communicative musicality has thus proved to be a very fruitful theory, expanding beyond its origins in adult-infant communication to be more widely applicable. While this widespread adoption points to its explanatory usefulness, it also suggests, possibly, some looseness in its core concepts if they can morph to many varied musical situations.

However, what I aim to do here is demonstrate how the theory of communicative musicality is based on sociocultural conceptions of infancy and infant upbringing and reflects social values that have a high currency in our society at the moment. This is not to deny the usefulness of the core theory for illuminating aspects of early childhood music education activity and for providing a set of structural ideas based in interactive improvisation that are important in generating models of practice in early childhood music. However, the widespread adoption of the theory and its expansion into many applied areas point to its resonance with an ideology of parenting and with a set of values that I propose are limited to WEIRD populations. It is also being adopted as a rationale for approaches that seek to intervene and instruct parents in how to interact with the babies in the belief and conviction that this is a universal pattern of parenting that all parents ought to adopt and that failure to do so will have detrimental consequences for the children, tying in to attachment and determinist ideas I discussed earlier. This is another clear example of how research has proposed something that 'could be', based on research with a limited group of mothers, which has then flipped over to become an '*ought to be*' for all mothers. I hark back to the Somali-born mothers and their passive non-participation in the community musician's session, where the children's centre workers were convinced they should be taking part in ways prescribed by the musical activities being offered. There is therefore an ethical position that underlies my explanation of how this is a specific cultural model of adult-infant interaction. There is also an important intersection here with the widespread beliefs about the importance of early intervention and critical periods which, as I have explained earlier, need to be challenged and carefully reconsidered.

Let us look more closely at anthropological studies of infant care. How mothers behave with their babies and young children is associated with variations of culture, socio-economic status, ethnicity and variations in educational background (Kağıtçıbaşi, 2007). They all provide sets of cultural scripts that govern the mother-infant relationship. Protoconversation between mother and baby is not a universal; mother-infant interaction is further varied by a wide range of culture-specific norms, some of which, for example, have no expectation that babies will engage in any form of protoconversational exchanges (Schieffelin & Ochs, 1986). The Somali-born mothers laughed and thought me quite odd for 'baby-talking' with their babies, telling me that it was futile as their babies could not speak yet. There are endless variations in how mothers may interpret and accommodate to, or are expected to interact with, their babies (see Bornstein, et al., 2015). Robert and Barbara LeVine (1994), for example, discovered that Gusii mothers in Kenya responded very quickly to sounds of their babies crying, but reacted to sounds of babbling and other little noises by ignoring them and even looking away. The Gusii mothers did not coo over or kiss their babies, and deliberately tried to keep them calm and quiet, neither distressed nor animated. By contrast, the American mothers the LeVines studied reacted positively to infant babble, responding as if it had meaning, creating pretend conversations and encouraging animated, excited responsiveness. Both sets of mothers were encouraging behaviours on the part of their infants that were socially appropriate within their own cultural contexts. Elinor Ochs (1983:188) makes a key point that 'when an American mother responds to her infant in a particular way, she is doing so not because of innate biological patterning, but because she is acting on cultural assumptions about the qualities and capacities of young children'. Recall that communicative musicality is assumed to have its origins in early adult–infant interaction, in particular in protoconversations when the mother attributes meaning to the child's vocalisations and gestures and seeks to extend exchanges. It is therefore a culturally constructed behaviour based on a culturally constructed image of babies and young children, rather than a universal behaviour with biological origins. David Lancy (2007) goes beyond mother–infant interaction in the earliest months and suggests that the emphasis on mother–baby and mother–child play is a modern, recent development, not found in the majority of the world's societies, and represents therefore a 'non-normative behaviour' found among what he provocatively calls 'a curious minority of the world's mothers'. Thus, where verbal communication is the most salient form of interaction and is emphasised, particularly in minority-world societies with early verbal-based schooling, interaction and sensitive responsiveness to babies is likely to be verbal, vocal and animated, in an attempt to promote precocious verbal abilities (Blum, 2017).

This knowledge does not diminish the value of theories of mother–infant interaction, communicative musicality and the like, but it should make us very cautious about the strong claims for innate, biologically 'hard-wired' propensities for music based on adult–infant interaction and shared play between mothers and small children, and much more alert to the variations in cultural practices and corresponding variations in how children are first engaged with musically. What anthropology can show us is that forms of vocalising between mothers and their babies are widespread, that there are some core similarities and, moreover, that vocalising sets foundations for verbal and musical development. But what anthropological study also tells us is that if we have better knowledge of the variability of practices, then we are less inclined to see our own practices as fixed and the right way, but can evaluate them and be more open-minded to a wide range of possible ways of interacting (LeVine & LeVine, 2016).

Taking this discussion to another level, anthropologists and cross-cultural psychologists have arrived at a two-dimensional concept of individualism and collectivism. It is important to point out from the start that this two-part conception is now thought to be oversimplistic, and certainly we would want to avoid the dualistic opposition it implies, but for the purposes of explanation it is a useful starting point. In societies that emphasise individualism, such as those of Europe and North America, children are brought up to be autonomous. By contrast, societies that emphasise collectivism, such as the Somali-born mothers I came to know with their strong affiliations to clan and extended family, children are brought up to know their place within a set of relationships and to conform and abide by the family expectations. So the mother who intends to develop independence and individualism engages in more distal behaviours – that is, separate sleeping and putting to sleep with particular routines aimed at smoothing the transition to sleep, limited breastfeeding, transporting in special carriers separate from her body and, significantly, engaging in face-to-face vocalisation and lively, pretend conversations that include playsongs and rhymes. The mother who intends to develop interdependence engages in more proximal behaviours – co-sleeping, breastfeeding, bodily carrying, bodily contact and embodied interaction rather than vocal interaction. She is still very sensitively responsive to her child, but using different modes of contact and embodied interaction (Mesman, et al., 2017). The Somali-born mothers popped their babies and toddlers under their voluminous Islamic clothing to breastfeed at the slightest tremble of upset or need, barely pausing in their conversations to do so.

These contrasts in mothering styles are presented here as distinct, whereas the reality is much more blurred and nuanced. Indeed, in my own work with the Somali-born mothers I was interested in the changes that result from migration, when different cultural traditions of child-rearing start to mix (Young, 2016b). Equally, there are mothers now in the Western world who practise attachment parenting, deliberately adopting extended breastfeeding, the use of slings and co-sleeping, as well as incorporating animated interactions, singing and vocalising (cf. Faircloth, 2010).

Continuing from babyhood into the first two years, this period is assumed to be critical for attachment and the mother is expected to show 'sensitive responsiveness' to her child, to give devoted, exclusive attention to her infant. Within this model of parenting, singing to and emotional regulation via music are promoted as valuable strategies. But, as ethnographic studies reveal, this model of intensive mothering is a very recent invention that is still only available to a small handful of mothers. When and where infant mortality rates are high, resources are in short supply and mothers must work hard, care by siblings and extended family members is common, and intensive mothering as in the Western model is rare. Indeed, we only have to go a short while back in our own history to find similar circumstances. My own father was the last of seven (surviving) children and his oldest sisters cared for him in place of their busy and partially invalid mother. Lancy describes how in many cultures babies were – and still are – kept in a 'liminal' space, not quite here (2014b). Many of the world's babies are hidden, in their mother's clothing, or in cradles, baskets or tiny hammocks, between two worlds, kept calm, restrained, quiet. My Greek friend, Angeliki, adopted the Greek tradition of not addressing her beautiful baby by name until his first birthday when babies have survived the fragile first year and can at last be named at a christening.

To have given such attention to parenting culture and diversity of babyhoods in a book intended for early childhood music educators may seem to have been an unusual diversion. Yet pages and pages are devoted to the ins and outs of infant musical psychology in weighty textbooks without any recourse to the very culturally specific nature of those musical babyhoods and how they are thus narrowly determined. I am also attempting to shift dominant ideas about music with babies and young children that are deeply rooted and invested with strong emotions and also increasingly tied in to commercial, profit-making ventures in early childhood music, and so I need to assemble a strong and well-worked argument. I stress that I do not deny the value of talking with, singing with and playing movement games with babies and toddlers. But we need to recognise these activities as culturally specific, not intuitive, hard-wired or biological. We can then recognise that we are closing down our opportunities to be inclusive and open to a wider range of possibilities for how to do music with young children. I have no problem with digitised music adding to humanly made music, as seems to be the emerging practice; I do not see it as threatening but enriching. I see no need for highly animated, sensory-enriched music sessions for babies; indeed, they seem to me to be often rather alarming and intrusive, although it is of course valuable to provide imaginative, playful activities for little children. I very much enjoy the imaginative theatre and arts performances for babies, but they risk reifying a precious image of innocent babyhood and early childhood. I see no need for a special repertoire of lullabies just for babies or all this commodified musical stuff; let them join in with community musical events – and stay up late on their father's shoulders at pop festivals. And, at the risk of overstating a fundamental idea of this chapter, it is important that we recognise that what we may take for granted, or assume to be 'normal', may indeed be merely a reflection of our own cultural upbringing and should not be foisted on others beyond our own social class or ethnic group with an air of 'we know best'. This brings me neatly to my next and final topic.

Diversity

Restating a key point that I have been making in this book, in order to step off from it in a new direction, early childhood music education has been dominated by developmentalism drawn mainly from psychological perspectives that neglect wider society and culture. As a result, pedagogical practices have been oversimplified. Sociocultural approaches to learning that have recently been influential on practice – those that seek to apply relational approaches drawn from Vygotskian theorising or theories of adult-infant interaction, for example – usefully draw attention to the social and communicative processes of learning at the 'micro level'. But they still fail to emphasise, on another plane (recalling Georgina Born's four planes (2011) that I introduced in the previous chapter), how cultural values shape those social processes, how they shape the pedagogy, how children are spoken to, how they are expected to behave and participate, what is valued in the upbringing of children and so on. My example of the Somali-born mothers sought to illustrate just that and my follow-on discussions have provided the theoretical backing.

Over recent years the demography of many countries has changed dramatically due to the arrival of immigrants and refugees from many corners of the world. Although the presence and mix of immigrant children varies from country to country, educators have a common responsibility to work towards inclusion and integration for the benefit of *all* children, whether newly arrived or not. In some urban settings the proportion of children who have immigrant backgrounds can be very high indeed. So music educators are working with mixed groups of children and need tools for understanding and managing this complexity (Karlsen, 2011:7). Claudia Gluschankof (2008), drawing on ethnographic study of children music-making in Arab and Jewish kindergartens in Israel, pointed out that the differences the children encountered were not only between home, setting and community, but also resided in the contexts created by the adults as a result of their beliefs about childhood, music, play and education, and how these beliefs were manifest in the practices of the setting.

Arriving in preschool is when immigrant children first meet the differences between their home culture and that of their country of arrival. These children can be described as 'border crossers', who move back and forth each day between the differing and sometimes discordant worlds of preschool education and home. The Somali families who accompany us through this chapter illustrate 'border crossing' even for babies and toddlers. Kathryn Marsh, who has made extensive studies of children's playground games and songs in many different countries and among immigrant children, talks of 'bicultural' children who, as a result of migration into English-speaking Australia, UK and US, have musical influences both from home and their countries of arrival (2015, 2017). She emphasises how for these children social integration, 'identity construction and cultural maintenance and change must be negotiated on a continual basis' and she demonstrates how children's self-initiated playground musical activities can contribute to the process of social integration.

While the children of Kathryn Marsh's study are recently arrived, some societies have long been assimilations of different ethnic groups: North America and Singapore are prime examples. Singapore is a city state with a long history of blended ethnic populations, religions, languages and a colonial history. Its children, Chee-Hoo Lum writes, enjoy colourful, multicultural musical lives (Lum, 2012). In an interesting account of the musical lives of Malay/Muslim children in Singapore (2012) he describes the varied musical environment of a family that includes two children aged one and two. The family musical environment includes Disney songs and children's karaoke discs, some with an educational aim to teach the Arabic alphabet. Via their parents' interests in traditional martial arts the children get to see performances of traditional Malay music and dance. Their home has many instruments: a piano, guitar, kulintang, gendang, child-sized kompang and maracas. So the children's musical lives interweave Western and Asian music, popular and traditional, children's music and adult's, and offer a range of different ways of participating that includes listening, karaoke singing, looking on, performing and playing. It seems to me that Lum's family offers an image of how a diverse, intercultural, musical childhood could be.

However, in spite of the growing musical diversity of the children we teach, early childhood music education practice, broadly speaking, remains persistently monocultural, rather than multicultural or intercultural. The rationales for why early childhood music education should become more interculturally responsive, both in its pedagogical processes and in content, are clear. The overriding reason, as Sidsel Karlsen (2011) emphasises, is to validate and accommodate the diversity of populations – a reason that is underpinned by a commitment to building democratic societies that welcome and embrace pluralism. Through the study of music from various cultures, particularly of music belonging to immigrant communities, children can build a better understanding of their own identity and of the different people who make up our society. Music thus becomes a tool for achieving other non-musical, social and political aims such as tolerance towards others, equality and democracy. While I tend to be critical of the push to claim non-musical benefits for music in terms of individual gains for children such as improved academic performance, gains in terms of community cohesion through sociable sensitivity to others capitalises on what music is best at and on what it was made for: music brings people together, plain and simple. Another reason is to reduce the dominance of Western musical styles and forms and to enrich and broaden the musical palette of the children we work with. Patricia Shehan Campbell, an eminent scholar working across both fields of music education and ethnomusicology (e.g. 2003, 2010, 2011), endorses these reasons. She calls for music education to move from its current narrow focus on the preparation of conventional musicians working within the traditions of Western art music to a holistic view of musical study that incorporates worldwide perspectives of musical knowledge, both in terms of content and of process. Young children are already encountering some variety of musical styles via the technologies that are embedded in their everyday lives – although this musical diet is probably not very varied in terms of world musics, traditional folk musics, or even classical music for that matter – but we can start with what they bring with them and expand on this variety, rather than narrow it down. If teaching musical concepts and skills is a priority (although I would ask educators to reflect on what concepts and skills and why), then diverse musical resources can expand musical understanding and stretch musical skills. In addition, as I have emphasised earlier in this chapter, indigenous learning strategies often found in traditional musics around the world are in many ways more suited to the holistic and participatory ways that children learn.

A Somali tale

To conclude this chapter and to provide an illustration of intercultural practice I return to the mothers we met at the start of this chapter and tell the story of the paper sheep and camels. Sandra also worked with groups of Somali-born mothers and nursery-age children in this same city. Instead of starting by delivering off-the-peg music activities in a typical circle time, she began with conversations, driven by a commitment to a dialogic approach in which her work would evolve through collaboration. By talking and listening to the mothers she discovered that Somali cultural traditions have a rich heritage of poetry and story. One mother, Farsaan, had a particular talent for story-telling and language skills allowing her to tell her traditional stories in both Somali and English. Sandra made paper sheep and camel puppets for the animals in Farsaan's story, and improvised musical ditties and songs in English for the animals and their adventures. Farsaan listened, learned and joined in the songs, too. In this way a blended, hybrid, bicultural form of activity evolved through their collaborations, made up of a traditional Somali story, rhyme, poetry leading into song, rich with dual language learning. The song and story-telling satisfied the educational expectations of the early childhood setting, bridging the two worlds of home (Somali cultural background) and the English educational system. Sandra's work affirmed the mothers' and children's cultural heritage, but at the same time transformed it and reworked it in order to bring it into the context of an English preschool setting.

Afterword

What now? This book, as I warned at the outset, does not aim to provide simple answers or easy solutions. If I have complicated things, messed them up, left you puzzling, mulling over paradoxes and dilemmas, then I have achieved my aim. We need a wide range of possibilities for young children's musical experiences, not 'one size fits all' methods, curricula, lesson plans and assessment scales. Some issues require us to be bold, to take the responsibility to confront and provoke. Some issues require us to explore our own positions, backgrounds, attitudes and feelings. Some issues require us to work much harder to understand what is going on, both with the children in front of us and their families, but also, importantly, with the wider social, cultural and political contexts within which our work is nested. I wish it were possible to lay out simply and clearly what should be done in practical terms. But that task must be taken up by individual educators, in individual settings and adapted to specific groups of babies, toddlers, small children, parents and adults who come together in those places for music.

This book has explored the idea that certain images, ways of understanding music in children's lives, and the images of musical childhoods that lie beneath need to be revealed, recognised and understood if we are to create an early childhood music for today's children living in their present. I have sought to show how these images and stories of musical childhood may affect children in ways that are not necessarily beneficial and may stereotype, restrict and continue to contribute to the marginalisation and neglect of early childhood by mainstream music education, both in policy and in the allocation of resources. The book has explored certain key themes broadly encapsulated in the idea of contemporary children's lives: the new technologies; the return to essentialist ideas of gender; the new configurations of family life; changing attitudes towards children in terms of fears, anxieties that go hand-in-hand with an intensification of child-rearing practices; the commodification of music in childhood; increasing diversity alongside the differentiations between childhoods in terms of class and race. I have tried to show how adults regulate children's musicality by holding rigidly to conservative methods; by turning music into a commodified, for-profit product or into an intervention for selected children and mothers; by holding onto impoverished ideas of children as musical drawn from developmentalism and now, increasingly, from neuroscience; by selecting songs activities and resources that restrict children according to limiting images of childhood; and through the reinforcement of a very specific style of middle-class upbringing and musicality.

I will, nevertheless, try to set out a broad manifesto for change. I would like to see music approaches that maximise opportunities for young children, and for their parents, by removing stereotypical expectations determined by gender, race, age and all the other categories which pigeonhole children and parents and limit the opportunities available to them. I would like to see music approaches that diversify musical opportunities by incorporating new, multi-modal/multimedia musical practices enabled by new technologies and new performance-theatre approaches; by incorporating wider musical practices drawn from an expanding palette of styles and world-music traditions; and by recognition of the sociable, affective and subjective experiences of music for young children. I would like to see music that expands the agency of young children and their parents through dialogic rather than didactic pedagogical approaches and by making room for a diversity of parenting styles and cultures. And, finally, I would like to see approaches to music based on children's rights and entitlements for their enjoyable and sociable 'being' musically in the present and 'becoming' into their futures, and on the intrinsic qualities of musical experience first and foremost.

My route to drawing attention to the changes that I think need to happen has been to expand the theoretical lens through which we view musical childhoods and to propose an interdisciplinary approach. My response has been to introduce alternative images of musical childhoods, mainly drawing on my new-found enthusiasm for anthropological perspectives in doing so; but these comparative images help to reveal where our own blind spots may lie. My response has been to employ critical approaches, digging around and challenging, at times confronting where the idealisation of young children and our own invested emotions may be clouding our view and judgement. These may not be the most effective ways to bring about changes to improve practice for all young children, and they are certainly not the only approach – but this is the best I can do.

References

Abad, V. & Edwards, J. (2004). Strengthening families: A role for music therapy in contributing to family centered care, *Australian Journal of Music Therapy*, 15, 3–17.

Adachi, M. (1994). The role of the adult in the child's early musical socialization, *The Quarterly Journal of Music Teaching and Learning*, 5(3), 26–35.

Adachi, M. (2012). Incorporating formal lesson materials into spontaneous musical play: A window for how young children learn music. In C.H. Lum & P. Whiteman (Eds.), *Musical Childhoods of Asia and the Pacific*. Charlotte, NC: Information Age Publishing, pp. 133–160.

Addessi, A.R. (2009). The musical dimension of daily routines with under-four children during diaper change, bedtime and free-play, *Early Childhood Development and Care*, 179(6), 747–768.

Agomuoh, F. (2015, February 2). Are smartphones helping or harming children under 2? 'Shut-up toys' widespread, but impact poorly understood, *International Business Times*.

Alanen, L. (1992). *Modern childhood? Exploring the 'child question' in sociology*. Jyväskylä: Jyväskylä Institute for Educational Research.

Alanen, L. (2012). Disciplinarity, interdisciplinarity and childhood studies, *Childhood*, 19(4), 419–422.

Allen, G. (2011). *Early Intervention: Smart investment, massive savings*. London: Department for Work and Pensions and Cabinet Office.

American Academy of Pediatrics (2011). Policy statement: Media use by children younger than 2 years, *Pediatrics*, 128(5), 1040–1045.

Apple, M. (2013). *Knowledge, Power, and Education: The selected works of Michael W. Apple*. New York: Routledge.

Arculus, C. (2013). *What is the nature of communication between two-year-olds in a musical free play environment?* (unpublished Master's thesis), University of Central England, Birmingham, UK.

Arendt, H. (1958). *The Human Condition*. Chicago: University of Chicago Press.

Baker, F. & Mackinlay, E. (2006). Sing, soothe and sleep: A lullaby education programme for first-time mothers, *British Journal of Music Education*, 23(2), 147–160.

Bamberger, J. (2005). What develops in musical development? In G. McPherson (Ed.), *The Child as Musician*. Oxford: Oxford University Press, pp. 69–92.

Barrett, M.S. (2009). Sounding lives in and through music: A narrative inquiry of the 'everyday' musical engagement of a young child, *Journal of Early Childhood Research*, 7(2), 115–134.

Barrett, M.S. (2011). Towards a cultural psychology of music education. In M.S. Barrett (Ed.), *A Cultural Psychology of Music Education*. Oxford: Oxford University Press, pp. 1–16.

Barrett, M.S. (2012). Belonging, being and becoming musical: An introduction to children's musical worlds. In S. Wright (Ed.), *Children, Meaning-making and the Arts, 2nd Edition*. Frenchs Forest, NSW: Pearson Australia, pp. 57–81.

Bedford, R., de Urabain, I.R.S., Cheung, C.H., Karmiloff-Smith, A. & Smith, T.J. (2016). Toddlers' fine motor milestone achievement is associated with early touchscreen scrolling, *Frontiers in Psychology*, 7, 1108.

Bernard, R. (2016). ECE in a multicultural and inclusive society. Paper presented at the 27th EECERA Annual Conference *Social Justice, Solidarity and Children's Rights*, Bologna, Italy, 29th August to 1st September.

Beyer, E. (1996). The development of cognitive structures in infants: New approaches to music education. *Abstracts of 22nd ISME World Conference, Amsterdam*, pp. 20–21.

Biesta, G. (2006). *Beyond Learning: Democratic Education for a Human Future*. London: Routledge.

Bigand, E. & Poulin-Charronnat, B. (2006). Are we 'experienced listeners'? A review of the musical capacities that do not depend on formal musical training, *Cognition*, 100(1), 100–130.

Blacking, J. (1995). *Music, Culture and Experience: Selected papers of John Blacking*. Chicago: University of Chicago Press.

Blaise, M. (2005). *Playing it Straight: Uncovering gender discourses in the early childhood classroom*. London: Routledge.

Blum, S.D. (2017). Unseen WEIRD assumptions: The so-called language gap discourse and ideologies of language, childhood, and learning, *International Multilingual Research Journal*, 11(1), 23–38.

Boocock, S.S. & Scott, K.A. (2005). *Kids in Context: The sociological study of children and childhoods*. Lanham, MA: Rowman and Littlefield Publishers.

Born, G. (2011). Music and the materialization of identities, *Journal of Material Culture*, 16(4), 376–388.

Bornstein, M.H., Putnick, D.L., Cote, L.R., Haynes, O.M. & Suwalsky, J.T.D. (2015). Mother-infant contingent vocalizations in eleven countries, *Psychological Science*, 26(8), 1272–1284.

Bower, B. (2010). Birth of the beat: Music's roots may lie in melodic exchanges between mothers and babies, *Science News*, 178(4), 18–23.

Bowlby, J. (1988). *A Secure Base: Parent-Child Attachment and Healthy Human Development*. New York: Basic Books.

Braidotti, R. (2011). *Nomadic Theory: The portable Rosi Braidotti*. New York: Columbia University Press.

Bremmer, M. (2015). *What the Body Knows about Teaching Music: The specialist pre-school music teacher's pedagogical content knowing regarding teaching and learning rhythm skills viewed from an embodied cognition perspective* (unpublished PhD thesis), School of Education, University of Exeter, Exeter, UK.

Bronfenbrenner, U. (1979). *The Ecology of Human Development: Experiments by nature and design*. Cambridge, MA: Harvard University Press.

Brooks, W. (2016). Putting lullabies to bed: The effects of screened presentations on lullaby practices, *Australian Journal of Music Education*, 50(2), 83–97.

Brown, A.R. (2015). Engaging in a sound musicianship. In G. McPherson (Ed.), *The Child as Musician: A handbook of musical development*. New York: Oxford University Press, pp. 208–220.

Bruer, J.T. (1999). *The Myth of the First Three Years*. New York: The Free Press.

Bruer, J.T. (2011). Revisiting 'The Myth of the First Three Years': Special briefing paper written to accompany the event *Monitoring Parents: Science, evidence, experts and the new parenting culture*, Centre for Parenting Culture Studies, Kent University. blogs.kent. ac.uk/parentingculturestudies (accessed 26th October 2017).

Buckingham, D. (2009). New media. New childhood? Children's changing cultural environment in the age of digital technology. In M.J. Kehily (Ed.), *An Introduction to Childhood Studies, 2nd Edition*. Maidenhead: Open University Press, pp. 124–138.

Burman, E. (2017). *Deconstructing Developmental Psychology, 3rd Edition*. London: Routledge.

Burroughs, B. (2017). YouTube kids: The app economy and mobile parenting, *Social Media and Society*, 1–8.

Burton, S.L. & Pearsall, A. (2016). Music-based iPad app preferences of young children, *Research Studies in Music Education*, 38(1), 75–91.

Cain, M., Lindblom, S. & Walden, J. (2013). Initiate, create, activate: Practical solutions for making culturally diverse music education a reality, *Australian Journal of Music Education*, 2, 79–97.

Campbell, P.S. (2003). Ethnomusicology and music education: Crossroads for knowing music, education, and culture, *Research Studies in Music Education*, 21(1), 16–30.

Campbell, P.S. (2010). *Songs in Their Heads: Music and Its Meaning in Children's Lives, 2nd Edition*. New York: Oxford University Press.

Campbell, P.S. (2011). Musical enculturation: Sociocultural influences and meanings of children's experiences in and through music. In M.S. Barrett (Ed.), *A Cultural Psychology of Music Education*. Oxford: Oxford University Press, pp. 61–81.

Cannella, G.S. (1997). *Deconstructing Early Childhood Education: Social justice and revolution*. New York: Peter Lang.

Chaudron, S., Beutel, M.E., Černikova, M., Donoso Navarette, V., Dreier, M., Fletcher-Watson, B., Heikkilä, A.-S., Kontríková, V., Korkeamäki, R.-L., Livingstone, S., Marsh, J., Mascheroni, G., Micheli, M., Milesi, D., Müller, K.W., Myllylä-Nygård, T., Niska, M., Olkina, O., Ottovordemgentschenfelde, S., Plowman, L., Ribbens, W., Richardson, J., Schaack, C., Shlyapnikov, V., Šmahel, D., Soldatova, G. & Wölfling, K. (2015). *Young Children (0–8) and Digital Technology: A qualitative exploratory study across seven countries*. Joseph Rowntree Research Commission Publications Repository.

Chen-Hafteck, L. (2000). Discussing cross-cultural issues in children's song-learning and singing. In C. Woods, G. Luck, R. Brochard, F. Seddon & J.A. Sloboda (Eds.), *Proceedings of the Sixth International Conference on Music Perception and Cognition*. Keele: Keele University Department of Psychology. CD-ROM.

Cheung, C.H., Bedford, R., de Urabain, I.R.S., Karmiloff-Smith, A. & Smith, T.J. (2017). Daily touchscreen use in infants and toddlers is associated with reduced sleep and delayed sleep onset, *Scientific Reports*, 7. doi: 10.1038/srep46104

Cirelli, L.K., Wan, S.J. & Trainor, L.J. (2014). Fourteen-month-old infants use interpersonal synchrony as a cue to direct helpfulness, *Philosophical Transactions of the Royal Society B, Biological Sciences*, 369(1658).

Clark, A. (2005). 'Ways of seeing': Using the Mosaic approach to listen to young children's perspectives. In A. Clark, A.T. Kjørholt & P. Moss (Eds.), *Beyond Listening: Children's perspectives on early childhood services*. Bristol: Policy Press, pp. 29–49.

Cohen, A., Armstrong, V.L., Lannan M.S. & Coady J. (2009). A protocol for cross-cultural research on the acquisition of singing, *Annals of the New York Academy of Sciences*, 1169, 112–115.

Cohen, V. (1980). *The Emergence of Musical Gestures in Kindergarten Children* (unpublished PhD thesis), University of Illinois at Urbana-Champaign, Illinois, USA.

Corbeil, M., Trehub, S.E. & Peretz, I. (2016). Singing delays the onset of infant distress, *Infancy*, 21(3), 373–391.

Correa, A.N. (2013). *Bebês Produzem Música? O Brincar-Musical de Bebês em Berçário* [Do Babies Produce Music? The Musical Play of Babies in Nursery] (unpublished Doctor of Education thesis), Faculty of Education, Federal University of Rio Grande do Sul, Porto Alegre, Brazil.

Corrigall, K.A. & Trainor, L.J., (2014). Enculturation to musical pitch structure in young children: Evidence from behavioral and electrophysiological methods, *Developmental Science*, 17(1), 142–158.

Corsaro, W.A. (1992). Interpretive reproduction in children's peer cultures, *Social Psychology Quarterly*, 55(2), 160–177.

Corsaro, W.A. (1997). *The Sociology of Childhood*. Thousand Oaks, CA: Pine Forge Press.

Cox, G. (2015). Historical perspectives. In G.E. McPherson (Ed.), *The Child as Musician: A handbook of musical development*. Oxford: Oxford University Press, pp. 523–527.

Cross, G. (2016). Wondrous innocence, *Journal of Consumer Culture*, 4(2), 183–201.

Custodero, L.A. (2006). Singing practices in ten families with young children, *Journal of Research in Music Education*, 54(1), 37–56.

Custodero, L.A., Britto, P.R. & Brooks-Gunn, J. (2003). Musical lives: A collective portrait of American parents and their young children, *Applied Developmental Psychology*, 24(5), 553–572.

Dahlberg, G., Moss, P. & Pence, A. (2007). *Beyond Quality in Early Childhood Education and Care: Languages of evaluation*. Abingdon: Taylor & Francis.

Daily Mail Reporter (2013, 11th November). Pop songs at bedtime push out lullabies: Parents opt for lyrics from Adele and Rihanna to send babies off to sleep. *Daily Mail*.

Dansereau, D.R. (2014). Considering gender: Representation in early childhood songs and implications for practice perspectives, *Journal of the Early Childhood Music and Movement Association*, 9(3), 10–14.

Davidson, J.W. & Borthwick, S.J. (2002). Family dynamics and family scripts: A case study of musical development, *Psychology of Music*, 30, 121–136.

Davies, B. (2014). *Listening to Children: Being & becoming*. London: Routledge.

Dean, B. (2017). *A Hidden World of Song: Singing in the everyday home lives of 3–5-year-old children* (unpublished PhD thesis), School of Education, University of Exeter, Exeter, UK.

Dekker, S., Lee, N.C., Howard-Jones, P. & Jolles, J. (2012). Neuromyths in education: Prevalence and predictors of misconceptions among teachers, *Frontiers in Psychology*, 3, 429.

Delalande, F. (2015). *Naissance de la musique: Les explorations sonores de la première enfance* [The Birth of Music: Sound explorations in early childhood]. Rennes: Presses Universitaires de Rennes.

Deleuze, G. & Guattari, F. (1987/2004). *A Thousand Plateaus: Capitalism and schizophrenia*. London: Continuum.

Della Sala, S. & Anderson, M. (Eds.) (2012). *Neuroscience in Education: The good, the bad and the ugly*. Oxford: Oxford University Press.

DeNora, T. (2000). *Music in Everyday Life*. Cambridge: Cambridge University Press.

Deuze, M. (2012). *Media Life*. Cambridge: Polity Press.

de Vries, P. (2005). Lessons from home: Scaffolding vocal improvisation and song acquisition with a 2-year-old, *Early Childhood Education Journal*, 32(5), 307–312.

de Vries, P. (2009). Music at home with the under-fives: What is happening? *Early Child Development and Care*, 179(4), 395–405.

Dickson, J. (2016, September 20). What UK pre-schoolers want: Tablets, YouTube and Netflix. *Kidscreen.*

Dissanayake, E. (2008). If music is the food of love, what about survival and reproductive success? *Musicae Scientiae, Special Issue: Narrative in Music and Interaction,* 169–195.

Donaldson, M. (1978). *Children's Minds.* London: Fontana.

Donnelly, L. (2017, April 14). This is how your iPad could be hurting your baby's brain. *The Independent.*

Downing, S.L. (2008). *Arjuna's Angels: Girls learning gamelan music in Bali* (unpublished PhD thesis), University of California, Santa Barbara, CA, USA.

Duran, L. (2015). Growing into music in Mali: Perspectives on informal learning in West Africa. In N. Economidou & M. Stakelum (Eds.), *Every Learner Counts: Democracy and inclusion in music education.* Innsbruck: Helbling Verlag, pp. 49–64.

Duran, L. (undated). *Growing into Music: Mali. Da Kali. The Pledge to the Art of the Griot.* mali-cuba.com/video/malifilms/ (accessed 5th February 2018).

Dzansi, M. (2004). Playground music pedagogy of Ghanaian children, *Research Studies in Music Education,* 22(1), 83–92.

Edwards, J. (2011a). Music therapy and parent infant bonding. In J. Edwards (Ed.), *Music Therapy and Parent-infant Bonding.* Oxford: Oxford University Press, pp. 5–21.

Edwards, J. (2011b). Introduction. In J. Edwards (Ed.), *Music Therapy and Parent-infant Bonding.* Oxford: Oxford University Press, pp. 1–4.

Edwards, R., Gillies, V. & Horsley, N. (2015). Brain science and early years policy: Hopeful ethos or 'cruel optimism'? *Critical Social Policy,* 35(2), 167–187.

Emberly, A. (2014). Ethnomusicology and childhood: Studying children's music in the field, *College Music Symposium,* 54.

Ennis, L.R. (Ed.) (2015). *Intensive Mothering: The cultural contradictions of modern motherhood.* Bradford, ON: Demeter Press.

Ericsson, K.A., Krampe, R.T. & Tesch-Römer, C. (1993). The role of deliberate practice in the acquisition of expert performance, *Psychological Review,* 100, 363–406.

Faircloth, C. (2010). What science says is best: Parenting practices, scientific authority and maternal identity, *Sociological Research Online, Special Section on Changing Parenting Culture,* 15(4), 4.

Fawcett, C. & Liszkowski, U. (2012). Observation and initiation of joint action in infants, *Child Development,* 83, 434–441.

Fitch, W.T. (2015). Four principles of bio-musicology. *Philosophical Transactions of the Royal Society B, Biological Sciences,* 370(1664).

Fletcher-Watson, B. (2013). Apps for babies: implications for practice and policy. In B.T. Clegg, J. Scully & J. Bryson (Eds.), *ESRC Research Capacity Building Clusters; National Summit Conference 2013.* Birmingham: Aston Business School, pp. 58–65.

Fletcher-Watson, B., Fletcher-Watson, S., McNaughton, M.J. & Birch, A. (2014). From cradle to stage: how early years performing arts experiences are tailored to the developmental capabilities of babies and toddlers, *Youth Theatre Journal,* 28(2), 130–146.

Forrester, M.A. (2010). Emerging musicality during the pre-school years: A case study of one child. *Psychology of Music,* 38(2), 131–158.

Frost, J.L. (2009). *A History of Children's Play and Play Environments: Toward a contemporary child saving movement.* New York and London: Routledge.

Fujita, F. (2006). Musicality in Early Childhood: A case from Japan. In S.J. Reily (Ed.), *The Musical Human: Rethinking John Blacking's ethnomusicology in the twenty-first century.* Aldershot: Ashgate, pp. 87–106.

Gantley, M. (1994). *Cultural Constructions of Infancy: An anthropological study of infant care in Cardiff* (unpublished PhD thesis), London School of Hygiene & Tropical Medicine, London, UK.

Gibson, R.E. (2009). Musical Parenting: An ethnographic account of musical interactions of parents and young children (unpublished doctoral dissertation), University of Washington, Washington, USA.

Gillen, J. & Cameron, C.A. (2010). *International Perspectives on Early Childhood Research: A day in the life*. London: Palgrave Macmillan.

Gillies, V. (2014). Troubling families: Parenting and the politics of early intervention. In S. Wagg & J. Pilcher (Eds.), *Thatcher's Grandchildren? Politics and childhood in the twenty-first century*. Basingstoke: Palgrave Macmillan, pp. 204–224.

Gillis, J. (2009). Transitions to modernity. In J. Qvortrup, W.A. Corsaro & M-S. Honig (Eds.), *The Palgrave Handbook of Childhood Studies*. Basingstoke: Palgrave MacMillan, pp. 113–126.

Gingras, B., Honing, H., Peretz, I., Trainor, L.J. & Fisher, S.E. (2015). Defining the biological bases of individual differences in musicality, *Philosophical Transactions of the Royal Society B, Biological Sciences*, 370(1664).

Glover, J. (2000). *Children Composing 4–14*. London: Routledge/Falmer.

Gluschankof, C. (2007). Research and practice in early childhood music education: Do they run parallel and have no chance to meet? The case of preschool singing repertoire. In S. Young & N. Nicolau (Eds.), *Proceedings of European Network of Music Educators and Researchers of Young Children, Nicosia,* Cyprus, pp. 27–31.

Gluschankof, C. (2008). Musical expressions in kindergarten: An inter-cultural study? *Contemporary Issues in Early Childhood*, 9(4), 317–327.

Gluschankof, C. (2016). Public and secret musical worlds of children. In B. Ilari & S. Young (Eds.), *Home Musical Experiences of Children Across the World*. Bloomington: Indiana University Press.

Göncü, A. (1999). *Children's Engagement in the World: Sociocultural perspectives*. Cambridge: Cambridge University Press.

Gopnik, A. (2016). *The Gardener and the Carpenter: What the new science of child development tells us about the relationship between parents and children*. London: The Bodley Head.

Gopnik, A., Griffiths, T.L. & Lucas, C.G. (2015). When younger learners can be better (or at least more open-minded) than older ones, *Current Directions in Psychological Science*, 24(2), 87–92.

Goswami, U. (2006). Neuroscience and education: From research to practice? *Nature Reviews Neuroscience*, 7(5), 406–411.

Gottlieb, A. (2000). Where have all the babies gone? Toward an anthropology of infants, *Anthropological Quarterly*, 73(3), 121–132.

Gottlieb, A. (2004). *The Afterlife is Where we Come From*. Chicago: University of Chicago Press.

Gottlieb, A. (undated). press.uchicago.edu/books/gottlieb/gottlieb_videos.html

Gray, P. (2013). *Free to Learn: Why unleashing the instinct to play will make our children happier, more self-reliant and better students for life*. New York: Basic Books.

Green, L. (1997). *Music, Gender, Education*. Cambridge: Cambridge University Press.

Green, L. (1999). Research in the Sociology of Music Education: Some introductory concepts, *Music Education Research*, 1(2), 159–169.

Green, L. (2014). *Music Education as Critical Theory and Practice: Selected essays*. London: Routledge.

Greenhalgh, Z. (2018). *Music and Singing in the Early Years: A practical guide*. London: Routledge

Greenstreet, R. (2011, May 14). Lang Lang: 'I'd play the piano at 5am'. *Guardian Newspaper*.
Gudmundsdottir H.R. (forthcoming in 2018). Revisiting singing proficiency in 3-year-olds, *Psychology of Music*.
Gudmundsdottir, H.R. & Cohen, A.J. (2015). Advancing interdisciplinary research in singing through the AIRS Test Battery of Singing Skills, *Musicae Scientiae*, 19(3), 234–237.
Guldberg, H. (2013, July 16). The determinist myth of the early years. *Spiked*.
Habibi, A., Cahn, B.R., Damasio, A. & Damasio, H. (2016). Neural correlates of accelerated auditory processing in children engaged in music training, *Developmental Cognitive Neuroscience*, 21, 1–14.
Hall, C. (2005). Gender and boys' singing in early childhood, *British Journal of Music Education*, 22(1), 5–20.
Hannon, E.E. & Trainor, L.J. (2007). Music Acquisition: effects of enculturation and formal training on development, *Trends in Cognitive Sciences*, 11(11), 266–472.
Hargreaves, D.J. (1986). *The Developmental Psychology of Music*. Cambridge: Cambridge University Press.
Hargreaves, D.J. & Lamont, A. (2017). *The Psychology of Musical Development*. Cambridge: Cambridge University Press.
Hays, S. (1996). *The Cultural Contradictions of Motherhood*. New Haven: Yale University Press.
Hendrick, H. (1997). *Children, Childhood and English Society, 1990–1890*. Cambridge: Cambridge University Press.
Henrich J., Heine S.J. & Norenzayan, A. (2010). The weirdest people in the world? *Behavioral and Brain Sciences*, 33, 61–135.
Honig, A.S. (1983). Sex role socialization in early childhood, *Young Children*, 38(6), 57–70.
Honing, H., Cate, C.T., Peretz, I. & Trehub, S.E. (2015). Without it no music: Cognition, biology and evolution of musicality, *Philosophical Transactions of the Royal Society B, Biological Sciences*, 370(1664).
Hirschfeld, L.A. (2002). Why don't anthropologists like children? *American Anthropologist*, 104(2), 611–627.
Hirsh-Pasek, K. & Bruer, J. (2007). The brain/education barrier, *Science*, 317(5843), 1293.
Holloway, D.J., Green, L. & Stevenson, K. (2015). Digitods: Toddlers, touch screens and Australian family life. *M/C Journal: 'Beginnings' Issue*, 18(5).
Hourcade, J.P., Mascher, S.L., Wu, D. & Pantoja, L. (2015). Look, my baby is using an iPad! An analysis of YouTube videos of infants and toddlers using tablets. *Proceedings of the 33rd Annual ACM Conference on Human Factors in Computing Systems (CHI '15)*. New York: ACM, pp. 1915–1924.
Howe, M.J.A., Davidson, J.W., Moore, D.G. & Sloboda, J. (1995). Are there early childhood signs of musical ability? *Psychology of Music*, 23(2), 162–176.
Hughes, P. (2005). Baby, it's you: International capital discovers the under threes, *Contemporary Issues in Early Childhood*, 6(1), 30–40.
Huron, D. (2003). Is music an evolutionary adaptation? In I. Peretz & R.J. Zatorre (Eds.), *The Cognitive Neuroscience of Music*. Oxford: Oxford University Press, pp. 57–75.
Huttenlocher, P.R. (1979). Synaptic density in human frontal cortex – developmental changes and effects of aging, *Brain Research*, 163, 195–205.
Ilari, B. (2005). On musical parenting of young children: Musical beliefs and behaviors of mothers and infants, *Early Child Development & Care*, 175(7/8), 647–660.
Ilari, B. (2013a). Musical cultures of girls in the Brazilian Amazon. In P.S. Campbell & T. Wiggins (Eds.), *The Oxford Handbook of Children's Musical Cultures*. New York: Oxford University Press, pp. 131–146.

Ilari, B. (2013b). Concerted cultivation and music learning: Global issues and local variations, *Research Studies in Music Education*, 35(2), 179–196.

Ilari, B. & Habibi, A. (2015). Favorite songs, melodic elements, and a familiar tune: Performance of children from Brazil and the United States on components of the ATBSS, *Musicae Scientiae*, 19(3), 265–281.

Ilari. B.S., Keller P., Damasio H. & Habibi A. (2016). The development of musical skills of underprivileged children over the course of one year: A study in the context of an El Sistema-inspired program. *Frontiers in Psychology*, **7**, 62.

Ilari, B. & Young, S. (Eds.) (2016). *Home Musical Experiences of Children Across the World*. Bloomington: Indiana University Press.

James, A., Jenks, C. & Prout, A. (1998). *Theorising Childhood*. Cambridge: Polity Press.

James, A. & Prout, A. (Eds.) (1990). *Constructing and Reconstructing Childhood: Contemporary issues in the sociological study of childhood, 1st Edition*. London: Falmer Press.

Jaques-Dalcroze, E. (1967/1921). *Rhythm, Music & Education*. London & Whitstable: The Riverside Press Ltd.

Jenks, C. (2005). *Childhood, 2nd Edition*. London: Routledge.

Jones, L. & Duncan, J. (2013). Deleuze and early years education: Explorations in theory and lived experiences, *Global Studies of Childhood*, 3(3), 203–207.

Jones, M. (2015). *Adults' Constructions of an Early Childhood Music Class: Lived experience and cultural reproduction* (unpublished Master of Research thesis), Macquarie University, Sydney, Australia.

Jones, P. (2009). *Rethinking Childhood: Attitudes in contemporary society*. London: Continuum.

Juvančič, K. (2010). 'Singing in the Dark': Applied ethnomusicology and the study of lullabies. In K. Harrison, E. Mackinlay & S. Pettan (Eds.), *Applied Ethnomusicology: Historical and contemporary approaches*. Newcastle upon Tyne: Cambridge Scholars Publishing, pp. 116–132.

Kabali, H., Irigoyen, M., Nunez-Davis, R., Budacki, J., Mohanty, S., Leister, K. & Bonner Jr., R. (2015). Exposure and use of mobile media devices by young children, *Pediatrics*, 136(6), 1044–1050.

Kagan, J. (2000). *Three Seductive Ideas*. Cambridge, MA: Harvard University Press.

Kağıtçıbaşı, Ç. (2007). *Family, Self, and Human Development Across Cultures: Theory and applications, 2nd Edition*. London: Routledge.

Kane, E. (2006). 'No way my boys are going to be like that!' Parents' responses to children's gender noncomformity, *Gender and Society*, 20, 149–176.

Karlsen, S. (2011). *Music Education in Multicultural Schools*. Report from the Nordic research project 'Exploring democracy: Conceptions of immigrant students' development of musical agency'. www5.siba.fi/documents/10157/79c1858e-2dc7-41ac-9feb-90adbb04c2af (accessed 5th February 2018).

Katz, M. (2010). *Capturing Sound: How technology has changed music*. Berkeley: University of California Press.

Kehily, M.J. (Ed.) (2009). *An Introduction to Childhood Studies, 2nd Edition*. Maidenhead: Open University Press.

Keller, H. (2012). Attachment and culture, *Journal of Cross-Cultural Psychology*, 44(2), 175–194.

Keller, H. (2014). Introduction: Understanding relationships – what we would need to know to conceptualize attachment as the cultural solution of a universal developmental task. In H. Otto & H. Keller (Eds.), *Different Faces of Attachment: Cultural variations on a universal human need*. Cambridge: Cambridge University Press, pp. 1–26.

Kertz-Welzel, A. (2016). Sociological implications of English as an international language in music education, *Action, Criticism & Theory for Music Education*, 15(3), 53–66.

Kierstead, J.K. (2006). *Listening to the Spontaneous Music-making of Preschool Children in Play: Living a pedagogy of wonder* (unpublished Doctor of Philosophy thesis), Department of Education Policy and Leadership, University of Maryland College Park, Maryland, USA.

Kincheloe, J.L. (2002). The complex politics of McDonald's and the new childhood: Colonizing kidzworld. In G.S. Cannella & J.L. Kincheloe (Eds.), *Kidworld, Childhood Studies, Global Perspectives, and Education*. New York: Peter Lang Publishing, pp. 75–122.

Kinsky, V., Smetana, M., Ulm-Aram, M. & Koeniger, E. (2017). The Viennese approach of elemental music making, *Proceedings of the 8th Conference of the European Network of Music Educators and Researchers of Young Children: Creating musical spaces, origins, cultures and childhoods*, 20th to 24th June, p. 345.

Kirschner, S. & Tomasello, M. (2010). Joint music making promotes prosocial behavior in 4-year-old children, *Evolution and Human Behaviour*, 31(5), 354–364.

Kodály, Z. (1974). *The Selected Writings of Zoltán Kodály* (L. Halapy & F. Macnicol, Trans.). London: Boosey and Hawkes.

Koops, L.H. (2010a). 'Deñuy jàngal seen bopp' (They teach themselves): Children's music learning in the Gambia, *The Journal of Research in Music Education*, 58(1), 20–36.

Koops, L.H. (2010b). 'Can't we just change the words?' The role of authenticity in culturally informed music education, *Music Educators Journal*, 97(1), 23–28.

Koops, L.H. (2014). Songs from the car seat: Exploring the early childhood music-making place of the family vehicle, *Journal of Research in Music Education*, 62(1), 52–65.

Kratus, J. (1989). A time analysis of the compositional processes used by children ages seven to eleven, *Journal of Research in Music Education*, 37(1), 5–20.

Kucirkova, N. & Zuckerman, B. (2017). A guiding framework for considering touchscreens in children under two, *International Journal of Child-Computer Interaction*, 12, 46–49.

Lamont, A.M. (2016). Musical development from the early years onwards. In S. Hallam, I. Cross & M. Thaut (Eds.), *Oxford Handbook of Music Psychology*, 2nd Edition. Oxford: Oxford University Press.

Lancy, D.F. (2007). Accounting for the presence/absence of mother-child play, *American Anthropologist*, 109, 273–284.

Lancy, D.F. (2014a). *The Anthropology of Childhood: Cherubs, chattel, changelings*, 2nd Edition. Cambridge: Cambridge University Press.

Lancy, D.F. (2014b). 'Babies aren't persons:' A survey of delayed personhood. In H. Otto & H. Keller (Eds.), *Different Faces of Attachment: Cultural variations of a universal human need*. Cambridge: Cambridge University Press, pp. 66–109.

Lancy, D.F. (2016). Ethnographic perspectives on culture acquisition. In C.L. Mehan & A. Crittenden (Eds.), *Childhood: Origins, evolution, and implications*. Albuquerque, NM: University of New Mexico Press.

Lancy, D.F. (2017). *Raising Children: Surprising insights from other cultures*. Cambridge: Cambridge University Press.

Lancy, D.F., Bock, J.C. & Gaskins, S. (Eds.) (2010). *The Anthropology of Learning in Childhood*. Lanham, MA: Rowman & Littlefield.

Lareau, A. (2003). *Unequal childhoods: Class, race and family life*. Berkeley: University of California Press.

Lee, D. (1961). *Autonomous Motivation*, Journal of Humanistic Psychology, 1(2), 12–22.
Lee, N. (2001). *Childhood and Society: Growing up in an age of uncertainty*. Buckingham: Open University Press.
Legrenzi, P. & Ulmitá, C. (2011). *Neuromania: On the limits of brain science*. Oxford: Oxford University Press.
Lenz-Taguchi, H. (2010). *Going Beyond the Theory/Practice Divide in Early Childhood Education*. London: Routledge.
Leppänen, T. (2011). Babies, music and gender: Music playschools in Finland as multimodal participatory spaces. *Policy Futures in Education*, 9(4), 474–484.
LeVine, R.A. (1998). Child psychology and anthropology: An environmental view. In C. Panter-Brick (Ed.), *Biosocial Perspectives on Children*. Cambridge: Cambridge University Press, pp. 102–130.
LeVine, R.A. & LeVine, S. (2016). *Do Parents Matter? Why Japanese Babies Sleep Soundly, Mexican Siblings Don't Fight and American Families Should Just Relax*. New York: Public Affairs.
LeVine, R.A., Dixon, S., LeVine, S., Richman, A., Leiderman, P.H., Keefer, C.H. & Brazelton, T.B. (1994). *Child Care and Culture: Lessons from Africa*. New York: Cambridge University Press.
LeVine, R.A. & White, M. (1986). *Human Conditions: The cultural basis of educational development*. London: Routledge and Kegan.
Lewis, J. (2013) A cross-cultural perspective on the significance of music and dance to culture and society, with insight from BaYaka Pygmies. In M. Arbib (Ed.), *Language, Music, and the Brain: A mysterious relationship*. Cambridge, MA: MIT Press, pp. 45–65.
Liedloff, J. (1975). *The Continuum Concept*. Boston: Da Capo Press.
Lum, C.-H. (2012). Hanging out with Britney and Raihan: The colorful musical lives of Malay/Muslim children in Singapore. In C.-H. Lum & P. Whiteman, (Eds.), *Musical Childhoods of Asia and the Pacific*. Charlotte, NC: Information Age Publishing, pp. 57–74.
Mackinlay, E. (2010). Music and mothering. In A. O'Reilly (Ed.), *Encyclopedia of Motherhood*. Thousand Oaks, CA: Sage, pp. 1–5.
Mackinlay, E. (2012). Yi Lull, *Australian Kodály Journal*, 31–36.
MacNaughton, G. (2005). *Doing Foucault in Early Childhood Studies*. London: Routledge.
MacRae, C. (2017). Telling 'lively stories': Slow research into being two. Paper presented at the 27th EECERA Annual Conference *Social Justice, Solidarity and Children's Rights*, Bologna, Italy, 29th August to 1st September.
Macvarish, J. (2016). *Neuroparenting: The expert invasion of family life*. London: Palgrave.
Maestripieri, D. & Call, J. (1996). Mother-infant communication in primates, *Advances in the Study of Behavior*, 25, 613–642.
Malloch, S.N. & Trevarthen, C. (1999). Mothers and infants and communicative musicality, *Musicae Scientiae*, 3(1), 29–57.
Malloch, S. & Trevarthen, C. (Eds.) (2010). *Communicative Musicality*. Oxford: Oxford University Press.
Mang, E. (2001). Intermediate vocalizations: An investigation of the boundary between speech and songs in young children's vocalizations, *Bulletin of the Council for Research in Music Education*, 147, 116–122.
Marsh, J., Brooks, G., Hughes, J., Ritchie, L., Roberts, S. & Wright, K. (2005). *Digital beginnings: Young children's use of popular culture, media and new technologies*. Report of the 'Young Children's Use of Popular Culture, Media and New Technologies' Study, Literacy Research Centre, University of Sheffield.

Marsh, J., Mascheroni, G., Carrington, V., Árnadóttir, H., Brito, R., Dias, R., Kupiainen, R. & Trueltzsch-Wijnen, C. (2017). The online and offline digital literacy practices of young children: A review of the literature. COST ACTION IS1410. http://digilitey.eu (accessed 5th February 2018).

Marsh, K. (2008). *The Musical Playground: Global tradition and change in children's songs and games*. Oxford: Oxford University Press.

Marsh, K. (2015). Music, social justice, and social inclusion: The role of collaborative music activities in supporting young refugees and newly arrived immigrants in Australia. In C. Benedict, P. Schmidt, G. Spruce & P. Woodford (Eds.), *The Oxford Handbook of Social Justice in Music Education*. Oxford: Oxford University Press, pp. 173–189.

Marsh, K. (2017). Creating bridges: Music, play and well-being in the lives of refugee and immigrant children and young people, *Music Education Research*, 19(1), 33–46.

Maxted, A. (2014, March 15). High-investment parenting – the HIP way to bring up your kids. *The Times Newspaper*.

McCabe, D.P. & Castel, A.D. (2008). Seeing is believing: The effect of brain images on judgments of scientific reasoning, *Cognition*, 107(1), 343–352.

McDermott, J. & Hauser, M.D. (2007). Nonhuman primates prefer slow tempos but dislike music overall, *Cognition*, 104(3), 654–668.

Mehr, S.A. (2015). Miscommunication of science: Music cognition research in the popular press, *Frontiers in Psychology*, 6, 988.

Mehr, S.A., Schachner A., Katz R.C. & Spelke, E.S. (2013). Two randomized trials provide no consistent evidence for nonmusical cognitive benefits of brief preschool music enrichment, *PLoS ONE* 8(12), e82007.

Meloni, M. (2014). The social brain meets the reactive genome: Neuroscience, epigenetics and the new social biology, *Frontiers in Human Neuroscience*, 8, 309.

Merriam, A. (1967/2017). *Ethnomusicology of the Flathead Indians*. London: Routledge.

Mesman, J., Minter, T., Angnged, A., Cissé, I.A.H., Salali, G.D. & Migliano, A.B. (2017). Universality without uniformity: A culturally inclusive approach to sensitive responsiveness in infant caregiving, *Child Development*. doi: 10.1111/cdev.12795

Minks, A. (2002). From children's song to expressive practices: Old and new directions in the ethnomusicological study of children, *Ethnomusicology*, 46(3), 379–408.

Minks, A. (2008). Performing gender in song games among Nicaraguan Miskitu children, *Language & Communication*, 28, 36–56.

Minks, A. (2013). *Voices of Play: Miskitu Children's Speech and Song on the Atlantic Coast of Nicaragua*. Tucson: University of Arizona Press.

Miya, F.N. (2007). Using African indigenous knowledge systems in early childhood music education. In K. Smithrim & R. Upitis (Eds.), *Listen to their Voices: Research and practice in early childhood music*. Waterloo, ON: Canadian Music Educators' Association, pp. 161–180.

Moog, H. (1968). *The Musical Experience of the Pre-school Child* (C. Clarke, Trans.). Mainz: Schott.

Moore, D. (2015). *The Developing Genome: An introduction to behavioural epigenetics*. Oxford: Oxford University Press.

Moorhead, G.E. & Pond, D. (1977). *Music of Young Children*. Santa Barbara: Pillsbury Foundation for Advancement of Music Education.

Morley, I. (2014). A multi-disciplinary approach to the origins of music: Perspectives from anthropology, archaeology, cognition and behaviour, *Journal of Anthropological Sciences*, 92, 147–177.

Moss, P. (2014). *Transformative Change and Real Utopias in Early Childhood Education: A story of democracy, experimentation and potentiality.* London: Routledge.

Murris, K. (2016). *The Posthuman Child: Educational transformation through philosophy with picturebooks.* London: Routledge.

Nansen, B. (2015). Accidental, assisted, automated: An emerging repertoire of infant mobile media techniques, *M/C Journal: 'Beginnings' Issue*, 18(5).

Nansen, B. & Jayemanne, D. (2016). Infants, interfaces, and intermediation: Digital parenting and the production of 'iPad Baby' videos on YouTube, *Journal of Broadcasting and Electronic Media*, 60(2), 587–603.

Nardo, R. (2008). Music technology in the preschool? Absolutely! *General Music Today*, 22(1), 38–39.

Nicholson, J.M., Berthelsen, D., Williams, K.E. & Abad, V. (2010). National study of an early parenting intervention: Implementation differences on parent and child outcomes, *Prevention Science*, 11(4), 360–370.

Niland, A. (2009). The power of musical play: The value of play-based, child-centered curriculum in early childhood music education, *General Music Today*, 23(1), 17–21.

Niland, A. (2012). Exploring the lives of songs in the context of young children's musical cultures, *Min-Ad: Israel Studies in Musicology Online*, 10, 27–46.

Nome, D. (2016). The sound of the children: Social life among toddlers in kindergarten as a song and a dance. Paper presented at the 26th EECERA Annual Conference *Happiness, Relationships, Emotion and Deep-level Learning*, Dublin, Ireland, 31st August to 3rd September.

Ochs, E. & Schieffelin, B. (1983). *Acquisition of Conversational Competence.* London: Routledge, Kegan & Paul.

Olsen, D. (1996). *Music of the Warao of Venezuela: Song people of the rain forest.* Gainesville: University Press of Florida.

Olsson, L.M. (2009). *Movement and Experimentation in Young Children's Learning: Deleuze and Guattari in early childhood education.* London: Routledge.

Organisation for Economic Co-operation and Development, (2002). *Understanding the Brain: Towards a new learning science.* Paris: OECD.

Osgood, J. (2017). Opening Pandora's box: Post-modern perspectives of childhood. In S. Powell, S & K. Smith (Eds.), *An Introduction to Early Childhood Studies, 4th Edition.* London: Sage.

Osgood, J., Albon, D., Allen, K. & Hollingworth, S. (2013). 'Hard to reach' or nomadic resistance? Families 'choosing' not to participate in early childhood services, *Global Studies of Childhood*, 3(3), 208–220.

Osgood, J. & Robinson, K.H. (2017). Celebrating pioneering and contemporary feminist approaches to the study of gender in early childhood. In K. Smith, K. Alexander & S. Campbell (Eds.), *Feminism(s) in Early Childhood: Using feminist theories in research and practice.* New York: Springer, pp. 35–48.

Palmer, S. (2016). *Toxic Childhood: How the modern world is damaging our children and what we can do about it*, New Edition. London: Orion Books.

Paoletti, J.B. (2012). *Pink and Blue: Telling the boys from the girls in America.* Bloomington: Indiana University Press.

Panter-Brick, C. (Ed.) (2008). *Biosocial Perspectives on Children*, Biosocial Society Symposium Series, no. 10. Cambridge: Cambridge University Press.

Papoušek, M. & Papoušek, H. (1981). Musical elements in infant's vocalisations: Their significance for communication, cognition and creativity, *Advances in Infancy Research*, 1, 163–224.

Paradise, R. & Rogoff, B. (2009). Side by side: Learning by observing and pitching in, *ETHOS, Journal of the Society for Psychological Anthropology*, 37(1), 102–138.

Pecker P.C. (2014). Models of practice from university to real life: What I have learned with Esther Beyer. *Proceedings of the International Society for Music Education Early Childhood Commission Seminar Listening to Diverse Musical Beginnings*, Universidade de Brasilia, Brazil, 15th to 19th July, pp. 68–72.

Penn, H. (2005). *Unequal Childhoods*. Abingdon: Routledge.

Penn, H. (2014). *Understanding Early Childhood: Issues and controversies, 3rd Edition*. Abingdon: Routledge.

Penn, H. (2017). Anything to divert attention from poverty. In M. Vandenbroeck with J. De Vos, W. Gias, L.M. Olsson, H. Peen, D. Wastell & S. White, *Constructions of Neuroscience in Early Childhood Education*. London: Routledge, pp. 54–67.

Peretz, I., Cummings, S. & Dubé, M-P. (2007). The genetics of congenital amusia (tone deafness): A family-aggregation study, *American Journal of Human Genetics*, 81(3), 582–588.

Peretz, I. & Vuvan D.T. (2017). Prevalence of congenital amusia, *European Journal of Human Genetics*, 25(5), 625–630.

Peterson, D. (2016). The baby factory: Difficult research objects, disciplinary standards, and the production of statistical significance, *Socius*, 2, 1–10.

Pettit, A.J. (2014). *Passing Traditions: Child-directed music as an index of cultural change in metropolitan India* (unpublished PhD thesis), University of California, Los Angeles, USA.

Piaget, J. (1954). *The Construction of Reality in the Child* (M. Cook, Trans.). London: Routledge and Kegan Paul.

Pieridou Skoutella, A. (2015) *Small Musical Worlds in the Mediterranean: Ethnicity, globalisation and Greek Cypriot children's musical identities*. London: Routledge.

Prensky, M. (2001). Digital natives, digital immigrants, *On the Horizon*, 9(5), 1–6.

Prout, A. (2005). *The Future of Childhood*. London: Routledge.

Prout, A. (2011). Taking a step away from modernity: Reconsidering the new sociology of childhood, *Global Studies of Childhood*, 1(1), 4–14.

Prout, A. & James, A. (1990). A new paradigm for the sociology of childhood? Provenance, promise and problems. In A. James & A. Prout (Eds.), *Constructing and Reconstructing Childhood: Contemporary issues in the sociological study of childhood, 1st Edition*. London: The Falmer Press, pp. 7–33.

Punch, S. (2016). Cross-world and cross-disciplinary dialogue: A more integrated, global approach to childhood studies, *Global Studies of Childhood*, 6(3), 1–12.

Rabinowitch T.-C. & Meltzoff, A.N. (2017). Joint rhythmic movement increases 4-year-old children's prosocial sharing and fairness toward peers, Frontiers in Psychology, 8, 1050.

Radesky, J.S., Schumacher, J. & Zuckerman, B. (2015). Mobile and interactive media use by young children: The good, the bad, and the unknown, *Pediatrics*, 135(1), 1–3.

Raju, M. (2015). *Some aspects of singing development, the song creating process and favorite songs of Estonian children*. Estonian Academy of Music and Theatre, Tallinn. www.ema.edu.ee/vaitekirjad/doktor

Raju, M. & Ross, J. (2012). Adaption to Estonian children of the protocol for cross-cultural research in singing, *TRAMES, A Journal of the Humanities and Social Sciences*, 16(2), 125–144.

Rauduvaite. A., Lasauskiene J., Abramauskiene J. & Chuang, M-J. (2017). Children's singing: Reflections on vocal teaching in Lithuania and Taiwan, *People: International Journal of Social Sciences*, Special Issue, 853–869.

Regelski, T. (2002). On 'methodolatry' and music teaching as critical and reflective praxis, *Philosophy of Music Education Review*, 10(2), 102–123.

Retra, J. (2010). *Music is Movement: A study into aspects of movement representation of musical activities among preschool children in a Dutch music education setting* (unpublished PhD thesis), School of Education, University of Exeter, Exeter, UK.

Rogoff, B. (2003). *The Cultural Nature of Human Development*. Oxford: Oxford University Press.

Rogoff, B., Moore, L., Najafi, B., Dexter, A., Correa-Chávez, M. & Solis, J. (2007). Children's development of cultural repertoires through participation. In J. Grusec & P. Hastings (Eds.), *Everyday Routines and Practices: Handbook of socialization*. New York: Guilford, pp. 490–515.

Rose, H & Rose, S. (2014). *Genes, Cells and Brains: The Promethean promises of the new biology*. London: Verso Books.

Rose, N. (2013). The human sciences in a biological age, *Theory, Culture & Society*, 30(1), 3–34.

Rose, N. & Abi-Rached, J.M. (2013). *Neuro: The new brain sciences and the management of the mind*. Princeton: Princeton University Press.

Rose, S.E. (1995). *The effects of Dalcroze eurhythmics on beat competency performance skills of kindergarten, first-, and second-grade children*, (unpublished PhD thesis), University of North Carolina, Greensboro, USA.

Roulston, K. & Misawa, M. (2011). Music teachers' constructions of gender in elementary education, *Music Education Research*, 13(1), 3–28.

Rutkowski, J. & Chen-Hafteck, L. (2001). The singing voice within every child: A cross-cultural comparison of first graders' use of singing voice, *Early Childhood Connections: Journal of Music- and Movement-Based Learning*, 7(1), 37–42.

Rutkowski, J., Chen-Hafteck, L. & Gluschankof, C. (2002). Children's vocal connections: A cross-cultural study of the relationship between first graders' use of singing voice and their speaking ranges. In *Proceedings of the 10th International Conference of the ISME Early Childhood Conference*. Copenhagen: Danish University of Education, pp. 39–50.

Ryan, K.W. (2011). The new wave of childhood studies: Breaking the grip of bio-social dualism? *Childhood*, 19, 439–452.

Sanders, L. (2009). Trawling the brain: New findings raise questions about reliability of fMRI as gauge of neural activity, *Science News*, 176(13), 16.

Schieffelin, B. & Ochs, E. (Eds.) (1986). *Language Socialization Across Cultures*. Cambridge: Cambridge University Press.

Shelley, S. (1981). Investigating the musical capabilities of young children, *Bulletin of the Council for Research in Music Education*, 68, 26–54.

Skelton, C. & Francis, B. (2003). *Boys and Girls in the Primary Classroom*. Maidenhead: Open University Press.

Sloboda, J.A., Davidson, J.W. & Howe, M.J.A. (1994). Is everyone musical? *The Psychologist*, 7, 349–354.

Small, C. (1977). *Music, Society and Education*. Middletown, CO: Wesleyan University Press.

Sole, M. (2014). *Songs from the Crib: Toddlers' private bedtime vocalizations – A collective case study* (unpublished Doctor of Education thesis), Teachers College, Columbia University, New York, USA.

Soley, G. & Hannon, E.E. (2010). Infants prefer the musical meter of their own culture: A cross-cultural comparison, *Developmental Psychology*, 46(1), 286–292.

Sommer, D. (2012). *A Childhood Psychology: Young children in changing times*. London: Palgrave Macmillan.

St. John, P.A. (2006). Finding and making meaning: Young children as musical collaborators, *Psychology of Music*, 34(2), 239–262.

Stadler Elmer, S. (2012). *Infant Vocal Productions Challenge Music Education: A case study on the transition between speaking and singing at age 14 months*. Paper presented at the Twenty-fourth International Seminar on Research in Music Education, Thessaloniki.

Stevens C. (2012). Music perception and cognition: A review of recent cross-cultural research, *Topics in Cognitive Science*, 4(4), 653–667.

Street A. (2006). *The Role of Singing within Mother-Infant Interactions* (unpublished PhD thesis), School of Education, University of Roehampton, London, UK.

Sulkin, I. & Brodsky, W. (2013). Parental preferences to music stimuli of devices and playthings for babies, infants, and toddlers, *Psychology of Music*, 43(3), 307–320.

Suthers, L. (2004). Music experiences for toddlers in day care centres, *Australian Journal of Early Childhood*, 29(4), 45–49.

Swanwick, K. & Tillman, J. (1986). The sequence of musical development, *British Journal of Music Education*, 3(3), 305–339.

Tafuri, J. (2008). *Infant Musicality: New research for educators and parents*. Farnham: Ashgate Publishing Ltd.

Tan, Y.T., McPherson, G.E., Peretz, I., Berkovic, S.F. & Wilson, S.J. (2014). The genetic basis of music ability, *Frontiers in Psychology*, 5, 658.

Tang, P. (2006). Telling histories: Memory, childhood, and the construction of modern Griot identity. In S. Boynton & R. Kok (Eds.), *Musical Childhoods and the Cultures of Youth*. Middletown, CT: Wesleyan University Press, pp. 105–120.

Taylor, A. (2013). *Reconfiguring the Natures of Childhood*. Abingdon: Routledge.

Thelen, E. & Smith, L.B. (2007). Dynamic systems theories, *Handbook of Child Psychology*, I(6).

Thomas, N. (2004). Sociology of childhood. In T. Maynard & N. Thomas (Eds.), *An Introduction to Early Childhood Studies*. London: Sage, pp. 75–86.

Thorne, B. (2007). Editorial: Crafting the interdisciplinary field of childhood studies, *Childhood*, 14(2), 147–152.

Tisdall, E.K.M. (2012). The challenge and challenging of childhood studies? Learning from disability studies and research with disabled children, *Children and Society*, 26(3),181–191.

Tisdall, E.K.M. & Punch, S. (2012). Not so 'new'? Looking critically at childhood studies, *Children's Geographies*, 10(3), 249–264.

Tobin, J., Wu, D. & Davidson, D. (1989). *Preschool in Three Cultures*. New Haven: Yale University Press.

Toren, C. (2004). Do babies have culture? *Anthropological Quarterly*, 77(1), 167–179.

Trehub, S.E. (2010). In the beginning: A brief history of infant music perception, *Musicae Scientiae*, 14(2), 71–87.

Trehub, S.E. (2015). Infant musicality. In S. Hallam, I. Cross & M. Thaut, (Eds.), *The Oxford Handbook of Music Psychology, 2nd Edition*. Oxford: Oxford University Press.

Trehub S.E., Becker J. & Morley I. (2015). Cross-cultural perspectives on music and musicality, *Philosophical Transactions Royal Society, Series B, Biological Sciences*, 370(1664).

Trehub, S.E. & Trainor, L. (1998). Singing to Infants: Lullabies and playsongs. In C. Rovee-Collier, L.P. Lipsitt & H. Hayne (Eds.), *Advances in Infancy Research, Volume 12*. Stamford, CT: Ablex Publishing, pp. 42–77.

Trevarthen, C., (2008). The musical art of infant conversation: Narrating in the time of sympathetic experience, without rational interpretation, before words, *Musicae Scientiae*, 12(1), 15–46.

Tudge, J.R.H. (2008). *The Everyday Lives of Young Children: Culture, class, and child-rearing in diverse societies*. New York: Cambridge University Press.

Uprichard, E. (2008). Children as being and becomings: Children, childhood and temporality, *Children and Society*, 22(4), 303–313.

Valentine, G. (2004). *Public Space and the Culture of Childhood*. Aldershot: Ashgate Publishing Ltd.

Vandenbroeck, M. (2014). The brainification of early childhood education and other challenges to academic rigour, *European Early Childhood Education Research Journal*, 22(1), 1–3.

Vandenbroeck, M. (2017). Introduction. Constructions of truth in early childhood education: A history of the present abuse of neurosciences. In M. Vandenbroeck with J. De Vos, W. Gias, L.M. Olsson, H. Peen, D. Wastell & S. White, *Constructions of Neuroscience in Early Childhood Education*. London: Routledge, pp. 1–19.

Vansieleghem, N. (2010). The Residual Parent to Come: On the need for parental expertise and advice, *Educational Theory*, 6(3), 341–355.

Vestad, I.L. (2010). To play a soundtrack. How children use recorded music in their everyday lives, *Music Education Research*, 12(3), 243–255.

Vestad, I.L. (2014). Children's subject positions in discourses of music in everyday life: Rethinking conceptions of the child in and for music education, *Action, Criticism, and Theory for Music Education*, 13(1), 248–278.

Vincent, C. & Maxwell, C. (2016). Parenting priorities and pressures: Further understanding of 'concerted cultivation', *Discourse: Studies in the Cultural Politics of Education*, 37(2), 269–281.

Vygotsky, L. (1978). *Mind in Society: The development of higher psychological processes* (M. Cole, Trans.). Boston: Harvard University Press.

Walkerdine, V. (1993). Beyond developmentalism? *Theory and Psychology*, 3(4), 451–469.

Ward, V. (2013, April 21). Toddlers becoming so addicted to iPads they require therapy, *The Telegraph Newspaper*.

Warzecha M. (2013). Boys' perceptions of singing: A review of literature, *Update: Applications of Research in Music Education*, 32(1), 43–51.

Wassrin, M. (2016). *Towards Musicking in a Public Sphere: 1–3 year olds and music pedagogies negotiating a music didactic identity in a Swedish preschool*. Stockholm: Stockholm University.

Wastell, D. & White, S. (2017). *Blinded by Science: The social implications of epigenetics and neuroscience*. Bristol: Policy Press.

Weisberg, D.S., Keil, F.C., Goodstein, J., Rawon, E. & Gray, J.R. (2008). The seductive allure of neuroscience explanations, *Journal of Cognitive Neuroscience*, 20(3), 470–477.

Welch, G.F. (1986). A developmental view of children's singing, *British Journal of Music Education*, 3(3), 295–303.

Welch, G.F., Sergeant, D.C. & White, P. (1996). The singing competences of five-year-old developing singers, *Bulletin of the Council for Research in Music Education*, 127, 155–162.

Werle, K. & Bellochio, C.R. (2014). Childhood, music and experience: Fragments of making music and playing. Paper presented at the annual meeting of ISME, Pontifical Catholic University of Rio Grande do Sul, Porto Alegre, Brazil, 20th July.

Wells, K. (2018). *Childhood Studies: Making young subjects*. Cambridge: Polity Press.

Whiteman, P. (2001). *How the bananas got their pyjamas: A study of the metamorphosis of preschoolers' spontaneous singing as viewed through Vygotsky's Zone of Proximal Development* (unpublished PhD thesis), University of New South Wales, Sydney, Australia.

Whiteman, P. (2009). Type, function and musical features of preschool children's spontaneous songs. In L.K. Thompson & M.R. Campbell (Eds.), *Research Perspectives: Thought and practice in music education, Volume 2*. Charlotte, NC: Information Age Publishing, pp. 37–62.

Whiteman, P. & Campbell, P.S. (2012). Picture it! Young children conceptualizing music. In C.-H. Lum & P. Whiteman (Eds.), *Musical Childhoods of Asia and the Pacific*. Charlotte, NC: Information Age Publishing, pp. 161–189.

Williams, K.E., Barrett, M.S., Welch, G.F., Abad, V. & Broughton, M. (2015). Associations between early shared music activities in the home and later child outcomes: Findings from the Longitudinal Study of Australian Children, *Early Childhood Research Quarterly*, 31, 113–124.

Wright, R. (Ed.). (2016). *Sociology and Music Education*. London: Routledge.

Wyness, M. (2006). *Childhood and Society: An introduction to the sociology of childhood*. Basingstoke: Palgrave.

Yelland, N. (Ed.) (2005). *Critical issues in Early Childhood Education*. Maidenhead: Open University Press.

Young, S. (2003a). *Music with the Under-Fours*. London: Routledge.

Young, S. (2003b). The interpersonal dimension: A potential source of musical creativity for young children?, *Musicae Scientiae*, 10th Anniversary Special Issue, 175–179.

Young, S. (2006). Seen but not heard: Young children, improvised singing and educational practice, *Contemporary Issues in Early Childhood*, 7(3), 270–280.

Young, S. (2008). Lullaby light shows: Everyday musical experience among under-two-year-olds, *International Journal of Music Education*, 26(1), 33–46.

Young, S. (2012). Theorizing musical childhoods with illustrations from a study of girls' Karaoke use at home, *Research Studies in Music Education*, 34(2), 113–127.

Young, S. (2016a). Early childhood music education research: An overview. *Research Studies in Music Education*, 34(1), 29–44.

Young, S. (2016b). *Infant feeding practices among Somali-born women now resident in Bristol* (unpublished MLitt thesis), Department of Archaeology and Anthropology, University of Bristol, Bristol, UK.

Young, S. (2017a). The branded product and the funded project: Neoliberal policies creating musical spaces in early childhood. Paper presented at the EuNet MERYC conference, Homerton College, Cambridge, UK, 20th to 24th June.

Young, S. (2017b). Diverse parenting goals and community music in early childhood, *International Journal of Community Music*, 10(3), 261–272.

Young, S. & Gillen, J. (2010). Musicality. In J. Gillen & C.A. Cameron (Eds.), *International Perspectives on Early Childhood Research: A day in the life*. London: Palgrave Macmillan, pp. 59–67.

Young, S. & Ilari, B. (2012). Musical participation from birth to three: Towards a global perspective. In G. McPherson & G. Welch (Eds.), *Oxford Handbook of Music Education*. Oxford: Oxford University Press, pp. 279–295.

Young, S. & Powers, N. (2009). *See theatre: Play theatre*, Edinburgh: Starcatchers. http://starcatchers.org.uk/downloads/research_report.pdf

Young, S. & Street, A. (2009) Time to Play: Developing inter-culturally sensitive approaches to music in children's centres serving predominantly Muslim communities. In A.R. Addessi & S. Young (Eds.), *Proceedings of the 4th Conference of the European Network of Music Educators and Researchers of Young Children*, 22nd to 25th July, Bologna Italy. Bononia University Press, pp. 32–39.

Young, S., Street, A. & Davies, E. (2007). The Music One-to-One Project: Developing approaches to music with parents and under-two-year-olds, *European Early Childhood Education Research Journal*, 15(2), 253–267.

Zelizer, V.A. (1985). *Pricing the Priceless Child: The changing social value of children.* New York: Basic Books.

Zevenbergen, R. (2007). Digital natives come to preschool: Implications for early childhood Practice, *Contemporary Issues in Early Childhood*, 8(1), 19–29.

Zhao, C.T. & Kuhl, P.K. (2016). Musical intervention enhances infants' neural processing of temporal structure in music and speech, *Proceedings of the National Academy of Sciences of the United States of America*, 113(19), 5212–5217.

Zimmerman, M.P. (1991). Psychological theory and music learning. In R.J. Colwell (Ed.), *Basic Concepts in Music Education*. Niwot: University Press of Colorado, pp. 157–174.

Zur, S.S. (2018). Children's use of music in understanding time: Perspectives from Singapore, Australia and the US. In A. Twum-Danso Imoh, S.M. Meichsner & M. Bourdillon (Eds.), *Global Childhoods Beyond the North-South Divide*. Basingstoke: Palgrave MacMillan.

Index

accomplishment of natural growth 96
Adachi, M. 83
Addessi, A-R. 93
'Advancing Interdisciplinary Research in Singing' (AIRS) 112
age segregation 117
ageism 30
agency 24, 31, 33–34, 37, 62, 79, 88, 134; and babies 66; and gender 103; musical 120–121
AIRS *see* 'Advancing Interdisciplinary Research in Singing' (AIRS)
Alanen, L. 32
amusia 43, 44
anthropology 19, 23, 31, 108, 110, 111, 114, 122, 127; biological 125; of music 74, 91
Apple, M. 89
assemblage 40–41, 72
assimilation and accommodation 76
attachment 10, 126; and parenting 52, 88, 128; theory 49–52, 55–56, 60
authenticity 124

babyhood 123; and care 51; developmental milestones 108; diversity of 129; musical 9, 23, 27, 47, 61; *see also* determinism; infant musicality
Bamberger, J. 72–73, 81
Barrett, M. 85, 94
BaYaka Pygmies 122
Beng babies 34, 114
Beyer, E. 11, 34, 76
Biesta, G. 8, 108
biological: capabilities 64; explanations 20, 40, 61; maturation 72, 82; processes 42, 65, 84; theories of music 10, 44, 45, 125, 127; *see also* determinism
Born, G. 88, 106, 130
Bowlby, J. 49
Braidotti, R. 4
brain development 52, 54–56, 61
Bremmer, M. 117
Bronfenbrenner, U. 81
Brooks, W. 123
Brown, A. 5
Burman, E. 26, 60
Burton, S. 102

Campbell, P.S. 131
Chen-Hafteck, L. 113
childcare 6, 35, 70, 95; majority world 118; Western practices 110
child-centred approaches 33, 79
childhood studies 2, 4, 18–21, 23–26, 32–35, 98, 105; 'new wave' 38–41, 84
children/childhood 2, 15, 32, 40, 62–63; in changing times 4–6, 9, 98, 123; ideologies of 27; intercultural 131; musical 2, 4–5, 29, 80, 89, 93, 124; from psychological perspective 65–66, 75; as recapitulation 78; traditional image of 8; 'useful'/'useless' 26–27; *see also* commodified music for children; constructions of childhood
children's music 115–117
children's music-making 29, 33, 35–36, 66, 73, 77, 90–92, 118, 130
cognition 76; musical 41, 81
Cohen, V. 81
collectivism 128
commodified music for children 6, 24, 28, 92, 94–95, 115, 133

communicative musicality 49, 51, 74, 124–127
composition 98, 75
concerted cultivation 96
concrete operations 75
conservatism 12–15, 22, 78
constructions of childhood 26–29, 32, 61, 74, 83, 101, 123; as musical 78–80, 124
Corsaro, W.A. 36, 37, 78
co-sleeping 108–109, 128
creativity 73, 78–80, 82
critical theory 3, 15, 19, 29, 39, 81, 85
cross-cultural studies 111–113

Dalcroze eurhythmics 41, 77
Dean, B. 33, 94
Delalande, F. 76
determinism 60–61
Deuze, M. 101
developmental psychology 2, 13; in context 82; models of 67; theories of 3, 19, 63, 66, 80; *see also* musical development; Piaget; Vygotsky
Developmental Psychology of Music, The 80
developmentalism 18, 31, 65–67, 129, 134
digital technology 5, 7, 97, 98, 100–102
digitisation of music 5
Disney 64, 72, 88, 89, 131
diversity 8, 23, 24, 62, 85, 111, 129–132
Donaldson, M. 75
Downing, S. 117
Duran, L. 117–118, 120

ecology of human development 81
Emberly, A. 113
embodiment 41, 77, 80
epigenetics 45, 85
ethnomusicology 108, 115, 116, 124
everyday music 2, 4, 8, 33, 35, 44–45, 86, 90–93, 99–102, 118–119
evolutionary biology 42, 52; and mothering, 88
evolutionary theories of music 10, 46–47, 119

family music 92
folklore studies 91

franchises 6, 12, 14
Fujita, F. 116

Gamelan instruments 77, 78; children learning 117
gender 24, 30, 64, 71, 87, 89, 103–106, 110, 123, 134
Gibson, R. 93
Gillen, J. 93
Gluschankof, C. 94, 130
Gottlieb, A. 106, 114
Gudmundsdottir, H. 70, 75, 112

Hargreaves, D. 80
Hays, S. 25
historical perspective 17, 23, 30, 83
the home: cultural background 2, 90, 130–131; music in 5–7, 29, 33, 43, 64, 71, 87–88, 92, 113; and parenting 92–97; and technology, 99, 101, 102; *see also* family music
Hughes, P. 6
human capital theory 10

identity 88, 130, 131; musical 65, 94, 121; professional 14
Ilari, B. 71, 82, 96, 105
immigrant children 130–131
indigenous processes of learning in music 114–121
infant musicality 14, 69, 113, 125–127; *see also* communicative musicality
instruments 25, 83; and gender 105–106; in nursery environment 77; and play 38, 41, 126; and sociality 47; and tuition 44, 53, 120
interdisciplinarity 18–20, 32, 38–40, 60, 63, 84, 86, 134
internalisation 83
interpretive reproduction 36–37, 78
iPad 99–100, 102

Jones, M. 89
Jones, P. 25, 103

Kagan, J. 96
karaoke 7, 87–89, 92–93, 102, 104–105, 131
Karlsen, S. 131
Kertz-Welzel, A. 22–23
Kodály, 14, 76–78, 80
Koops, L. 95, 96, 118, 119, 124
Kratus, J. 75

Lamont, A. 71, 81
Lancy, D. 50, 106, 110, 119, 127, 129
Lareau, A. 6, 96
learning in music 14, 36, 46, 60, 65, 71–72, 79; through bodily movement 77; through discovery 75; embedded 119; everyday 44; formal 120; observational 118–119; as participation 82–83, 112, 116; relational approaches 130; and singing 20, 64; and technologies, 97, 99, 102–103; transfer 53; *see also* indigenous processes of learning in music
Lee, N. 4
Leppänen, T. 27
LeVine, R. 26, 69, 109, 127, 128
lullaby 95, 121–123, 125
Lum, C-H. 96, 130

Mackinlay, E. 113
Macvarish, J. 9, 51
Malloch, S. 125
Marsh, K. 130
material turn 39, 40, 41
Mehr, S. 16
Merriam, A. 122
methodolatry 14
migration 4, 35, 130
Minks, A. 116, 118
model of practice 126; in private music classes 15, 49; traditional 12, 13
Monitor Preschool Report 98
Moore, D. 45
mother-baby interaction 48–49, 51, 126–128
motivation: autonomous 119–120
multimodal: expressions 49, 116; media 5, 98, 117, 121; processes 121
music as social process 88–90
music classes: baby 11, 59; private 12, 15, 27
musical development 29, 68, 71–74, 85–86; *see also* recapitulation theory; singing
musicking 87, 89

Nansen, B. 102–103
neuromyths 54–56
neuroscience 16, 42, 52–57, 59–60, 85, 134; research methods 57–59
Niland, A. 37, 47

Ochs, E. 127
Olsen, D. 122
Orff Schulwerk 14, 76, 78
Osgood, J. 104

Papoušek, M. 49
paradigm 17–19, 79; shift 45
parenting: culturally defined 50, 107; culture 124–125, 129; goals 96; high investment 27, 148; intensive 6, 96, 128; middle-class 7, 28; musical 6, 9, 117, 93–94, 122; skills 109; styles 134; values 126; Western 94–95; *see also* attachment
peer culture 36, 37–38, 70, 84, 91; and gender 104, 106
Peterson, D. 69
Pettit, A. 122–123
philosophical approaches 76–79
Piaget 41, 65, 75–77, 80, 82, 112
Pillsbury Nursery study 68, 77
play 26, 30–31; musical 33, 35, 37, 48, 68, 77, 79; solitary 7
playground games 89, 91, 118, 130
Pond, D. 68, 77
positivism 18, 80
postfeminism 104
poverty 8, 26, 36, 89
problem-solving 81
prosocial behaviours 42, 48, 96, 119, 126
protoconversation 126–127
Prout, A. 20, 30, 31, 32, 40

rapping 65
recapitulation theory 78, 79
Regelski, T. 14
Reggio Emilia 79
research: with babies 35; cross-cultural 111–112; early childhood music 12, 13, 16, 18, 22, 50, 67, 70; infant auditory perception 69; longitudinal 74; musical development 63, 68, 73, 97; and technology 97, 98, 100, 102; and 'toddler gap' 71
Retra, J. 81
'risk' society 7, 8, 25
Rogoff, B. 82, 112, 118, 119
Rose, S. 53, 57, 58
Rutkowski, J. 112

Save Childhood Movement 7
sentimental idealization 26

Singapore 96, 130
singing: to babies 125, 128–129; at bedtime 94–95; in car 64, 89, 96; cross-cultural studies 112–113, 115; development 1, 64, 66, 68–70, 72–74, 80; games 35, 91, 118; groups 47; in home and family life 33, 93, 94; in nursery settings 1–3, 37, 20, 83; spontaneous 84; *see also* karaoke; lullaby
Small, C. 87
smartphone 5, 89, 94, 98–99, 123
sociocultural: approaches to learning 129; as context 30, 46, 63, 81–82; theory 83–84, 126; *see also* Vygotsky
sociology: of music 88, 91, 127; of music education 90
sociology of childhood 18–19, 31–33, 36–39, 62–63, 76, 81, 90
Sole, M. 94, 96
Soley, G. 113
Somali-born mothers 27, 108–111, 125–128, 130, 132
Sommer, D. 8
Street, A. 125
Suzuki method 120
Swanwick, K. 80
Swanwick and Tillman spiral 68
systems theories 84–85

tablets *see* touchscreen technology/tablets
Tafuri, J. 68, 74, 96
TAP *see* Technology and Play (TAP) report
Technology and Play (TAP) report 98
Thorne, B. 39
Tillman, J. 80
Tobin, J. 111
touchscreen technology/tablets 5, 6, 98, 99
toys 5, 83, 89, 123; pink and blue 103–104, 106; 'shut-up' 99; as sleep aids 94, 13
traditional cultures 116
Trevarthen, C. 49, 74, 125

Vansieleghem, N. 9
Vygotsky 74, 75, 81, 82–83, 85

Warao, The 122
Wassrin, M. 20, 35, 36, 38
Wastell, D. 54
Western, Educated, Industrialised, Rich and Democratic (WEIRD) populations 50, 52, 59, 67, 71, 85, 114, 126
Whiteman, P. 84

YouTube 98; apps 123; clips 7, 65, 70, 98

Zimmerman, M. 81
zone of proximal development 83, 84

Printed in Great Britain
by Amazon